REPORT OF THE COMMISSION OF INQUIRY INTO ENGLISH

*Balancing Literature, Language and Media
in the National Curriculum*

Edited by

CARY BAZALGETTE

BRITISH FILM INSTITUTE

bfi

BFI PUBLISHING

First published in 1994 by the
British Film Institute
21 Stephen Street
London W1P 1PL

The British Film Institute exists to encourage the development
of film, television and video in the United Kingdom, and to
promote knowledge, understanding and enjoyment of the culture
of the moving image. Its activities include the National Film and
Television Archive; the National Film Theatre; the Museum of the
Moving Image; the London Film Festival; the production and
distribution of film and video; funding and support for regional
activities; Library and Information Services; Stills, Posters and
Designs; Research; Publishing and Education; and the monthly
Sight and Sound magazine.

British Library Cataloguing in Publication Data.
A catalogue record for this book is available from the
British Library

ISBN: 0-85170-425-5

Cover by Sam Holmes

Set in 9.5/11.5 pt Times by
D R Bungay Associates, Burghfield, Berks
Printed in Great Britain by
The Eastern Press Ltd, Reading

Contents

Introduction

This book represents an attempt to broaden the public dimension of debates about education. It is the report of a Commission of Inquiry into English, set up by the British Film Institute in association with the *Times Educational Supplement,* which investigated the balance between literature, language and media in the National Curriculum for England and Wales. The Commission took place at the National Film Theatre, London, over two days in November 1993, and was preceded by a public debate entitled 'Competition, Coherence and Control: Education in the Next Ten Years'.

Why should a cultural institution like the BFI, which is supported by the Department for National Heritage to foster the development of film and television, get involved in discussions about formal education?

The BFI was set up in 1933 as a result of lobbying by a group called the Commission on Educational and Cultural Films, who were active in the early 1930s. They called for an institute to be formed 'with wide powers over the whole realm of cinema, comparable to those exercised by the BBC in the realm of wireless'. The aims and objectives of the BFI do not quite have that breathtaking ambition, but the founder members, who included John Buchan, HG Wells and George Bernard Shaw, made it clear that a key component of the BFI's mission should be to find out more about the 20th century's own art form, cinema.

Since the 1930s it has remained a central part of our aims to foster study and appreciation of cinema, and of television and video, on the basis that these media are, now more than ever, immensely significant forces in our national culture.

That is why, since 1988, we have been pressing for the Government to include a consideration of the moving image media in its plans for the National Curriculum. Because the Government was planning a curriculum of ten separate subjects, we argued pragmatically for media education to be included within English, since that was where most media teaching was already going on.

This argument was initially accepted. The Statutory Order of March 1990, which lays down what English teachers must do, contains a small element that requires them to ensure that children study 'media texts'. This is different, in an essential and significant way, from saying that the media can be used to illustrate aspects of English or to motivate the study of literature. It is a requirement to study the media themselves.

It is, however, a limited one, and quite properly so: studying audiovisual texts requires skills and concepts which most English teachers do not have, and any change in this direction must happen gradually, accompanied by additional training and by rigorous evaluation. Such evaluation would, in an ideal world, help us to reflect upon what children ought to learn about the media and whether this could, or should, be provided entirely within English. Elements within other subjects, and cross-curricular planning, might also be appropriate.

These developments have not taken place. In fact, the tiny changes made so far have been threatened with reversal: ministers have castigated the efforts of teachers to incorporate media work, and proposals for a new English curriculum were published in April 1993, which removed the requirement to study media texts in their own right.

Objections to these proposals were widespread. Even if they had not been, the BFI does not see it as appropriate merely to beg for another little space in the curriculum. If it is contentious to ask whether audiovisual media have any space at all in the curriculum, however small, then much larger issues of principle are opened up. What is the curriculum for? How are subject boundaries justified and maintained? Who has a stake in these debates?

It was these questions and others like them that prompted our initiation of this project, and our decision to look at the issue of overall balance in the curriculum, rather than the more parochial problem of whether media education should be 'in' or 'out'. We were delighted to find that the editor and staff of the *Times Educational Supplement* shared our concerns and our proposals for addressing them through a Commission of Inquiry.

Our intention was to initiate better informed, more responsible debate among the widest possible range of positions, in the hope of setting a new agenda through which consensus might be found. We started from the proposition that English is not and never has been a fixed, known quantity. Debates about what it is for, and what it should include, are inevitable. Its legitimation as an academic subject, with literature at its heart, has happened within the last 100 years. By validating the vernacular it became, firstly, a route for working men and for women to gain access to the national literary heritage; secondly, a haven for personal expression through speech and writing. Relevance to the lives of ordinary people has remained a crucial, though contentious, motivation.

Attempts to define the subject tend therefore to become embroiled in argument about high and low culture, past and present, imagination and utility. These questions cannot and should not be avoided. However, we must recognise that they can never be definitively answered. A subject that engages with language must also engage with social change, and with the technologies through which communications are made. As society and technologies change, there will inevitably be changes in the meanings that language can generate, the pleasures it can make available, and the identities it can express.

Reaching agreement about how these changes should affect the school curriculum is never going to be easy. It is bound to knock against political and cultural commitments and provoke ideological confrontation. But this should be the grounds of healthy - indeed passionate - debate, not entrenched opposition between enemy camps.

It was therefore important to set up a formal structure for the Inquiry that would discourage confrontation. Following the format of the Commission of Inquiry into the Future of the BBC, organised by the BFI and BAFTA in March 1993, we invited a Chair and a panel of four Commissioners to hear evidence from sixteen witnesses over four sessions. Each witness was asked to give a presentation of no more than five minutes, the substance of which had to be submitted in writing in advance. They were each cross-examined by the Commissioners, with one Commissioner leading the questions for each session. Members of the audience were invited to make comments and ask further questions in each session, once all the witnesses had spoken and been questioned by the Commissioners. The proceedings were recorded on video and audio, and the main part of this book consists of the lightly edited transcripts of the whole event.

The result, in the opinion of all those involved, is a fascinating, thought-provoking and often entertaining panorama of ideas about our schools and about our national culture. The Commissioners have undertaken a daunting and remarkable task in distilling what they feel to be the key issues that must inform all current and future debate about English. Everyone involved in education should feel indebted to their achievement.

A crucial factor which set the terms of the Commission's work from the outset was the Public Debate held on the evening before the Commission itself opened. Anna Ford chaired Sir Malcolm Thornton, Eric Bolton and Alan Smithers in a hard-hitting analysis of the present state of education. The themes of their discussion recurred again and again through the Commission itself: the need for a new consensus; the proposition that debate should precede legislation; the failure of educational debate to win public understanding and participation; the importance of a balanced historical perspective. The Debate's proceedings were, again, fully transcribed and form a further section of this book.

The overall success of the Commission and the Debate is due to the commitment and hard work of many people. Wilf Stevenson, Director of the BFI, and Colin MacCabe, Head of BFI Research and Education, backed the project from the start. The support of Patricia Rowan, editor of the *Times Educational Supplement*, was a vital factor, as was that of her staff, particularly Helen Priday, Heather Neil, Sean Coughlan and the designer, David Hinds. The front of house, box office, catering and technical staff of BFI South Bank were untiringly efficient and helpful in their management of immensely complex logistical arrangements. Kate Stables and Joan Woods, later joined by Natasha Murray, resourcefully shouldered the secretarial and administrative burden generated by the event in BFI Research and Education. We are also grateful to Samuelsons for providing the audiovisual record of the event, and to Barnett, Lenton & Co for the transcripts. For the video extracts which formed such an appropriate opening to each session and which ensured that children's voices were also heard, we are indebted to Ann Brogan of BBC Schools,

Colin Izod and Andrew Bethell of Double Exposure, and to Media Education Wales, Cardiff. But the biggest 'thank you' must go to Giselle Dye as co-ordinator of the whole event, whose resolution, ingenuity, skill and unfailing good humour were an example to us all.

Cary Bazalgette
Principal Education Officer, BFI Research and Education
Director of the Commission of Inquiry

Participants in the Commission

THE CHAIR

Mary Warnock
DBE
Former Mistress of Girton College, Cambridge. She was a member of the IBA (1973-81), Chair of the Committee of Inquiry into Special Education (1974-78); a member of the Committee of Inquiry into the Validation of Public Sector Higher Education (1984) and Chair of the Committee on Teaching Quality (1990). She has written extensively on ethics, philosophy and education.

THE COMMISSIONERS

Robin Alexander
Professor of Primary Education at the University of Leeds and a member of CATE, the national advisory and accrediting council for teacher training. He has taught in schools and higher education and has researched and written extensively about the primary phases. His recent work includes the 1991 study of primary education in Leeds and membership of the 1992 DES inquiry into primary school teaching methods.

Marilyn Butler
Rector of Exeter College, Oxford; formerly King Edward VII Professor of English Literature, King's College, Cambridge. She is a literary and cultural historian, specialising in the Romantic period.

Alan Howarth
CBE MP
Member of Parliament for Statford-upon-Avon since 1983. He taught English at Westminster School from 1968-74. As Parliamentary Under-Secretary of State, Department of Education and Science, between 1989 and 1992, he worked as Schools Minister and was responsible for Higher Education and Science. He is currently a member of the Select Committee on National Heritage.

Anthony Smith
CBE
President of Magdalen College, Oxford. He was a BBC producer in the 1960s, and has written a number of books on the media. He worked for the Annan Committee on the Future of Broadcasting and played a key role in the national debates

that led to the foundation of Channel Four, of which he was a Board Director (1981-85). Between 1979 and 1988 he was Director of the British Film Institute.

THE WITNESSES

Michael Armstrong Head of Harwell Primary School, Didcot, Oxfordshire.

Jennifer Chew Teacher of English with responsibility for Special Needs, Strode's College, Egham, Surrey.

Brian Cox Formerly Professor of English, University of Manchester (1966-93); Chairman, National Curriculum Working Group (1988-9).

Farrukh Dhondy Writer, Commissioning Editor for Multi-cultural Programming, Channel Four.

Phillippa Giles Executive Producer, responsible for series and serials derived from existing material (literary adaptations, and so on), BBC Drama.

Stuart Hall Professor of Sociology, The Open University; writer and academic specialising in the field of cultural studies.

John Hickman Head of English, Forest Gate School, London.

Elspeth Howe Chair, Broadcasting Standards Council.

Margaret Hubbard Principal Teacher of English and Media Studies, Craigroyston Community High School, Edinburgh.

Colin MacCabe Head of BFI Research and Education Division.

Margaret Maden County Education Officer, Warwickshire.

John Richmond Deputy Commissioning Editor for Schools programmes, Channel Four.

Susy Rogers Executive Committee member, National Confederation of Parent Teacher Associations.

Roger Scruton Writer and philosopher, currently Professor at Boston University, USA.

Sally Tweddle Senior Programme Officer, Vision for Schools unit, National Council for Educational Technology.

Andrew Webber English and Media Studies teacher, Chatham Grammar School for Girls, Kent.

6

Participants in the Debate

THE CHAIR
Anna Ford   Journalist and Broadcaster

THE SPEAKERS
Sir Malcolm Thornton Conservative MP for Crosby since 1983; Chairman of the Parliamentary Select Committee on Education, Science and the Arts since 1989.

Eric Bolton   Professor of Teacher Education, University of London Institute of Education; formerly Senior Chief Inspector of Schools, 1983-91.

Alan Smithers   Director, Centre for Educational Employment Research, University of Manchester; formerly member of the National Curriculum Council.

Key Dates 1960-1993

1960   National Union of Teachers (NUT) Special Conference 'Popular Culture and Personal Responsibility'.

1963   The Newsom Report, *Half Our Future,* on the education of pupils aged thirteen to sixteen of average and less than average ability, recommends the raising of the school-leaving age to sixteen, the allocation of more resources to these pupils, and 'the study of film and television in their own right, as powerful forces in our culture and significant sources of language and ideas' (paragraph 475).

1967   The Plowden Report, *Children and their Primary Schools,* commends a balance of traditional and progressive teaching, but is subsequently characterised as advocating only the latter.

1974   The Bullock Report, *A Language for Life,* stresses the need for teachers and pupils to be competent in respect of knowledge of and about English language, and the importance of teacher training; recommends an extension of the film and television study proposals by Newsom.

1976   The Prime Minister, James Callaghan, calls for a 'great debate' about education, in a speech at Ruskin College.

April 1983   A Department of Education and Science (DES) report commissioned from 'a group of teachers' and entitled *Popular TV and Schoolchildren,* recommends that 'all teachers should be involved in examining and discussing television programmes with young people'.

1984   *In English from 5 to 16* (Curriculum Matters I), Her Majesty's Inspectorate (HMI) propose learning objectives for children at ages seven, eleven and sixteen, under the headings Listening, Speaking, Reading, Writing and knowledge about Language.

1985 Government White Paper *Better Schools* proposes more attention be given to the full ability range and more active methods of teaching and learning be developed.

Jan 1985 Planning begins for the General Certificate of Secondary Education (GCSE), to replace CSE and O Level GCE, with the publication of General Criteria: examinations to be available to the majority of pupils at sixteen-plus and seven criterion-related grades to be awarded.

May 1986 Kenneth Baker succeeds Sir Keith Joseph as Secretary of State for Education.

July 1986 The Technical and Vocational Education Initiative (TVEI), funded by the Manpower Services Commission (MSC), offers large-scale funding to local education authorities (LEAs) to develop fourteen to eighteen curricula.

July 1987 *The National Curriculum 5-16: A Consultation Document* issued by the Department for Education and Science (DES) announces a ten-subject national curriculum for England and Wales which is to be 'broad and balanced': English, Mathematics and Science to be the core subjects.

Dec 1987 The Task Group on Assessment and Testing, set up in July under Professor Paul Black, produces recommendations for assessment including a ten-level scale for measuring pupil achievement.

March 1988 The Kingman Report: Committee of Inquiry into the teaching of English Language under Sir John Kingman offers a model of the English language *in use* and proposals for attainment targets in learning about language.

April 1988 Working Group to advise on attainment targets and programmes of study for English set up under Professor Brian Cox; briefing includes requirement to make recommendations for teaching media studies through English.

1988 Education Reform Act establishes the National Curriculum Council (NCC, chaired by Duncan Graham), the Curriculum Council for Wales (CCW) and the School Examinations and Assessment Council (SEAC, chaired by Philip Halsey);

provides for the delegation of budgetary and staffing responsibility to schools, and the establishment of grant-maintained schools.

Nov 1988   Cox working group issues first report, *English for Ages 5-11*.

Feb 1989   NCC circular defines system for numbering school years and grouping into Key Stage 1 (ages five to seven), Key Stage 2 (eight to eleven), Key Stage 3 (eleven to fourteen) and Key Stage 4 (fourteen to sixteen).

April 1989   Language in the National Curriculum (LINC) project set up to follow up the implications of the Kingman Report and develop teaching materials to improve learning about language.

June 1989   Cox working group final report, *English for Ages 5-16*.

July 1989   John MacGregor succeeds Kenneth Baker as Secretary of State for Education.

March 1990   DES issues Statutory Order, *English in the National Curriculum*, to be phased into schools over years 1990-1994. Includes requirement to study 'media texts' from Key Stage 3 onwards.

Nov 1990   Kenneth Clarke succeeds John MacGregor as Secretary of State for Education.

June 1991   LINC teaching materials completed but withheld from publication by Tim Eggar (Minister of State).

Aug 1991   David Pascall succeeds Duncan Graham as chair of NCC.

Jan 1992   The DES Discussion Paper, *Curriculum Organisation and Classroom Practice in Primary Schools,* by Robin Alexander, Jim Rose and Chris Woodhead, argues that effective delivery of the National Curriculum requires a mixture of teaching methods and fuller exploitation of teachers' subject strengths.

March 1992   Education (Schools) Act reduces numbers of HMI and reconstitutes them to form new Office for Standards in Education (OFSTED); school inspections to be open to tender.

April 1992   Conservatives win General Election.

April 1992	John Patten succeeds Kenneth Clarke as Secretary of State for Education.
July 1992	NCC presents case for early revision of the Statutory Order for English, asserting that knowledge and skills need to be defined more explicitly and rigorously.
April 1993	DFE issues proposals for revision of the Order in *English for Ages 5-16 (1993)*, containing controversial requirements in relation to Standard English and lists of required reading, but excludes specific requirement to study media texts in their own right.
April 1993	Sir Ron Dearing appointed as chair designate of School Curriculum and Assessment Authority (SCAA) and commissioned to undertake a review of the national curriculum and assessment arrangements.
May 1993	Widespread boycott of the arrangements for testing of fourteen-year-olds in English.
July 1993	Education Act 1993 accelerates programme for establishing grant maintained schools; sets up SCAA to replace NCC and SEAC.
Aug 1993	Sir Ron Dearing issues Interim Report recommending a reduction in the numbers of statements of attainment defining each subject, a reduction of the amount of time taken in testing, the abolition of 'league table' test results, and a postponement of the English and Technology revisions until at least 1995/6.
Sept 1993	Publication by NCC of the *Consultation Report* on the proposals for the revision of English: clarifies requirements on standard English, reduces number of titles for required reading, and references to audiovisual media remain marginal.
Dec 1993	Publication of *The National Curriculum and its Assessment:* final report by Sir Ron Dearing.

THE COMMISSIONERS' FINDINGS

PREAMBLE

'English' as a school subject will be debated once again in the summer of 1994, following the publication of the latest proposals for a revised curriculum. But it will also be debated during the five years following September 1995, as the new curriculum is consolidated and evaluated in practice. We wish to propose an agenda for both of these processes by describing the issues which we felt were of paramount importance, after hearing all the evidence that was presented to us.

Perhaps the most striking feature of the evidence we have received, at the Inquiry and thereafter, has been the contrast between it and the general tenor of political and media debates about education. Two points have struck us as making a significant difference to the ways in which ideas are formed and decisions are taken.

Most of the issues faced in education today are not new. They have emerged time and again, in many guises, over the last 100 years. The invocation of terms such as 'traditional' and 'basic' too often betrays a lack of historical awareness. In the evidence that we heard, we were impressed by the witnesses whose arguments were effective and convincing because they were contextualised historically.

However, our predominant concern is with the confrontational nature of public debate about education in Britain. It is characterised by simplistic dichotomies: 'traditional' versus 'progressive'; 'phonics' versus 'look and say'; 'Shakespeare' versus 'soap opera'. But despite the wide range of values expressed by the witnesses we heard, we found no evidence of entrenched opposition or irreconcilable polarities; there was, in fact, a large measure of agreement. In our view it is a caricature to portray education as dominated by sectarianism.

We found six issues which we believe must be resolved in any curricular reform involving the areas of teaching and learning presently covered by English. We think that they can be discussed in new and more productive ways.

1 Basic Skills

1.1 The politicisation of the debate about English has re-defined as mutually exclusive educational purposes which are in fact complementary and interdependent. It is not just that there is no practical necessity for schools to feel that they must choose, for example, between teaching the basic skills and fostering creativity; but that a 'basic skill' has little practical meaning divorced from its application. Part of the problem here, we suggest, is often

12

an excessively narrow definition of 'skill'. We were given compelling evidence from a wide range of witnesses that illustrated how children and young people acquired basic skills most effectively when they could see their purpose as essential to communication.

1.2 The Commission did not hear any arguments against the proposition that the basic skills of reading and writing should be given high priority, especially in the early years. They did hear, however, a suggestion that arguments about phonics are arguments about educational values rather than about techniques. That phonics, like 'basics', have become politically emblematic is not in doubt. That most teachers use a mixture of methods in teaching reading, and that they are most likely to achieve success with their pupils when doing so, is also well-documented. Yet it is also clear that this eclectic and pragmatic approach is sometimes construed politically as a less than wholehearted commitment to 'the basics'.

1.3 We wish to argue that debates about the teaching of reading and writing should be rescued from this morass. If there is universal acceptance of the need for children to acquire, as early as possible, the skills of reading fluently and with understanding and discrimination, and of writing clearly and accurately (this was certainly what we heard in evidence), then the question to be addressed is simply that of how these skills are best acquired. That is a pedagogical question, not a political one.

2 Progression and Standards

2.1 It was noticeable that we were given little evidence about how learning should progress through different key stages, and about how the balance between different aspects of the curriculum might change from one key stage to another. We were given convincing arguments that investigation of ideas about language and its workings, as well as critical and creative work with media, can start with very young children. But there is an unnecessarily sharp split between the concerns of primary and secondary teaching in discussions about the curriculum. We think this is dangerous and unhelpful: more ways must be found of bridging this gap and of encouraging teachers in different phases to listen to and learn from one another. The formulations of the National Curriculum may be resulting in arbitrary notions of what is 'appropriate' for primary or secondary pupils, denying the former access to ideas, experiences and skills which they are capable of handling and from which they can benefit.

2.2 'Standards', frequently referred to in discussions about the teaching of English, are perhaps a more prominent issue in the primary school, where we can see an amalgam of two contrasting traditions: the nineteenth-century elementary system's emphasis on the so-called 'basic skills' of reading, writing, spelling and handwriting; and progressivism's concern for creativity, for language as response to 'felt' experience, and the importance of starting with and building on what the child already knows. One was primarily concerned with preparation for a narrow spectrum of adult employment; the other with the rounded development of the individual. It is important to acknowledge that the two positions are not incompatible: both are needed and they reinforce each other. For the majority of primary teachers and schools the primacy of reading and writing has never been in question, even during the 1960s and 70s, when progressivism had its strongest impact.

3 Heritage

3.1 We heard no evidence to suggest that anyone wants to discard or undervalue the literary heritage of English. Nor, however, did we see any likelihood that consensus might be reached upon the content of a literary canon. We believe that a historical perspective is important here: the notion that literature was once taught more purposefully and more widely is a myth. Good boys' schools taught Latin and Greek to scholarship standard; English Literature, always identifed with middle class girls, became comparably rigorous only in the mid-20th century, as the numbers of girls interested in A Levels and university places rose. Schoolchildren in general were not drilled in canonical literature, apart from those primary children who learned poetry by heart. The number introduced to a serious study of literature remained a minority - perhaps twenty per cent of fifteen-year-olds - until the introduction of GCSE in the 1980s.

3.2 Our society as a whole has few shared assumptions about the nature and value of culture. There is no body of agreed knowledge about literature, or indeed agreement that such knowledge is desirable as part of the equipment of an educated person. The absence of agreed assumptions must be addressed, and we believe that the English curriculum is one of the places to address them. But the production of a canonical list will not achieve this. It is inappropriate for government or for agencies acting on its behalf to impose such a list. Judgments about what texts should be used in schools should not be politicised: to do so is inappropriate in a democracy, and undermines the professionalism of teachers.

3.3 It is more important to establish the 'idea' of a canon than its content. From their earliest years in school, pupils should learn that individuals and groups always have valued certain texts as an essential, irreducible part of their heritage. This idea should be investigated and debated, and it is the business of both primary and secondary teachers to ensure that the range and quality of texts to which pupils have access enables them to develop and share a genuine sense of cultural value, born of experience, not imposition. In the public sphere, continuing debate about what constitutes 'heritage' is essential, and must include the recognition that it can never be a fixed category. As time passes, texts from different cultures and from different media will lay claim to being considered as essential elements of the national culture.

3.4 At the same time, and as a means to ensuring that such debate is interesting and purposeful, we should be much clearer about what ought to constitute knowledge about literature, and indeed about all kinds of text, including those from other cultures and from non-print media. Critical concepts such as genre and narrative can be explored by pupils of any age, and curricular guidance on these will be of value to teachers.

4   Global Language and Standard English

4.1 In the evidence presented to us, we were aware of a constant tension between cultural unity and diversity, standard English and other dialects, purity and pluralism. Although the negotiation of these tensions is undoubtedly a challenge to teachers, we heard very little to suggest that they constitute a fatal weakness, or a set of oppositions that must be resolved. On the contrary, we believe that such tensions are necessary and productive. None of our witnesses said anything to undermine the case for standard English as an essential medium of communication which every child is entitled to understand and be able to use. The fact that many of them saw this as something that must be learned about in relation to dialects, historical forms and home languages did not, in our view, affect the status ascribed to standard English. We were however impressed by the numerous calls we heard for better materials and guidance to support the teaching of knowledge about language.

4.2 We also heard about the realities of multi-ethnic schools where large numbers of pupils may be learning English as a second language. We acknowledge the challenges involved in ensuring that children who need to gain competence in English do so as quickly as possible, and here we noted, again with concern, the reductions due to be made to funding support for teaching English as a second language. But we wish to remember that British cultural history is a history of incursions. We are, and always have been, a cultural crossroads. A common culture is not the same thing as a uniform culture: but a potential danger posed by a 'National' curriculum is that it may allow some people to deny this truth. We live, it was pointed out to us, in 'a world irrevocably in translation'. The tensions between centre and periphery, commonality and diversity, may pose powerful threats to social stability, but at the same time they offer rich imaginative and communicative possibilities. Understanding and rejoicing in the plurality of our culture is not a 'therapy' for the 'problem' of the multi-cultural classroom: it must be an essential feature of all children's learning.

5   Shared Culture and the Media

5.1 The Commission heard strong and convincing arguments for the established combination of language and literature to be extended to include the study of film, television and other audiovisual media. The justifications offered included the following: English is about exploring the making of meaning, and media texts have as strong a claim as literary texts in this regard; audio-visual media are ubiquitous and must therefore be studied critically; the media provide for today's children and adults a common experience of language in use which is pervasive, powerful and very diverse; the combination of the visual image and the spoken word is a highly accessible route into the study of established literature and drama, and indeed can enable many pupils to encounter this material who would not otherwise be able or inclined to do so.

5.2 It appears from the evidence that the idea of learning about the media as a general entitlement is now a widely-accepted principle, which we would endorse. We can also see that this principle carries with it many problems which will require further investigation. Although English has a strong claim to be the subject base for critical analysis of media, it seems unreasonable to confine media education entirely to English. Other aspects of the curriculum can also contribute effectively to the ways in which children can learn about the media, just as they can, and should, contribute to children's gaining competence in the English language. While media education may be relatively easy to integrate into the primary curriculum, there is a danger of inconsistent and uneven approaches in the secondary school; curriculum overload is also a potential problem. Existing boundaries within secondary English, and between English and other subjects, may come to be questioned as media education is incorporated. The question of definition also arises, when 'media' may be taken to mean only audiovisual forms, or may be extended to include computer software, visual arts and music. Our response to some of the evidence we heard was that the popular, commercial forms of media are too often accepted as appropriate objects of study without any discussion as to whether significant works of cinema or television – which might well be regarded as worthy additions to our cultural heritage – might have equal or greater claims upon pupils' attention. Finally, we are concerned that there is at present too little in the way of teaching material or training to support a large-scale incorporation of media education into the curriculum.

5.3 None of these problems constitutes a valid reason for rejecting the principle that the diversity of children's and young people's experience of communication, which inevitably includes the media, should be reflected in the curriculum. We recommend that flexible and gradual ways be found to ensure that the curriculum begins to incorporate both critical and creative work with media, starting from modest beginnings, and subject to careful monitoring.

6   The Boundaries of English

6.1 In establishing a national curriculum, the struggle over definitions of language, literature and heritage can look like a struggle for the soul of the nation. There are, indeed, vital debates to be had. English has drawn to itself a vast range of responsibilities, and the principles on which these should be prioritised are not always apparent to outsiders.

6.2 As we move towards the millennium, it is clear that the ways in which we use information technologies and the media, and the ways in which we think about them, will continue to change and to affect more traditional modes of communication. Reading, writing, speaking and listening are already acquiring new dimensions that cannot easily be accommodated within a subject based purely upon verbal, mainly written, language. We believe that it is already time to start looking ahead and to contemplate the possibility that curricular boundaries may have to be re-drawn. Communication through language, which constitutes our relationship with the worlds of both science and art, will always be of fundamental concern. It is possible, however, that in the future this central aspect of education may have to be given a new title. 'English' may already have become too ambiguous and too controversial for what is crucial to all education.

MINUTES OF EVIDENCE

Day One: 26 November 1993

Session One

Cultural Heritage and Cultural Analysis: What is English For?

Mary Warnock Everybody feels that they have a stake in what is taught under the heading of English in schools, and that it is absolutely central to all stages of education from nursery education onwards. It is not something that we want to be totally in the hands of professionals, where it has, regrettably, become a rather polarised issue.

I think the great thing about this Commission is that we shall be able to have a wholly rational discussion, not from any entrenched points of view. That is why I feel so very pleased that this Commission has come into existence and I feel extremely glad to be here as the Chair.

The Commission has been asked to address a quite specific issue, which is the balance between literature, language and media in the National Curriculum. We will be hearing evidence from a wide range of people, some of whom are professionals in the teaching of English, and others of whom are not. We will be ranging through four main topics, rather roughly divided and which may overlap. The question of balance within the curriculum is the centre of our discussions today.

The first session is entitled 'Cultural Heritage and Cultural Analysis'. Those two terms were used in the report of the English Subject Working Group to characterise two views of what English in schools is about, so this session is going to look at the crucial questions: what is English for when it is taught in schools; why should texts be studied at all; on what basis should texts be selected for study; and how should the study of texts relate to the actual production of texts such as writing or making films.

The session was introduced by a five-minute video made by BBC Education at Winton School, Islington. It showed young children talking about English language, about the books they liked, and about the films and television programmes they liked.

Mary Warnock   Our first witness is Professor Brian Cox, who chaired the English Subject Working Group that was set up in 1988 when Kenneth Baker was Secretary of State. He retired this year as Professor of English at Manchester University. He was also one of the contributors to the so-called Black Papers on education which were published in the late 1960s and which were critical of some aspects of teaching.

Brian Cox   I believe that a National Curriculum for English must create a balance – a word that has already been used·this morning – between unity and diversity, between a common culture for all children and respect for local or ethnic differences. Briefly I will describe what I mean by that.

I believe the present English curriculum, established by my Working Group in 1989, has been very popular with teachers for a number of reasons, and partly because it does reflect a balance which was thought to work in schools.

In language work, all children are entitled to be helped to write and speak standard English. At the same time, dialects must be treated with respect. In the classroom, children who speak dialect at home should not be told their usage is incorrect. They should understand that standard English is an addition, essential for many purposes. We also need to welcome bilingualism in the classroom and the enrichment that that provides in knowledge about language. But children need to understand the importance of standard English, and if they do not have access to standard English, many important opportunities are closed to them in cultural activities, in further and higher education and in industry, commerce and the professions. Those educationalists – there are not many of them these days – who deny children these opportunities are confining them to the ghetto, to a restricted discourse which will close to them access not only to the professions but also to leadership in national politics. So first of all, I want to balance them with all children entitled to write and speak standard English by the age of sixteen, and at the same time, respect for bilingualism and for the originality of dialect.

Knowledge of English literature is, I believe, of central importance in providing us with a common range of reference, and is of vital significance in developing linguistic skills in English. The Kingman Report of 1988 said:

> Wide reading, and as great an experience as possible of the best imaginative literature, are essential to the full development of an ear for language, and to a full knowledge of the range of possible patterns of thought and feeling made accessible by the power and range of language. Matching book to the pupil is an aspect of the English teacher's work which requires fine judgment and sensitivity to the needs of the child. It is good for children to respond to good contemporary works, written both for children and for adults. It is equally important for them to read and hear the great literature of the past. Our modern language and our modern writing have grown out of the language and literature of the past.
>
> *Report of the Committee of Inquiry into the Teaching of English Language,*
> HMSO, March 1988, Chapter 2, paragraph 21

The National Curriculum of 1989 says that my Working Group recommended these principles for the choice of texts for study:

1. All children should be given the opportunity to gain pleasure and critical awareness from the study of pre-twentieth-century English literature. Shakespeare is made compulsory and in the Statutory Order (March 1990), specific mention is made of the Authorised Version of the Bible, Wordsworth, Jane Austen, Dickens and the Brontës. There is no prescribed list, and teachers are left free to choose their own texts.
2. All children should encounter and find pleasure in literary works written in English – particularly new works – from different parts of the world. We were thinking of a great variety of authors such as Chinua Achebe, Ngugi, Toni Morrison, Alice Walker, Anita Desai, Derek Walcott, and so on.

Within this framework, however, we recommended that teachers must be left free to choose the texts which they think their students will enjoy. The task of helping young people to continue reading for pleasure after they leave school is daunting. We felt that prescribed lists of authors and books – the sort that were introduced in 1992 by the National Curriculum Council (NCC) and by the School Examinations and Assessment Council (SEAC) – are unnecessary and indeed might harm standards of literacy, because children will often be bored and put off reading, and teachers want to help children to enjoy reading by having the freedom to choose texts within this framework.

Any prescribed list of books for a national curriculum must to some extent reflect a concept of national identity. I agree very much with what Edward Said wrote in *Culture and Imperialism,* published early in 1993. He challenges static concepts of national identity and the barren dogmatism of 'us and them', which vitiates so much political discourse in West and non-West. He writes:

> Trying to say that this or that book is (or is not) part of 'our' tradition is one of the most debilitating exercises imaginable . . . I have no patience with the position that 'we' would only or mainly be concerned with what is 'ours' any more than I can condone reactions to such a view that requires Arabs to read Arab books, use Arab methods and the like.
>
> Edward W Said
> *Culture and Imperialism,* New York, Alfred A Knopf, 1993, p. xxv

In our multi-cultural society in Britain today, we must take this into account in choosing texts for study. Not only will children be introduced to a broader range of thought and feeling, but, through looking at literature from different points of view, pupils should also be able to gain a better understanding of the cultural heritage of English literature itself.

So we have a balance in language and a balance in literature put forward by the present Order now in place in schools.

The third point is that the National Curriculum, as we heard in the introduction, emphasises cultural analysis. In their study of texts, children should be helped to develop a critical understanding of the world and cultural environment in which they live. Children should know about the processes by which meanings are conveyed and about the ways in which print and other media carry values. We emphasise this strongly in attainment targets and programmes of study, that indeed analysis of the media is essential to an English curriculum.

To sum up, we need national unity for the development of literacy, for common understanding of standard English and for common values so we may live at peace with one another. We need to maintain our cultural heritage, which places great emphasis on freedom of expression and independence of mind. At the same time, we need to respect local differences and the need for diversity in our multi-cultural society, so that we may respect each other's dialects, each other's culture, each other's religion. This balance will not be easy to achieve, but it seems to me an essential aim for an English curriculum.

The present curriculum, for which my Working Group was responsible, is not perfect. It obviously has some weaknesses, but I believe that the success it has had in the classroom shows it does not need radical change at the present moment. It is concern for this fine balance between unity and diversity that must be at the centre of all our thinking about National Curriculum English.

Marilyn Butler   Professor Cox, in practice, I think your rhetoric today and in the report stresses diversity more strongly than unity. I think it has been felt to do so, since the report came out, by elements critical to it who want to stress unity more. Can you explain why there is a real advantage in a sort of localised diversity in the classroom of the kind that you appear to be recommending, as opposed, say, to simply leaving it to local examination boards to name particular texts? It could be felt that decentralisation is already met by leaving the titles of books to some other educational authority, but you seem to be stressing autonomy in the classroom.

Brian Cox   Not entirely by any means, because I am in favour of a national curriculum, and I am in favour of the framework which we put forward. I would have thought that many people have said, for example in Professor Bridie Raban's analysis of this curriculum[1], that it has led, for example, to more study of pre-1900 English literature. I think diversity had often led to an inadequacy in that respect which has been put right by the present curriculum.

But I think one answer to your question would be to think of the children we have been watching on the video, because they brought out overwhelmingly the diversity in the schools and the need for sensitivity in dealing with that. The diversity of our schools means that teachers, with their professional understanding, need to be free in many fundamental ways to develop curricula which will help such different kinds of children. What we are saying is that the difficult balance between unity and diversity is one that we need to address, and there has to be variety between schools in looking at that particular problem.

Marilyn Butler   Could I ask you as a follow-up, what do you see the roles of local examination boards as being? Presumably they do continue to nominate set books and set texts and indeed set media texts?

Brian Cox   Yes. I am very happy with that arrangement as it was before the proposals for a revised Order and the proposals for assessment came out in the latter half of 1992, because schools could choose between the boards, which gave some freedom, and at the same time I think the boards tried to provide a framework which was professionally acceptable. I agree with you that the boards could give, as the London board did about two years ago, an emphasis to multi-cultural texts which might be welcome in many schools. So I am very happy with that arrangement, except that I feel that in the framework I described there should be some pre-1900 English literature, because that is part of our heritage and our language, just as I do feel that on the other side there must be some texts in English from other cultures. Within that framework, I am happy with diversity.

Alan Howarth   Professor Cox, I think the video demonstrated that we have the elements of a common culture but the community of experience that the children were indicating to us is largely a community of experience of watching familiar television programmes. How do we make that leap into achieving a comparable community of experience as far as reading of books is concerned? What are your thoughts as to how teachers are to persuade children that they can delve back into the heritage in order for that to be a springboard for their quest into the future? Do you give us a clue in the report, where you make the one exception – I very much welcome the fact that you were against prescriptiveness – as far as Shakespeare is concerned? Can you tell us how we are to lead these children from their shared appreciation of *Neighbours* to a shared appreciation of Shakespeare and beyond?

Brian Cox   One of the great changes in the classroom of the last ten years or so which has been most enriching has been the emphasis on drama and film, and the teaching of Shakespeare under, say, the Shakespeare and Schools Project in Cambridge[2], has enabled children of all abilities to participate in enacting scenes from Shakespeare. This can be very successful indeed at introducing the kinds of children that we were watching on the screen to drama with great pleasure. Of course one also includes seeing film of Shakespeare. A recent production of *Much Ado About Nothing* has been incredibly successful with a wide variety of young people, so it can be done. What one does not want are the old-fashioned texts which were prescribed last year and which I had when I was at school which, as many people of my age have said, killed an appreciation of Shakespeare forever.

Robin Alexander   Following the controversy about the revision of the Order, as you know we now have the NCC's *Consultation Report* and the School

Curriculum and Assessment Authority (SCAA) could reasonably say that the very strong objections raised in respect of the earlier versions have now been attended to – and in fact they do say that. To what extent are you happy that the latest version actually meets your reservations and concerns?

Brian Cox I am not happy, and I think I speak for almost every teacher of English in the country in saying that. What has happened is that the revised Order that came out seven months ago was full of proposals which simply would have caused chaos in the classroom and which were very ill thought out. They have been much improved and I welcome the work that has been done after the consultation, so that the absurd proposals for spoken standard English at Key Stage 1 and such things have been improved. The definitions have been improved. The lists are not so prescriptive. So indeed the revised one is much better. However, what has happened, is that we went three steps backwards and now we have gone two steps backwards. But on the other hand, another overwhelming argument (and for me the crucial one) is that for teachers to introduce the National Curriculum in English demands an immense amount of work. Millions of pounds are being spent on textbooks, and in-service training. The system has been only a few years going through the schools, and as it has been so welcome and so popular, it does not seem sensible to change it for a curriculum which teachers feel is still in many ways lacking – and may I mention specifically, I do think that over spoken standard English, it has still not got it right. As we saw with the children on the video, you really cannot lay down rules except to say that children are entitled to speak standard English by the age of sixteen and that all schools have to devise their own policies according to their own backgrounds. There are many points of this kind where I think the proposed Order really does not have the richness of the present curriculum.

Anthony Smith Professor Cox, I was very struck in the video by the emphasis placed by the children on the use of English as an instrument. They all saw it as being something important in their lives very directly, and I find in your statement – perhaps I am misreading it – an under-emphasis on that. You are concerned with what is essentially a very laudable national political project in which again you are loading on to the poor old English teacher, no doubt with the help of other teachers in other parts of the curriculum, but it seems to me that you are not saying what the children were saying about the way they see the need for acquiring skills in the English language.

Brian Cox Certainly the Working Group's curriculum completely answers you, I think, in the five 'Views of English' that we put forward. An 'adult needs' view is one of the five: strongly emphasising the need for an English which will help children when they enter the workplace. In my document I said that written and spoken standard English are essential in higher education, the professions and indeed in national life. It was interesting that the children we saw were aware of the international dimension as well. So if I under-emphasised that, I am happy now to put that right.

23

Mary Warnock Our second witness is Susy Rogers, who is a member of the Executive Committee of the National Confederation of Parent Teacher Associations. She is currently studying for a Ph.D. at the University of Glamorgan and has studied educational management and computer science.

Susy Rogers I am very pleased to be here as a representative of the National Confederation of Parent Teacher Associations, but I would like to stress that many of these opinions are my own and do not necessarily reflect those of the entire membership of the NCPTA, which comprises over 10,000 parent teacher associations in England and Wales, with a staggering eight million parents.

I want to be certain that, as a parent, I am able to ensure that my children are growing up in an enriched environment, encouraging the development of their mother tongue within the home. Through developing natural language patterns, I expect my children to capture meaningful contexts within the cultural values held in the home, encouraging a sense of freedom to think powerful ideas, freedom to express impossible realities and freedom to be.

So what about natural language acquisition in the home? I believe, as I know many parents do, that it is vital to recognise that our children need to be encouraged to develop their cultural identity through interactive dialogues as they engage in their daily activities together where everyday values are respected, where creative play and pre-school nursery facilities develop both vital interpersonal communication behaviour and meaningful linguistic patterns as children explore and tune into the world, creating their own individual microcosms. To this end, my eager response to developing my children's cultural heritage must be matched by imaginative resources, early learning materials readily accessible through lending libraries and suitable television, radio programmes and films. It becomes more vital than ever before in today's society, for parents to share in their children's linguistic development through reading together, watching television together, sharing experiences through exploring ideas in videos and films, as well as listening and creating meaningful experiences through our rich cultural heritage especially inherent in radio broadcasting.

With this in mind, I need, as a parent, to gain a better understanding of how best to prepare my children not only with the traditions of the past but also with the tools of the future as we move into the 21st century. This is where partnership in our children's school and home life is so vital. This is where we believe in a home/school partnership.

Within the spirit of the National Curriculum, I know, as a parent, how important it is to encourage children to use their imagination through creative reading, writing and listening. While I accept that children need to have the freedom to express their own ideas, the discipline of accuracy and grammatical correctness is also paramount in sustaining meaningful dialogues, firstly for bringing together communities with the boundaries of a 'village map', and secondly to identify a far wider territory encompassed by the 'global village'.

We know as parents how important it is for children to develop problem-solving skills through fact-finding to engage more fully in logical debate. But what we also need to know is how well our children are progressing in school and what resources are available for developing linguistic skills so as to be able to share in our children's growth and maturity in search of a language for life. We need to know, as parents, how schools are preparing our children to engage in dialogues that will encompass inter-cultural issues. In our rapidly increasing technological age, schools have opportunities through multi-media and innovative information technologies to explore new ways so that children are learning to communicate, learning to exchange ideas and learning to create fragile worlds hitherto unknown and unexplored.

Can I just illustrate this point with a quotation from Alice's little dialogue with Humpty Dumpty:

'You see', said Humpty Dumpty, 'when I use a word . . . it means just what I choose it to mean. Neither more nor less.'

'The question is', said Alice, 'whether you can make words mean so many different things'.

'The question is,' said Humpty Dumpty, 'which is to be the master – that's all'.

Lewis Carroll, *Alice Through the Looking Glass,* 1872

So what are the cultural contexts of the 21st century? How do we prepare children for responsible life in a free society, hopefully in the spirit of understanding, tolerance, equality of sexes and friendship among ethnic, national and religious groups and those of indigenous origin? Language, we know, is powerful in drawing together cultural diversities into meaningful contexts. But enabling children to develop their language through unparalleled opportunities of learning at home and in school, their self expression through imaginative dialogues and creative ideas helps them to come to terms with complex global issues, as well as to interpret everyday events in their individual private lives.

We are increasingly aware that in this age of technological change our children need to understand critically the way in which information is handled and processed, how powerful ideas and meanings are created and crafted by writers, dramatists, poets and film-makers from the past and the present.

So in conclusion, we as parents recognise that through their language acquisition, children are better able to make meaningful relationships and become increasingly confident in communicating effectively as they grow up and reach adulthood. To this end we need to be sure that our children have opportunities for self expansion through discussion, debate and drama as well as designing their own productions, for potential broadcasting, video or film. We appreciate that children learn by doing; it is therefore by critically evaluating and examining what children read and what they watch on television, what they see on videos and films, that parents and teachers can engage in and share meaningful experiences that will enable children to tune into the world around them, enriched by a common, cultural heritage, to step confidently into the vision of the next century.

Marilyn Butler You've given a very eloquent view of the ideal in education; could I ask if you feel that your children – or the children you see around you at the moment – are getting an education like this? I mean, is this an ideal that you see is not being realised or promised or one that's actually happening in good schools now?

Susy Rogers In many schools I think the vision of teachers teaching English, the vision that teachers have in presenting materials to children, is very realistic and is very pertinent to the way in which children are growing up in this society. Teachers are working very hard towards bringing together the type of materials and the type of processes that children really do need. But I do think the materials and the resources to help teachers to bring about the education which our children deserve, are sadly lacking.

Alan Howarth Mrs Rogers, you have, as Professor Butler said, spoken very eloquently indeed in setting out your vision on behalf of the National Confederation of Parent Teachers Associations, and can I ask you a little bit more about your concept of partnership between the school and home, and in particular, two questions: one broader, one narrower. Do you consider that the advent of the National Curriculum has actually opened up new and better opportunities for partnership in teaching and learning between home and school, or does it, because of the technicalities involved and all the specifics in it, actually set barriers to that partnership? More particularly, does the emphasis in the National Curriculum on standard English create new difficulties, or do you see it as no particular barrier in the way of an effective partnership in teaching and learning between the school and home?

Susy Rogers I think it is a fundamental issue as to how parents can help their children understand a language which is understandable throughout Britain, which is the common language, a language which we can use to communicate internationally. Having the National Curriculum as it stands gives us a platform for debate. It is important that we have something that we can follow and that we can talk to staff in schools about – that we have something we can relate to. Inevitably I think what is worrying is the very rigid, prescriptive measures that indicate that our children should read certain texts even if they are not ready for it. The profession in teaching English knows when children are ready to move from one text to another, and I believe that the choice should be with parents and teachers, and that it should be made by a home/school partnership. Teachers do know what is best for children and likewise parents can share in the language development of their children.

Marilyn Butler You spoke of information coming out of schools and how important that is to parents. Do you mean by that the league tables?

Susy Rogers League tables can be very misleading, as we have heard. And if children are tested when they are not ready to show what they can do, it becomes crucial that parents recognise teachers as the best people to test children at their different stages of language development. It is good to have some prescription, but we should not rigidly follow this through as the one and only way in which children are going to speak their own mother tongue. It is important for parents to have materials to which they can refer and they can also provide a choice within the home to help children develop their language.

Robin Alexander You have offered a very large agenda informed by a very generous vision, and you have looked well ahead, which is what we all have to do in education. Professor Cox stressed that he did not want prescription. Nevertheless, there has to be selection, as you cannot do everything. I wonder if you have any advice to give to teachers about the basis on which they should make selections, given the enormous range of aspects of English that you have argued should be covered?

Susy Rogers I do not know if I would like to give teachers advice. I am a parent myself; I have four children, and I know from my own children's language development that as they grow up, they watch television, go to films and to the theatre. They explore the world in its reality, and they also have ideas that they think might make it a better place. The National Curriculum prescribes certain texts and if my children are not ready for them, I need to be able to make a selection and to add to what they are reading. It is a vital partnership between the home and the school.

Mary Warnock Our third witness is Andrew Webber, who is a teacher of English and Media Studies at Chatham Grammar School for Girls in Kent. He has also, in the past, taught in comprehensive schools, and he has been engaged in adult education, including education in prisons.

Andrew Webber I would like to start by reading some comments which appeared in the *Kent Today* newspaper, my local newspaper, on 29 October, 1993.

> Chatham Grammar School for Girls joined in a lunchtime debate and voted overwhelmingly to include the Australian soap *Neighbours* on the English National Curriculum. Presumably, if they had their say in it, they would include *Top of the Pops* on the music national curriculum. Perhaps it is all good fun, but it does not say much for so-called advanced thinking in schools when an English master can join in the debate and advocate trash like *Neighbours* to broaden pupils' education.

Since this article was published I have written and read poetry with year 9; listened to Bob Marley and Metallica with year 10; taken the whole school to see Kenneth Branagh's *Much Ado About Nothing*; gone with year 11 to see a touring production of *Hamlet*; watched Kathryn Bigelow's brilliant *Blue Steel* and *Near*

Dark and read and discussed both *King Lear* and *Wuthering Heights* with year 12; and studied the *Sunday Mirror* alongside year 13, and about ten million other people.

In addition to this I have taught four English and media classes each week; read at least three popular novels, approximately twenty-four newspapers, three monthly magazines and four NMEs; bought four CDs; watched about fifteen hours of television; listened to three hours of Radio 4 in my car; and seen *The Secret Garden* and *True Romance* at the cinema.

I am a consumer of the media and a product of the media. I am also, in my spare time, an advanced-thinking English master, and yes, I do advocate trash like *Neighbours*. The first thing that I would like to clarify is the fact that this particular Commission of Inquiry must not be seen as arising out of some misinformed notion that there is chaos in our classrooms. Although teachers have been beset by innumerable changes recently, certainly at my school enthusiasm has not waned. There is still much good practice and standards remain high. A recent OFSTED inspection reported that all of the English and media lessons at our school are at satisfactory level and above.

English teaching seems to me to be very much concerned with trying to understand our culture, whatever that may be, and the road to understanding is paved with texts. Texts used for study, therefore, should reflect the culture and also shape its future, if it has one. Culture of course is problematic, but English is less so. What is English is the written, the spoken and the read word. What can be read, however, does not only include the written word. Images, pop music, adverts, fashion, television, films and so on can all be read and indeed are being read at colleges, schools and universities around Britain.

Because course content has broadened recently, particularly in English-related subjects, this does not mean that standards have been lowered. It means, rather, that more variety is to be found within the range of texts studied and the emphasis of study, therefore, is not always the finished product but often the process and means whereby that product was produced.

Teaching empowers students. It provides them with a framework for thought and an opportunity to take cultural products and evaluate their effects in a classroom context. This means that the methods of teaching have also changed recently, and instead of leading from the front, teachers are now encouraged to facilitate or manage learning. Indeed, I feel that there is some veracity in the statement that there is no such thing as teaching any more, there is only learning, but the teachers do it!

Teaching then, like learning, is exciting, and the wide range of texts available for study makes it all the more exciting. In these days of customer satisfaction, this can be no bad thing. For this reason, in the classroom, Hamlet happily coexists with Henry from *Neighbours*. Metallica and Marley have their place next to Branagh and Blue Steel and so on. Quality is born out of variety.

In English lessons in my Utopian society, children are taught to read television alongside novels, poems and plays from an early age. Course work remains the only fair way of assessing, if assessment is necessary, students' contributions. Media studies is properly and effectively funded and resourced, free thinking is encouraged and confident, mature and lively minds are developed through study. Creativity is celebrated. In my Utopian society, the media welcome the opportunity to be taken seriously, to be centre stage in any debate which takes place about the nature of culture. In my Utopian society, politicians and educationalists agree that teachers are professionals, united not only by their expertise but also by their willingness to carry on developing and learning alongside their students; thus decisions about education are made inside, and not outside, the classroom. Teachers retain their integrity and their right to choose texts.

Education creates this Utopian vision, but it is early, it is London, it is November 1993. Fog permeates everything. I merely advocate trash like *Neighbours*. Thank you.

Marilyn Butler   Obviously there is a lot of fun going on at Chatham! I suppose the balanced question has to be that in all of this, there must be some question of priority in the light of the very limited amount of time you have available, so if one puts so strong an emphasis as you are doing on 'culture' as the essence of English, it could be argued that some sacrifice may be entailed in the notion of language as the centre of the syllabus. In terms of priority, there might just not be time for the kind of consideration of the written and literary language, because your variety is so very broadly conceived.

Andrew Webber   Not necessarily. I think that the language is at the heart of all the examples that I have given, so therefore, by studying *Much Ado About Nothing* in the cinema, or the *Daily Mirror,* language is being assessed in its different forms. So I cannot see that there is a problem.

Marilyn Butler   It is a matter of detail and of the additional vocabulary in literary language. I am making the point that if the general public hears you saying all of this, they might react, as your local newspaper did, by thinking that somehow only *Neighbours* is being talked about, because the stress appears to be drifting away from written language.

Andrew Webber   Well, again, I think in the examples that I gave, that is not the case. I think I mentioned four or five literary examples and four or five media examples in my list of things that I had done recently, so therefore I feel there is a balance.

Anthony Smith   Mr Webber, what do you think that Kent newspaper from which you quoted is frightened of?

Andrew Webber   Me!

Anthony Smith   I wanted to ask you how you actually reply to a newspaper, or to anyone not susceptible to your charisma, about how you get them to nail down this question of 'trash' and its use in the teaching of English.

Andrew Webber   Just as a personal anecdote, following that particular article, I sent the writer, who is the editor of a local newspaper, or a former editor of one, an invitation to come here. I sent him a copy of my statement and a letter outlining what I thought he had got wrong, and I did actually agree, ironically, that *Neighbours* perhaps was trash, but that is another issue. Unfortunately there was no feedback whatsoever from him, so that was rather a shame. So I did respond as far as I could, but I did also ask his permission to read the material, and because he didn't respond, I assume he has given me permission.

Alan Howarth I would almost have thought your motto was: 'I consume, therefore I am'.

Andrew Webber Yes.

Alan Howarth You gave us an enthusiastic vision of children saturated by market forces, you described yourself as a product of the media and you said: 'I do advocate trash'. Can I ask you one question about the cultural heritage view of teaching English, and another about the cultural analysis view of teaching English. First, do you see any scope for the canon? Are there writers of such genius that experience of their work should be part of every young person's experience? Secondly, you alluded to fog; so does Dickens at the start of *Bleak House,* and Dickens presents us with the awful example of the Circumlocution Office. Surely it is part of the function of English teaching to teach discrimination: to develop in children a capacity for survival based upon a capacity for discernment and sifting the bogus from the genuine and learning to resist the abuse of language, whether in advertising, in political rhetoric or in bureaucratic jargon. Is that, too, part of the role that you have as a teacher of English?

Andrew Webber There are obviously two parts to that particular issue. I know this is not the nature of this debate, because A Level is really a separate issue entirely, but I feel very strongly that students approaching their A Level choices should consider taking the traditional English literature A Level course alongside media studies A Level. I feel that then gives them very clearly the broad spectrum about which you speak, and obviously that would then entail that, during a two-year A Level course, students would encounter the work of Shakespeare in some detail, and the language analysis that you have spoken about, and also would encounter advertising and so on. That is my ideal student, I think.

In relation to the second part of the question, again I agree with you, and I take your point – although I cannot remember what you said, actually!

Robin Alexander Fairly recently, a Minister of State for Education said the following: 'I have no patience with the kind of cultural relativism, or perhaps the word should be nihilism, that holds that any kind of text is grist to the educational mill.'

I have two questions. The first is, are you happy to be characterised in this way? The second is, is it possible to claim that any kind of text is grist to the educational mill, because with reference to the question I posed to Mrs Rogers, you are necessarily making a selection of some kind, and I am interested to know, as I asked her, the basis on which you make a selection?

Andrew Webber As I think I tried to make clear in the statement, I feel there needs to be negotiation in the choice of texts, but I think that the teacher's role is perhaps to define some parameters for the choice of texts. In other words, I would be quite happy to negotiate what we were to study with students. Having said that, I would want to provide them with a framework for their choice.

Robin Alexander And what would that framework encompass? What would be the criteria?

Andrew Webber It would depend largely on what you were meant to be studying, whether you were studying literature or television or radio or whatever. I think you have to allow for the fact that the teachers are the ones with perhaps more experience of the media in a cultural context. I realised I was old when I said to some A Level students, I remember buying Kate Bush's 'Wuthering Heights' when it came out, and they looked at me and said: 'Well, we were two'. So I think I have, and most teachers who are older than me have, years of experience of observing the development of media, the development of literature – if they have taken a keen interest in it. Therefore, I think the framework provided by the teachers is the framework of a teacher who has wider and broader knowledge of the subject than the individual, specific knowledge of the student. So the framework comes from the teacher's awareness and love and enthusiasm for the subject.

Robin Alexander So are you or are you not one of Baroness Blatch's extreme cultural relativists?

Andrew Webber No comment, I think I would say to that one.

Mary Warnock Our last witness in this session is John Richmond, who now works for Channel Four television, but until recently he was an English adviser working in the Language in the National Curriculum project. Before that he worked as an English adviser in different parts of England, and he was an English teacher prior to that for many years.

John Richmond On balance I am pleased that I am not going to say anything new! I think what I am going to say reinforces the immense consensus that does exist both among professionals and also among a range of people who have taken an active interest in the development of English teaching. That consensus is there, holding a lot of people together, and I think it is a very good basis on which to go forward and it is something that government needs to listen to.

English teaching suffers from labels. It is not alone in that, but a constant handicap in the recent debate about the subject has been the desire of some to package into terms like 'traditional' or 'progressive' or 'trendy' whole complexes of attitude and practice which in fact defy such tagging. I prefer to base my view of what constitutes good English teaching on a perception of what the future citizens of our nation palpably need in order to function both as productive and as enjoying members of society.

This leads me, in discussions about the teaching of writing, for example, to conclude that the ability confidently to handle a range of forms – letters, stories, essays, poems, reports – for a range of purposes – to persuade, to inform, to entertain, to move, to criticise – is a fundamental competence which our future citizens need and which we should teach.

I take it that the teacher's most basic concern should be with the substance of what pupils write. The teacher should demonstrate a continuing interest in what the pupil is trying to say. If this basic concern for meaning is established between teacher and pupil, then the need for correctness in the conventions of the writing system – a need which I unambiguously acknowledge – is given a valid impetus from the beginning of schooling. I do not care whether this view makes me, in the eyes of the labellers, a traditionalist or a trendy. I have derived my view from my observation of what works in classrooms, and, as I say, from a sense of what mental equipment tomorrow's adults will need in this area.

The same method applies to the particular topic of this session, 'Cultural Heritage and Cultural Analysis'. It's important that we are talking about both and not one or the other. The spectacle of some politicians and some commentators caricaturing this debate as one between those who would confine reading to a line-by-line analysis of a limited number of works of English literature whose greatness has long been established, and those who would confine it to the study of episodes of *EastEnders,* is a good example of the unhelpful and indeed malicious sloganising and sneering to which English teachers have been subject in recent years.

In the face of this, all one can do is to continue carefully to state the obvious. The first part of the obvious is that of course English teachers must make a judicious selection from the vast, diverse and accumulating store of literature available in English, written over a period of six centuries, shall we say, and including, over the last century and a half, an increasing representation from countries outside Britain and Ireland. I am perfectly happy that advisory lists of authors' names be published for each age group. I do not mind at all that Shakespeare's unique status in our national culture – a dangerous phrase – national consciousness – but you know what I mean – be acknowledged by making it compulsory that one or two of his plays be read by the time pupils are sixteen. I would like to point out, to those of the 'Let's save our civilisation before it is too late' school of thought, that the situation before 1963, the year of the introduction of the CSE, and before comprehensive schools, was that literature was read by an elite of about twenty per cent of fifteen-year-olds, and that of the eighty per cent or so of fifteen-year-olds in secondary modern schools, the majority – and I know there were honourable exceptions – were taught basic English and not judged capable of appreciating literature.

The last thirty years have seen the reading of more literature by more pupils than at any time since the beginning of state education. The introduction of the GCSE and a National Curriculum for English were the most significant organisational encouragements to this development. I want this situation to continue. I want English teachers, using their professional judgment within broad guidelines laid down for them by government, to continue to engage pupils' sympathy and excitement in the reading of literature, and to search for new ways of doing this.

The second part of the obvious is that the world outside English classrooms, and therefore the world which pupils bring into English classrooms, is changing at an unprecedented rate. The most exotic sentence in the Kingman Report is: 'Around the city of Caxton, the electronic suburbs are rising.' English is the subject whose essential business is language, where the language, as it were, comes up front. For English to turn its back on the study of language as used by the immensely powerful instruments of the mass media, instruments which will affect the next century's citizens in ways which are not wholly clear but which we know will be profound: such an action is sentimental and self-deceiving. Our pupils have a right to some understanding of the ways in which language is employed across a range of the texts which they encounter and which shape them every day, and not just in the pages of imaginative literature.

Nor do I believe, in a simple way, that literature is where you get your cultural heritage and the study of the media is where you get your cultural analysis. Admiration, response, study, analysis: all these words, with their different connotations, representing their different parties, must be built into the way in which we help our pupils to read, in the broadest sense of the word. The practical job for English teachers like Andrew Webber, when the rest of us who talk about it but do not actually do it have taken our leave, is to construct, in time and space and with limited resources, a curriculum which recognises heritage and promotes analysis, and encourages pupils' active engagement in the absorbing and the making of the literature and the language of our culture.

Marilyn Butler   That seems to me to be an admirable general summary of a slightly idealised situation so far, and a very hopeful account of what should be going to happen next. So can I press you on practicalities. Are there specific things, particularly in relation to your last remarks on the importance of the media (and I quite agree with you that one should not assume that only the media involve any kind of critical analysis and the study of heritage does not). What specifically needs to be done to ensure that children do not merely and sometimes incidentally meet the media on the way to literature, but have the media in their teaching system?

John Richmond   I will name a book which professionals here will know and non-professionals may well not. There is a book by Jenny Grahame called *The English Curriculum: Media* published by the English and Media Centre in London, which lays out in admirably practical terms the way in which, in the 200 minutes or so – and I am talking about secondary schools now and I will say something about primary schools in a moment – that are available to an English teacher in an average week in a secondary English department, the study of a range of media texts and media industries and other kinds of media forms can be managed. It is done both by saying that for a period of four weeks here, let us say in the middle of year 9, we will spend all the time looking at the history of advertising; as well as saying that while we are looking at something else – let us say we are studying a particular work of literature – we will also pay attention to the way in which that work of literature is packaged and presented to the world of readers.

I use that book simply as an example of the fact that a lot of work has been done to say: 'All right. Fine. We accept this and accept the other things that people say: both/and, not either/or. Good. Now let's get on and see how it works in practice in time and space'. A good deal of work has already been done on that, and I think it is a matter of disseminating that kind of practical work more widely.

Marilyn Butler   Could that be done now at that level?

John Richmond   I think it could. Classroom-working colleagues might agree, but I do not know, gentleman of leisure as I am! I think that enough work has been done here and there, as it were, colouring in the map, to give us, in the practical ways that happen at a level of detail which we do not have time for here, a sense of how you fit these things in. But it will always be a judicious selection made by working practitioners from a range of choices that they have in front of them.

May I say one last thing, which I think is relevant to that question? One of the things which makes English teachers most fed up is the feeling from the powerful, from those who govern, that unless they are watched over very carefully they will descend to the lowest common denominator. They need a corset, and they are being told that they will fall through the stage unless they are watched. Now that is not what most English teachers are like. Most of them want to introduce their pupils to works of literature and other kinds of language which they regard as admirable and as well made, and they do not need to be constantly kept an eye on in that kind of way.

Alan Howarth   You said at the outset that there is an immense consensus among professionals as to what the task of English teaching is, and you just now said that English teachers can be relied on. So do we actually need a National Curriculum? Are there not quite a lot of risks in having a National Curriculum? Is not any National Curriculum, by definition, to a degree (and perhaps quite a large degree) authoritarian, imposing views, imposing decisions on professionals as to what the content of the English syllabus should be, and I think by implication inescapably having a fairly powerful influence on what the method of English teaching shall be? It was never previously the way we approached this task in this country. We have not had an Academy in Britain as the French have traditionally had. You have worked with the National Curriculum Council, I understand. Is this whole programme actually a good idea?

John Richmond   Certainly it is, yes. I do not think I need to emphasise my credentials as a supporter of English teachers further than I have, and I will now make some critical points. I have also been an English inspector in a local authority. There is some very bad English teaching going on. There are some lazy, complacent, narrow English teachers about, with low expectations of their students.

34

You can find still some English teachers who will say to you, as you question and criticise the narrowness and the tediousness of the curriculum that they put in front of students, 'What can you expect with children from round here'. If I were to caricature – or characterise, you decide – the bad English teacher, it would be a failed authoritarian relying on a narrow range of not very good texts, and teaching them by entirely transmissional methods. There are still quite a lot of them about.

That is one extremely good reason why we needed a National Curriculum, to yank those teachers kicking and screaming up to the level of the people for whom I have an undying admiration.

Another reason is to do with work-loads. Actually, as long as the government-provided framework allows for the degree of professional autonomy which Brian Cox and others have been insisting on, it is actually rather nice to have a broad framework established so that we all know what we are doing. I have believed in a National Curriculum since my second year of teaching when I collapsed in a fearful heat because I was having to spill out all my guts week in and out, and I remember feeling then that there must be some common themes that we as a nation can agree on.

Incidentally, of course the impetus for a National Curriculum is by no means the property of the political right. There are, and always have been, strong left-of-centre arguments in other European countries for a common curriculum. So I think it is something that everybody can possess.

Alan Howarth   It seems to me you have made a strong case for an English National Curriculum as a model, as an embodiment of the best aspirations, but why should that not be the product of strenuous debate and dialectic within the profession? I do not think you have made the case for a government-imposed National Curriculum.

John Richmond   Teachers do not exist in a closed environment. They are paid for by people's taxes. They are responsible for people's children. They bear a heavy responsibility for the development of a productive work-force and a group of people who will enjoy themselves and care for others and play an active part in the community of the future. I quite openly, and with no reluctance at all, grant government its right to have a broad say in the things that will be taught and learned in the schools for which it pays. I think it is unreasonable to deny that.

Actually, though, the truth of the matter would be that throughout the debate over the National Curriculum, there were moments when some people within the profession and some people within the unions said: 'You have absolutely no right to say anything at all about what is taught in classrooms'. Those voices have long since disappeared and the professional associations and the trade unions and individual teachers all now accept that there is a good case for this broad framework. The thing that enrages them is that an instrument which was ninety-two per cent good was in existence, and there was also a large consensus about the eight per cent that needed fixing. It was to do with inappropriately high demands on writing for six year olds; it was to do with the fact that knowledge about language only started at nine; and there were one or two other detailed things that were wrong that could have been fixed. The performance that we have been through in the last three years is a painful spectacle of government trying to get itself back off hooks which it has put itself on unnecessarily.

Anthony Smith   Can I go back for a moment to the history versus analysis issue? Is there not a perception among those who govern that media texts are not studied with the same narrow, critical attention as traditional texts, and is it not necessary to demonstrate that, whether the text is *Neighbours* or *Much Ado About Nothing,* it is equally capable of the same kinds of close reading and detailed analysis and specific kinds of study? Is it not the fear that this is impossible, that makes the people who govern want to interfere in this whole business rather more than they ought?

John Richmond   I do not think that the reading of a work of established literary genius and a relatively ephemeral episode of a popular soap opera is the same. I do not think that half an hour of *Neighbours* bears the same scrutiny as half an hour of *Much Ado About Nothing.* I do not know any English teacher – though there may be some and they may speak up – who does think that you go at *Neighbours* in the same way as you go at *Much Ado About Nothing.*

Anthony Smith   The point I was making was that those who advocate teaching about ephemeral media texts need to show that that range of study requires the same intellectual skills and the use of high-quality reading that others do. That is not to say there is no hierarchy between the texts that needs to be offered to students.

John Richmond   Perfectly true, and to go back to that particular book I mentioned before, there is, readily available and possibly on the bookstall outside, quite an impressive collection of working documents which contain the kind of intellectual rationales or working equipment which classroom teachers can draw on in order to know confidently how to approach these texts; there is a lot of that work done, and it is there. It is not just a question of saying that we have now admitted to the pantheon a number of *sans-culottes* that were not admitted before, and deciding what we are going to do about them. There has been twenty years of work, starting from very small and uncertain beginnings, and now rather impressively considered, which gives practitioners the equipment to do that with – to end on a preposition!

Robin Alexander   I am going to be the one who utters the A word – assessment. It is very interesting that we have not talked much about assessment so far, and yet out there, the word is never far from anyone's lips or minds.

You have endorsed the National Curriculum. You have expressed a strong concern for the raising of standards. You will know that in the current rhetoric, the National Curriculum is first about entitlement, and this morning we have talked about some aspects of entitlement. But also in that rhetoric, assessment is seen to be the thing which raises standards. I wonder if you would like to comment on the role of assessment, and particularly, but not exclusively, National Curriculum assessment, in raising standards in respect of the vision of English that you have offered.

John Richmond   Yes. Assessment is the flip side of learning. It is an essential and permanent responsibility of all teachers to be engaged in the assessment of their pupil's learning, but the point about assessment is that we assess in order to act. We do not assess for the sake of assessment. A good definition of assessment might be the having of conversations and the making of judgments on the basis of which pupils and teachers can then act. The reason for the hue and cry over assessment and testing recently has been that there needs to be a balance between methods of assessment that deliver reliable information on the basis of which those present and able to do something about it can act, and assessment or testing which gives the Government – the representative of the taxpayer – some broad sense of what they are getting for their money. Again I do not think there are many people now who would begrudge the right of government to some sense of what they are getting for their money. The question is how to strike that balance. My view is that you have to give a substantial amount of responsibility, within guidelines, to teachers to conduct their own assessment, with some externally provided tests (in the broad sense of the word), which would themselves be little elements of good teaching. So at seven, eleven, fourteen and sixteen, if you like, teachers would take children through some activities which are statistically reliable and which are themselves models of good teaching. These would be compulsory and would be taken from a range available to the teachers. So that balance again is not in itself a problem to accomplish.

COMMENTS AND QUESTIONS FROM THE FLOOR

Richard Hudson (Professor of Linguistics, University College, London)   I welcome very much the emphasis on the study of texts and the study of the language of texts as part of cultural analysis. One of the kinds of patterns that you find in the language of texts is grammatical structure. I am very much struck by the fact that most of our new students in our development know very little about the grammatical structure of their own language, do not have any easily applicable meta-language set of categories and typically do not know the difference between a preposition and a pronoun. Does this matter? And a question for Andrew Webber: would your work be more interesting or more fruitful if you could assume that you could talk about the grammatical structure of some of the texts and compare their grammatical structures?

Sarah Mumford (Advisory teacher for Media Education, Wakefield)   We have talked about the English language in terms of literature, language and media, which seems to me to be quite appropriate in that it is language we see as the central factor in these cases. We are looking at language as the way we drive meaning and how meaning is made in our culture, and that means high and low culture and valuing all culture equally. We think about language not just as written or spoken or sung, but visually as well. We think in terms of visual literacy as well as print literacy. We obviously derive meaning from all these forms, both written and visual, so it seems to me that the actual concept of language, the way we make meaning, is at the heart of this process. However, you can then begin to look at language and ask where we get language from. How do we make sense of the world we are in? It is not just by reading books. Yes, that is important, and we do derive meaning from reading books, but we also derive it today from the mass media. The mass media includes literature, newspapers, advertising, film, television, video, computers, and so on. English teaching necessarily encompasses all of those, and they should all be given equal value so that the high culture of literature in terms of Shakespeare is included, but is also understood as history, and we face the future. I endorse what Mr Richmond said, that the resources are there to do this. I am using them and a lot of teachers are using them already in their English teaching. Up until now we have had permission to do this because it has been written down in black and white. My research for the MA that I am doing now proves that teachers are interested. They believe that media education is important, but particularly down at the lower end, they say that unless it is written in black and white, they do not have time to do it. I am extremely concerned about this. While we have media studies at GCSE level, it is obvious to me that media education needs to play a major part and needs to be written into the National Curriculum as well. With language at the centre of our curricular model, and both literature and media stemming from that, we would actually be addressing the next century.

Sharon Sims King (Aston University, Birmingham Language Studies Unit) How can the value of regional dialects be preserved and their diversity appreciated when the implication is that these dialects, carried into adulthood, mean exclusion from various aspects of the national life, and professional and political life especially?

Brian Cox   The present National Curriculum English instituted by my Working Group in 1989, of course, has only been running for secondary schools for about three years now, and of course it did have a strong component in knowledge about language which was experimental and which included statements about the importance of a meta-language developing mainly through language in process, through discussion with the students. It is very unfortunate that the Government cut-back of the Language in the National Curriculum project (LINC) has not allowed that experiment to develop as it should have done, because I believe that there is a strong argument for students having a meta-language in which to talk about their texts. We talked a lot about linguistic terminology and had chapters explaining this in our original document.

Andrew Webber   I am totally sympathetic to the gentleman who commented on the fact that students do not know much about grammatical structures, and I definitely see that as a weakness in my methodology that I do not emphasise that. I am one of the guilty ones, and I confess I would like to know more about the grammatical structures of the language myself. So perhaps I should be one of those on your course!

John Richmond I do not think we should design a compulsory school curriculum for the benefit of students on Professor Hudson's course. I would not do it for that reason, and I do not think you were asking for that. The brief history of this passionate debate is that we had to get rid of the notion that children become speakers and writers and listeners and readers of their language as a result of being taught in advance a Latinate grammar. Having recognised that that did not work, we were left with the question, what should we teach about language, and as Brian Cox says, we made an effort to say, not just in the LINC project, but other bodies and individuals and writers also made an effort to say: 'How about this for a constituency of things which pupils should know about language? Yes, by all means, let us teach them at appropriate ages a basic minimum of meta-linguistic terms to describe the language at sentence level. Let us also teach some things about regional accents and dialects. Let us also teach them about how babies learn to talk. Let us also teach them – moving towards literature – about style and literature, or perhaps style and register in non-literary texts. Here is a collection of things which in practical terms it will be possible to teach'. I hope that when all the dust has settled, most teachers will include an element of the teaching of grammar as a part of what they do – but only as part of what they do, and not in response to the hysterical noises that say that unless you explain to a seven-year-old what a non-finite subordinate clause is, the seven-year-old will never be able to use one.

Susy Rogers I think that parents today would like to see that their children can write letters with correct punctuation and spelling without necessarily relying on computerised equipment to do the spell-checking for them. I think it is very important that children should have a very good grasp of the essentials of grammar and the accuracy of syntax. It is vital that our children can communicate and express themselves well in writing. Most parents would be very anxious if their children were unable to recognise an adjective or an adverb in the simplest sense. Any piece of written work that children are asked to produce, whether it be in English or science or any other subject, should be accurately written. I am pleased to say that the Welsh Joint Education Committee see that as being very important, and in fact take up to five per cent off examination marks for spelling and grammatical errors. It is important that we should stress the accuracy of grammar and syntax and accuracy in written work.

Andrew Webber Equally, if we take the comment about media education being more central than it actually appears to be, we could also put a strong argument forward about the fact that television is, in a sense, more important than the written word today, and therefore the grammatical structures of television and the grammatical language of film and newspapers and radio, are just as important. A study of the written word is only one aspect of the grammar that we should be investigating. Perhaps, coming back to the gentleman who said that students are arriving in linguistics courses without a basic knowledge in certain areas of the written and spoken word, that may be because they have developed knowledge of other modes of communication and have an understanding of editing techniques and camera movements, which are the language of the moving image and which need to be understood just as much, of course, as the grammar of the written word.

Shona Walton (Chair, National Association for the Teaching of English)   In the National Curriculum, art and music both have an equal balance between making and appraising of artistic and musical texts. In the Cox curriculum, as we commonly call it, we do have a balance between creative and critical work, the construction and conveying of meaning. One of the labels that gets attached to English teachers is the stereotype of the teacher who spends too much time looking at creative writing. I'm concerned that the current curriculum on the table as proposed is that 'the construction of meaning' has been removed from Attainment Target 3, Writing. It is not there. I wonder whether the witnesses see any danger in removing this from the English curriculum?

Elizabeth Atkinson (Senior lecturer in Early Years Language and Literacy, University of Sunderland)   I was fascinated by the panel's response to Andrew Webber's presentation. Clearly, as serious analysts of language, they were trying their very hardest to resist his charisma. What is interesting, though, is that both Marilyn Butler and Alan Howarth appear to be making the mistake that Professor Butler so rightly said some people might make. By ignoring the diversity of materials and approaches which he stressed so eloquently and reacting to him as though he does only teach *Neighbours*, they are criticising him for something he did not say. Presumably, the fact that Mr Webber delivered his description of the broad, balanced and relevant English curriculum which he delivers in his school, with passion, ardour and the fire and sparkle which brings teaching and learning alive in the classroom, puts it into the category of what Alan Howarth fascinatingly calls 'the abuse of language'. Surely Mr Webber's presentation is a vivid example of the use of living language, demonstrating admirably that what language is about, whether it is Shakespeare or media studies, Dickens or *Neighbours*, is not only what words are used but how they are used.

Cathy Midwinter (Development Education Association)   I think it is interesting that we have mentioned *Neighbours* a lot, but that *Neighbours,* in fact, could be seen as coming from another culture. Many media texts actually give a range of views and analyses of different parts of the world, and it is very important for children that that is addressed in the classroom. I would like to ask the panel, how does that link in with giving access to literature from many different cultures and different parts of the world?

Janet Gibson (Head of English, Devonport High School for Girls)   I strongly endorse everything that John Richmond said. He really is talking about classroom practitioners, and I welcome that. My point is about assessment of the National Curriculum and in particular assessment at Key Stage 4, which I am quite involved with. Teachers at present are finding it extremely difficult to manage. We are having to struggle to blend in course work, with which we have a great deal of experience, with the constraints of the terminal exam, and I would welcome his comments in particular on the model that he might see for assessment at GCSE.

Brian Cox I welcome Shona Walton's question, because I feel there has been a very exciting shift in the teaching of English towards the craft of writing, with a change of emphasis. That is one of the reasons I think the present curriculum has been so exciting. Children really are going to achieve the kind of accuracy that we have been hearing about when they are concerned to speak and write to real audiences and not to go through exercises. To see that reduced in the 'revised revised' curriculum makes one very angry. It goes against some of the aspects of good practice which are now taken for granted by good teachers, I so very much welcome that question.

John Richmond The construction of meaning is the essential driving force that causes people to write things. Once you underestimate that or take it away from the centre of the teacher's view, then the reason why anybody bothers to go through the dreadfully painful process of putting pen to paper rather disappears. It is the construction of meaning and the sense that you have understood something in a way that was not available to you before you began to write it which gives the deep pleasure and satisfaction and sense of strength and sense of control of the world which means that most of us go on writing. So I hope that we will continue to press for that understanding, or that element of understanding of the writing process, to remain in the National Curriculum documents.

Secondly, of course I welcome and absolutely agree with Cathy Midwinter's endorsement of the importance of including in our curriculum literature produced from a wide range of different nations and cultures and social backgrounds. It is one of our great privileges that we happen to share a language which is of such world-wide significance. I think we have gone beyond the stage now, which I feel I was probably at when I was an English teacher twenty years ago, which was to say: 'Oh, good. Here's a piece of writing from the Caribbean. I'm very glad of it because it is from the Caribbean'. Put that way, it is a deeply patronising attitude to take. I would probably put my hand on my heart and say I did take that attitude twenty years ago. We are now at a point where we must apply the same standards of judgment and discrimination to literature from whatever source around the world. It is equally essential that we say if we are not representing the whole of the English-speaking world somewhere in the selection that we make for students between five and sixteen or five and twenty-one, then we are giving a narrow view of what literature is in English.

Finally there was the question about assessment at Key Stage 4. The question was, how we can square the circle of teachers' demand for course work assessment against an implacable demand from government for some form of external

41

validation of that assessment. I was a member of a group which put together a little paper which went to a large number of people: all MPs, government, Opposition parties, the Employers' Federation and the TUC, public schools, Headmasters' Conference, girls' schools – in short, a very wide constituency of organisations and the educationalists, including presidents and secretaries of the National Association of the Teaching of English, the two maths associations and the Association of Science Education. This was over a year ago, and we have since sent an updated version. We said: 'Look, here is a way of having what you legitimately want, which is the valid sense of how standards are going nationally, and combining that with the best and most practical ways that we know to go about assessment'. On the specific point of how that is done at Key Stage 4, I think it is done by reconvening bodies in each of the core subjects, including English, who would put together a collection of pieces of work that would take a student perhaps as little as a week or as much as two or three weeks to complete, and from which English teachers would have to choose at least one or two pieces of work which they have to do at some point in the second year of the GCSE course. Those pieces of work would be, by common consensus, good examples of English teaching. They would be subject to special scrutiny by moderators and other outside standardising forces to see that the teacher's judgment of the standards achieved by the students within that piece of work meet the standards agreed nationally. It is perfectly possible to do that by the kind of modernisation standards I am sure you are familiar with. It would be possible to do that, and not terribly expensive. It would have the other beneficial effect of exemplifying the essential principle, which is that you put learning first and assessment second. If you have the assessment instrument as a good example of learning, then you are actually doing that.

I think that is a practical proposal. We have put it to government twice now. They have not answered back. But I do not want to end on a sarcastic note. I take that sourness back! I want doors to open. I want us to get to yes, in the dreadful management jargon. I think we could do that if there were a few more sensible people up there listening.

Susy Rogers   We have a wonderfully rich cultural heritage from which we can draw various texts and materials, but it is crucial that children should have an understanding of how to unravel the implicit and the explicit meanings of what they see, of what they read and of what they write. We are moving into the 21st century, where we will have more scientific innovation, medical exploration and a whole variety of new ethical considerations. Children must be able to express their own understanding of the world in terms that can be written down accurately, in the sense that they can make a meaningful analysis of what they have seen and heard and discussed. Through analysis of our cultural heritage, we can move into the 21st century with our children being able to communicate effectively and honestly with one another.

Andrew Webber   The creativity question is a valid one. Since we are talking about balance here, there may well be a road which we go down which encourages

creativity in producing media texts – let's all go out and make videos and radio programmes – but we should not forget to encourage youngsters and adults to write
creatively as well. I think that needs to be emphasised, and I certainly feel that over
the last few years my teaching of creative writing has certainly taken a bit of a back
seat. I feel that is a great shame. I totally endorse that point on creativity.

As an examiner, I believe that teachers should have a choice of texts for study
from a broad list provided either by government or by educationalists. I generally
examine centres from Northern Ireland and I often get very interesting responses
to books like Bernard McLaverty's *Lamb* and *Cal*. I see very exciting and interesting pieces of work that have been done, both in course work and under exam
conditions. It is wonderful that centres are choosing texts which are pertinent to
their students' experience. In terms of standards, those students from Northern
Ireland are producing more exciting essays, shall we say, than the typical *Animal
Farm* work. Dialect needs to be supported but the point there is also that teachers
need to have a choice of texts, so that they can respond to the needs or demands
of their community.

Finally – and this is where we move into rather radical beliefs – we have heard
that assessment is very problematic and again we have heard the notion that the
exam should be part of the learning process and that if there has to be an exam at
all, it should be something which can be learnt from. One wonders, of course,
how much is to be learnt from sitting in silence with 200 other people for two
hours trying to write essays on Keats or whatever. Therefore, my feeling is that
the way in which we assess needs to be seriously thought about, and I am aware
of an MA in the modern novel that is taught at the University of Kent which has,
as its second year exam, a paper which you take away with you, do in the library
and return a week later. That seems to me extremely sensible, and I would like to
see, particularly on media studies courses, more and more pre-released material,
and less and less emphasis upon the rigid system of sitting students down on a
given day and examining them.

Judith Garrahan (English and Media Studies teacher)   Andrew Webber advo-
cates the teaching of trash, and so do I. Probably, in the real classroom, so do
most teachers. I am saying that fairly cynically, and my use of the word 'trash' is
a cynical use. Basically what I am trying to come to terms with is how you can
get kids to discern what is good and what is trash unless they are actually allowed
to discuss programmes which we, from our positions of knowledge and power
and control, consider to be trash. We should not forget that when kids come into
the classroom in the real world, the stuff that we consider is good, they may
consider to be trash, and the stuff that we consider to be trash, they may consider
to be very good. It is a cultural matter and it needs to be addressed.

The other matter is the obsession that certain members of government and
their supporters have with the cultural heritage and the canon. The canon ends, I
think, in 1899 or possibly 1901. It could include, first of all, more poetry,
although because the First World War is so popular with most Key Stage

43

students, I would imagine that, pretty soon, that too will be trashed. What I would like to remind people who doubt what we are doing now, is that contemporary literature, films, television and everything that Andrew Webber was talking about will become the cultural heritage of our grandchildren and great grandchildren. What we consider now to be stuff which is probably not terribly good may well be considered in the future – the next fifty or sixty years – to be the canon.

Alan Newland (Lecturer in Primary Education, University of North London) Professor Cox said that we had the balance just about right, and I broadly agree with him, but I take up the comment that there should be a respect for dialect and bilingualism. I would have liked to hear (and I think that many teachers share this view) rather than a 'respect' for bilingualism, a support and promotion of bilingualism; not just the acknowledgment and value of it, but guidelines and support and resources to support and develop it. We heard from a contributor from the audience here that actually Punjabi is the second language of Britain now. I would like to ask Professor Cox to respond to my regret that he uses the word 'respect' for bilingualism rather than 'promotion' of it.

Secondly, Malcolm Thornton has previously refuted the suggestion that there was any kind of conspiracy to use English studies and cultural and national icons to reinforce national identity. When Anthony Smith asked Andrew Webber what people like those on the *Kent Today* newspaper are frightened of, I wanted to answer for him. I think they are frightened of not knowing who we are, as a nation, becoming. I think they are frightened as to who we are becoming culturally, ethnically and linguistically, and I believe there is a kind of conspiracy that includes newspaper editors and politicians and others who share that fear. What we know as English has always been influenced by outside traditions. The notion that our language and literary heritage is somehow constrained by the sea around the British Isles is simply ill-informed. I would like to ask Andrew Webber and John Richmond, as one-time victims of newspaper editors and politicians, do they share that view with me?

Paul Moore (Northern Ireland Film Council)   I would like to take up the issue of culture, if I may, and say something which I hope my colleagues from Wales and Scotland might relate to. There seems to be an assumption that there is a consensual notion about a common culture, and I would like to introduce the notion that, in fact, culture is about the study of difference as well as about the study of what is the same. As you might imagine, for people living in Northern Ireland, that is not just a matter of philosophical debate. The very proof of that is that I have a colleague here with me: if we send one person to conferences like this, we have to send two people who are from each side of the cultural divide. It is wonderful for travelling, as it gives you great company! But these are not just philosophical debates. Surely studying culture is about studying the differences about people and accepting that we need to look at notions of class, gender, race, nationality, ethnicity, sexual differences, age, and so on.

In Northern Ireland we have our own English curriculum, which I have to say right away is infinitely better than yours! We seem not to have some of the problems that you have. I would like the panel to assure me that this notion of cultural sameness is not cultural imperialism but can actually ensure my cultural autonomy.

Diane Metz (Head of English, Whitefields School) We have a very large multi-ethnic group. We have no ethnic majority in the school, but sixty-three nationalities. I would like to say to Mr Webber, that when you were engaged in bringing *Neighbours* into your curriculum, that was putting English culture into practice. You were not talking about it, but doing it. You were taking the children seriously. If we want our children to take the texts we want to present seriously, we must also take seriously the texts they actually choose to read and to study. It is a two-way process. If we are concerned for our culture in the future, we will have trained our children to take each other seriously, to listen to each other and to value what these children have to say. As an English teacher, I would think that at the end of the *Neighbours* debate, Mr Webber's pupils will have learned how to structure an argument, they will have learned a critical vocabulary and how to discuss the things they choose to read and choose to watch. They probably could end up writing a very well-organised essay. I can see them doing a lot of language development, and they will enjoy it because they have chosen the topic. And because Mr Webber has listened to them, they might listen to what he has to say about *Romeo and Juliet.*

Beverley Naidoo (Advisory teacher for Cultural Diversity and English, Dorset) Given the shifting political forces globally in relation to Europe and the rest of the world, I would like to know what the witnesses see as the political intent in the new revised English Order, and the likely political and social effect of making a very clear distinction between our literary heritage and other cultural traditions.

I noticed that Mrs Rogers, among others, used the words 'rich cultural heritage', and I have taken it that she is actually referring to a very wide heritage. John Richmond spoke about literature in the English-speaking world. In the revised Order we have a very clear distinction between our literary heritage and other cultural traditions. Are those just words, or is there some deeper and more significant political intent behind them? What is likely to be, in people's judgment, the political and social effect of creating those two different constructs?

Alison Sealy (Lecturer in English Studies, Department of Arts Education, University of Warwick) I want to ask the panel to comment on the role of texts as commercial commodities and what influence that has on this debate. I want to propose that the process of socialisation into the culture, which goes on with children who become pupils in· classrooms, is partly a socialisation into the whole phenomenon of consumerism in the context of market competition, and I would like to propose that we can consider texts as commodities. A few examples of that would be the way in which television programmes, when they are being proposed, have to be thought about in terms of the competition for viewers; the proposal to put VAT on books; the competition which authors face with best-selling authors; and the take-over of publishing houses and so on. Some of my students ask me what they are supposed to do about teaching children to spell 'correctly', when it is actually advertisers who are guilty of some of the misspellings for effect. I am interested in the panel's views on the relationship between texts as curriculum content and texts as commercial commodities, and the role of children as consumers of those.

Bethan Marshall (Member of Executive, National Association for the Teaching of English)   I want to pick up some comments that have been made, more by the audience than the panel, and to address part of the title of this session, which is, what is English actually for. It seems to me that that is at the heart of the dilemma in this debate. We have four witnesses here who seem fairly agreed on what English is for, and I think that they have the massive support of English teachers on their side and that they are advocating a broad and balanced curriculum. Nobody, when they really listen carefully to what they were saying, would in any way disagree with any of the points that were made. Nobody at any point has been saying that you should not teach Shakespeare or pre-twentieth century literature; nor should you deny children the opportunity to speak standard English; nor should you deny children gaining a knowledge about language.

All these things are absolutely vital, but on the other hand they are saying that we live in the end of the 20th century and that we must address the issue of a multi-media society. Many messages and much information come from the media and children are very subject to it. Thus there is a great deal of concern about how much information television provides and what influence it has, and to deny children access to that is to bury our heads in the sand. That would be folly indeed. But it seems to me that unfortunately those people who have power over the curriculum, and who are actually dictating what they should have, have a very different view of what English is for. Again to address the question, what are people afraid of when they look at Andrew Webber, it seems that there is a fear of cultural disintegration. There is a concern, particularly on the part of the Right, to make political capital out of a notion of cultural disintegration. They are looking back to a kind of mythical consensus, a kind of cultural hegemony which I firmly believe never actually existed. It seems to me a travesty of what English is actually for to impose that on latter-day twentieth-century children.

I am desperately worried, and I think part of the despair that English teachers feel, is that that mythical view of a consensus that never really existed is about to be imposed on the multi-cultural classes of Britain. It would be so disastrous as to not really bear thinking about.

Brian Cox   I accept the criticism that was made of me by Alan Newland. When I used the word 'respect' in reference to bilingualism, I hope I also used words about enrichment. Bilingualism is a marvellous asset in the classroom. I hope that I had not got that wrong in my presentation. I very much welcome the question from Beverley Naidoo because I was quoting Edward Said on that point. I think this concept of 'our' culture is really dangerous and probably wrong.

Judith Garrahan's question was about the way the canon keeps changing, and I would have thought a growing awareness of the wideness of a culture in English, the global consciousness which Said talks about in that book, is what we are looking for as an idea. Therefore, the revised Order, by imposing a narrow and, as Bethan Marshall has said, mythical view of our culture is going to be most damaging to all sorts of relationships in our community in the future.

Susy Rogers   I was very pleased to hear Diane Metz say that her school had sixty-three cultures. I am very much aware that we have come from a village map, and the understanding of our village, into the understanding of the global village. We not only have a small area of understanding in terms of local community, but also, through information technology and multi-media, we are coming to grapple with far wider issues. Our children will need to come to terms with these if they are going to survive in the 21st century. If children are exploring powerful ideas in an increasingly technological age, some ideas and issues will be brought to them through other forms than verbal language, because language may in itself be too limiting for children to understand the context of the world in which they are living.

Andrew Webber   There have been so many valid points and useful and exciting observations. We cannot address all of them in this particular set-up. All I can say is that I totally agree with the majority of points that have been made. The only thing I can perhaps say practically is that because there are so many diverse issues about the teaching of English that we have already raised and that are going to be raised during this Commission, perhaps there is a strong argument for more time to do that, not in terms of this debate but in terms of classroom time. The problem with English is that it is competing for classroom time with other subjects. From the nature of the debates that have been raised, it is important that we are given more time with our students.

John Richmond   I have one or two very brief thoughts. Bilingualism absolutely must be supported, and of course we must be very vigilant about the possibility of the withdrawal or reduction of government funding to support the education of children for whom English is not the first language[3].

I would want to agree with our colleague from Northern Ireland, and no doubt with his colleague sitting next to him, that common culture is not the same as uniform culture. The use of the word 'common' there is something to do with mutual understanding and respect and interest and curiosity, and not to do with submerging differences, but celebrating them.

I think the answer to Beverley Naidoo's rhetorical question is that the division in the proposed new Order between 'our heritage' and 'other cultural traditions' is significant. It would be much better if we could use a common language giving equal status to the literature and other cultural forms which we bring into our classrooms. But I will say one practical thing about this: when we have embraced so many things from such a long period of time, from such a vast geographical area and including such a diversity of forms, the selection gets harder and harder. That is the job that classroom teachers have to do when we have all gone home. They have to say that there is, as never before, a collection of things to choose from, and they need tools, books, resources, ideas and conferences to help them to make that judicious selection from the great mass that is now available.

On Alison Sealy's point about texts as cultural commodities, I hope that we can continue to allow texts to spellbind, at the same time as recognising that they are cultural commodities. Thus a book is produced for profit by a commercial organisation, usually, and when you start to read it you can often forget all about that completely, because that is not what you are thinking about. I hope we can keep the magic as well as the more prosaic and politically conscious sense of where books come from.

On the point about what I think linguists call 'sensational spellings' or deliberately wrong spellings, I would say that that is not necessarily a problem as long as teachers point it out. 'Buy Right', spelt B-Y-R-I-T-E, could actually be a teaching point rather than a confusing point.

Mary Warnock   I would like finally in this session to again raise a question by Bethan Marshall. Is there a huge gap between the views of what we refer to as a nostalgia brigade for whom Andrew Webber is a real and fearful enemy, and the kind of consensus which, on the whole, we have felt here? If there is that gap, how can it be bridged or what can we do about it?

Brian Cox   I very much welcome what John Richmond said about the curriculum of my working group being ninety-two per cent right. He precisely indicated some of the faults in what we had done, but that had an extraordinary success in bringing the profession together, and it seems to me that the 'revised revised' Order, whatever happens in the Dearing Report, must not damage that. That is why I think teachers almost unanimously have been so angry during the last year or so, and I would hope that out of a debate like this it will be possible for people not involved in the profession to see clearly how much consensus actually exists in the profession at the moment. That creates a massive goodwill, if only it is properly exploited.

Andrew Webber   The only thing I would say in answer to the question, what is English for, is that it is for this!

John Richmond   I think we all know that we have been through a period where policy making by 'calling into the presence' a tiny and unrepresentative number of like-minded courtiers has been the order of the day. That has dealt an awful blow and caused an immense waste of time and an immense bowlful of unhappiness to a very large number of people, and it has distracted English teachers' attention from the main job they are trying to get on with. I hope that the Secretary of State has learned from the embarrassing reverses of the last eighteen months. I hope that if he has done, he will not encounter an excessive degree of triumphalism, even from those of us who feel that we have been most abused; and that if we can get this tiny elite of cultural hegemonists out of their dining clubs – or perhaps rather back into them and out of the Department for Education – we can re-introduce to the Department for Education a range of the very experienced and very distinguished people who have been sidelined by the East German manners of recent years, we might be able to get the whole project back on track.

Notes

1. Bridie Raban, Ursula Clark and Joanna McIntyre, University of Warwick, *Evaluation of the Implementation of English in the National Curriculum at Key Stages 1, 2 and 3, 1991-1993,* Final Report, National Curriculum Council, November 1993.
2. The Shakespeare and Schools Project is funded by the Leverhulme Trust, directed by Rex Gibson, and based at the Cambridge Institute of Education (inquiries to Dr Gibson on 0223 69631). The Cambridge School Shakespeare series of editions of the plays are published by Cambridge University Press.
3. Section 11 Funding is money made available by the Home Office to pay seventy-five per cent of the costs of paying additional teachers of English as a second language in schools where there are sufficient numbers of ethnic minority children needing such help. From April 1994 the proportion of costs paid by the Home Office drops to fifty-seven per cent, and to fifty per cent in 1995.

Day One: 26 November 1993

Session Two

Whose English? Can English Unite a Fractured Society?

Mary Warnock   In this session, Alan Howarth is the lead Commissioner. The thesis here is that English is one of the most widely used languages in the world, and its international presence is very powerfully maintained through films and television exported by the United States. It is universally (or nearly universally) used. Why then, is there so much confusion about a definition for standard English?

We must also enquire as to what is at stake in ensuring children's access to standard English. What are the relationships between the English taught in schools and regional, national, ethnic and class identities within the United Kingdom? We have already touched on some of these matters in session one, but we will come back to them now as the main focus of our discussion.

The session began with a five-minute extract from a Double Exposure programme directed by Andrew Bethell and produced by Colin Izod for the BBC Schools English File series 'New Approaches to Short Stories'. It depicted fifteen and sixteen-year-olds at Forest Gate School, London, discussing 'Another Evening at the Club' by Alifa Rifaat.

Mary Warnock   I would like now to introduce our first witness. He is Roger Scruton, who is currently Professor of Philosophy at Boston University in the United States. He is also a visiting Professor of Philosophy at Birkbeck College in London, and editor of the *Salisbury Review*.

Roger Scruton   I am going to speak as a defender of standard English, but of course that places on me the obligation to say exactly what standard English is. I would venture the following definition: standard English is the English used by competent speakers of the language and recognised as such by them. However, there is a great problem now of defining what a 'competent speaker' is. I believe that in the conditions in which we find ourselves, we ought to turn to writing as our principal criterion of competence. When people have to write down their thoughts, they make their best possible effort to say what they mean. It is the language which emerges from this best possible effort which defines competence, so writing has become an indispensable means of access to standard English, as I would define it, and as I think ordinary people recognise it.

The rules of grammar are the rules which describe this standard English. They describe it in the sense that they show how sentences are constructed, which sentences are recognised as correct and which are deviant. But a description of this kind becomes a prescription. As soon as a language is sufficiently settled to be the common property of a community, then the description of what that community regards as best will also become a prescription for new members, for children, for all those who are learning to take part in the complex game of communication. This is like many other customs in human society, beginning as mere mutual adjustments between people so that they can get on with each other and understand each other's ways, which become in time the rules of the game. The customs that we know as good manners are just like this, and so are customs in dress and other forms of behaviour. That which begins life as a series of adjustments between people becomes, in the end, a series of rules.

I believe that this standard English, although it may be quite hard to say what it consists of at any particular moment, is what ought to be taught in schools, primarily because there is an enormous disadvantage to those who do not know it: the disadvantage, first of all, of not knowing whether they can effectively communicate with their fellows; secondly, the disadvantage of having to look for words, phrases and sentences which could all have been generated by a simple mastery of grammar; and finally, the inability that so many people nowadays have to write something down coherently and be sure that they themselves know what they mean. So I think mastery of standard English is one of the great benefits that education in the English language can bestow. Not to know it is to be at a permanent social disadvantage.

This does not mean that standard English is fixed for all time. Like all customs, language too develops, but it must develop in such a way that the participants in it can continue to understand each other and also to articulate their thoughts, as they have them, to the best effect and with a proper view to communication.

Of course there are other forms of English than the standard which have their own expressive virtues. Idiolects and dialects, on the whole, are part of what make a language interesting, and the literature of the language will often try to record them. But these, I think, should be passed on through families or on the street and not in the classroom. If they are passed on in the classroom, they have an inevitable tendency to become standard and to be regarded as the sacrosanct things which the central and principal form of the language ought to be.

There are, I believe, three reasons for teaching English language in schools. The first is to give pupils a grasp of the standard English which I would defend, without which they will be permanently disadvantaged. That means giving them a grasp of grammar, sentence structure, the parts of speech and so on. The second reason for teaching English is to give some kind of theoretical grasp of grammar; not simply to teach it as a practice, which I think is the first duty of the English teacher, but to teach it also as an incipient theory of human thought. This is something which I am particularly interested in as a philosopher, since I have to teach my subject to students who are often ignorant of the fundamental distinctions in language which make it possible to understand philosophical ideas. Not to be aware of the distinction between subject and predicate is to be deprived of a vital piece of metaphysical knowledge. To be ignorant of verbs, objects, adverbial phrases and subordinate clauses is, I think, to have a deficient grasp of reality, for our language is our primary way of receiving and storing information about the world. The world is not merely a collection of objects. It contains facts, events, possibilities, probabilities, qualities, relations, aspects, laws, rights, duties, excuses. All these have their counterparts in grammar, and the grammar must be mastered if you are to think about them cogently.

Someone who has not grasped the subjunctive mood, for example, has difficulty in perceiving the distinction between the sentence: 'If she were to fall, she would hurt herself,' and the sentence: 'If she falls, she hurts herself'. The information contained in the first of those is information about unrealised possibilities and it is not fully available to someone who does not know the subjunctive. This information gap is revealed in philosophical speculation, and it may also intrude into daily life. Literal mindedness, I believe, is the fate of those who have no grammar. They do not speculate about imagined worlds. They merely shunt familiar objects around a narrow field of fact.

The third reason for teaching English, I believe, is to make people familiar with the literature of the language. I believe that people do not fully know their own language until they are able to distinguish good from bad writing in it. Great writers take liberties with grammar, as Shakespeare notoriously did, and thereby often achieve great effects; but this would be impossible if they did not have a grasp of the distinction between correct and deviant usage.

In conclusion, I would like to say that there really is such a thing as deviant usage and deviance is a form of ignorance; ignorance of grammar or of meaning or of the basic devices of style. There is no reason why, of course, people should not cultivate alternative modes of expression, dialects and the language of the street, and it can become an important part of literature. But still, why not know that other thing, the standard English, which makes it possible to understand other forms of life than your own.

Alan Howarth   Professor Scruton, if I do not paraphrase you too crudely, you put it to us that grammar is the indispensable means by which we apprehend and claim our community, and that if you misuse grammar you are a deviant. If you do not understand grammar, you cannot think, and you are thereby disqualified from full citizenship and self-evidently incompetent to exercise your responsibilities as a democrat. I want to ask you a bit more about your vision of this community of good grammarians. Does it consist of a clerisy of those who have had the good fortune to master the pluperfect subjunctive? What of those who speak other forms of English than standard English? Are they also members of the same society? What of those of our neighbours for whom English is not their first language? What of those who are not our neighbours immediately, geographically and physically, but for whom English is their first language? What is this society that you conjure for us?

Roger Scruton   There are so many different questions in all that, that I cannot answer them all at once. I would say that we are talking about primarily Britain and those people who live in it, and my sense of its identity is that it is first of all formed by the language through which people communicate with each other in all their transactions; that there is a difference between a successful transaction and an unsuccessful one; and that as the language develops, in order to make all the many human transactions possible, the standard emerges. It emerges because people recognise the difference between successful and unsuccessful communication.

I am not saying, as I said in my remarks previously, that I could not clearly identify for you what the standard presently is. It is a moving thing always, but nevertheless, all of us have a pretty reasonable grasp of it. I am now speaking this standard English and communicating with you at quite a high level – a level which is perhaps not easy if you do not command, as you said, the pluperfect subjunctive. After all, we are talking about possible worlds at the moment, and not actual ones.

Alan Howarth   And you used the phrases 'successful' and 'unsuccessful' communication. Do you hold that there is good writing, there is bad writing, that it is objectively identifiable and that the purpose of teaching of the grammar upon which you have laid such emphasis is to enable people to have access to a range of high-quality imaginative experiences, or would you indeed say that the virtue of their experience of studying literature (and I do not know what your views are on studying media texts) is that they should thereby be enabled to have access to grammar, because grammar is really what it is all for?

Roger Scruton   I would say it is perfectly possible to have a grasp of standard English and be totally uninterested in imaginative literature. Lamentable though that may be, this is perhaps the normal case among the average undergraduate that I teach. I try indeed to remedy it, and one way of remedying it is to confront people with literature which is not in standard English and hope that the shock will do some good to them. But on the whole, standard English does prepare one to read more widely in imaginative literature than other forms of English, for the reason that, being the standard, it is the one which gives the maximum scope of grammatical inflection.

Robin Alexander   Professor Scruton, I am interested in this notion of the teaching of the English language for survival, to enable people as pupils and adults to make their way successfully in the world. I wonder if you are saying that pupils will make their way successfully in the modern world solely on the basis of that particular kind of language? Is that so?

Roger Scruton   I think it is very difficult to generalise. The only time when one should generalise is when one is given five minutes in which to summarise one's complete philosophy of language. But I would say that, of course, one is more likely to negotiate one's way through all the many encounters that one has to negotiate one's way through, if one has a grasp of the linguistic expectations by which one is surrounded. Standards emerge; they are not laid down by a central body like the *Academie Française*. They emerge from the attempts of people to communicate with each other and they embody a repeated pattern of success. That is why, if we do not teach them, we cannot be fully sure that we are enabling our students to negotiate their way through the modern world successfully.

Robin Alexander   I am sorry, perhaps I did not make myself clear. You are rightly concerned with access, but is this access to only a particular part of the modern world as you define it – the professions, perhaps? Clearly the business of survival involves a whole range of linguistic contexts and I wonder how you feel about that?

Roger Scruton   Yes, I suppose the purpose of education, if it has a purpose other than keeping children off the streets, is to give access to the professions primarily. After all, other things are better prepared for perhaps out of the classroom. I employ one groom and one secretary. The groom is all the better for having left school early. If only she had been able to leave school when she could and learn what she had to, then she would have been exactly what she wants to be. But if we keep people locked in classrooms until they are sixteen, we ought at least to think of the higher possibilities in the form of employment and also remuneration which might be made available to them by imposing this on them. That is why, of course, we must think of giving them access to those jobs and forms of security which they might otherwise not have obtained.

Anthony Smith   May I say to Roger Scruton that I think he is not being as transgressional as he makes it sound, because I think he is saying, at least in part, what we seemed to agree in session one, which was that all students are entitled (to use the bureaucratic terms of the governmental documents) to a knowledge of standard English, and presumably that teachers are obliged to teach it. There did not seem to be an objection to that. But what I think he is implying is that in order to speak grammatically, one has to have a conscious knowledge of the rather sophisticated terminology of grammar. I wonder whether that is true. Surely standard English, which is the name we give to it, that you want taught, is what is being taught. The difference is that a lot of the members of the teaching profession here (and I bow to their superior knowledge and experience of this), think that it is no longer practical to teach people that there is a thing called the pluperfect subjunctive. That does not mean to say that the students should not learn how to use the pluperfect subjunctive.

Roger Scruton   I tried to make the distinction which you are wisely making at greater length, and I agree that there are two different things that can be taught by way of teaching grammar. First of all, there is the practical skill of speaking correctly according to the standard which teachers can teach without too much difficulty, even in modern conditions; and the second is the theoretical thing that you are referring to, the meditation on the rules of grammar, and the attempts to give some kind of theory of them. That is not something which it is necessarily possible to teach at every level, but I think it is a good thing to teach generally.

My own prejudice, however, is that one should not teach it in relation to one's own language, but rather in relation to a dead language. But the reasons for that I think are difficult for people now to grasp.

But going back to the actual practice, I have formed the habit of correcting my own pupils' usage at university level, and I tell them that, for instance, they are not to split their infinitives. Of course, after a while, they begin to see that not only does it sound better if they do not, but the ambiguities are removed by obeying this rule. I teach them to try and match up verbs with prepositions and with auxiliaries and so on. And on the whole, people do begin to learn. I had a student who submitted an essay which contained the following phrase: 'On the foundations which he built off', and that was a reference to something in Spinoza. Now clearly this student, as I pointed out to him, did not really have a clear conception of what role foundations play in a philosopher's thinking and he did not know whether you built on them, off them, from them, with them, whether they were to be justified at a later stage or whether they were things that were merely assumed. So I introduced him to the wonderful construction 'upon which', and he said: 'That is terrific, I am going to use that in my next essay'.

Marilyn Butler   That is a rather interesting story, because what it describes is a teacher liberating a student into more meaning, and I was wondering why it was that you had not put more emphasis on the liberatory aspects of learning language rather than on prescription and deviance and rules, as though they are the central and most appropriate metaphors, because it seems to me that metaphors are very emotive. I cannot imagine why anyone wants to start from here. It seems to me that the single thing that children are learning all the time when they are learning language is more and more words. To be proficient in the use of language, you have to enrich your knowledge of language, and so the more they experience books and talk and write and listen, the more they are actually using language, the more their ability to mean anything is amplified. It seems to me that this excessive emphasis on observing some invisible standard in which, for instance, the split infinitive is always changing, is just a mistaken emphasis.

Roger Scruton   I would say in reply to that, that while there are rules of grammar, they are, as I said, summaries of existing practice rather than prescriptions. They become prescriptions only in the teaching process, and I agree with what you are implying that they have essentially an historical and evolutionary character. On the other hand, the emphasis that you place on freedom, while it is legitimate, ought to be seen as simply the other side of rule-following. The freedom, for instance, that Beethoven achieved in his style, was made possible by the rules which Haydn and Mozart laid down for him. It is only through rule-guided activity that true creative freedom is obtainable. Of course, it comes sometimes with breaking the rules, but you cannot break rules which do not exist. I think if you look at the greatest creative achievements of our civilisation, you will see this confirmed again and again.

I do not accept what you are saying about children, that they are constantly learning new words through using their language. It depends how they are using it and with whom. Children who are spending their time shouting abuse at each other in the playground may be actually effectively narrowing their vocabulary down to those few street-wise expressions that enable one to get through to the other end without one's head being knocked off. There are so many different ways of employing language, and like any aspect of physical exercise, you can be both enhancing your freedom or diminishing it.

Mary Warnock I would now like to call our second witness, who is Colin MacCabe. He is Head of the British Film Institute Research and Education Division. He was formerly Head of British Film Institute Production and he was Professor of English at Strathclyde University in the early 1980s.

Colin MacCabe The history of English as language, as literature, as education, is a continuous debate about what shall or shall not count as English. This debate has never been limited to the universities or schools. It has always been peculiarly linked to notions of the nation. When Sidney wrote the 'Apology for Poetry', he concluded his general defence of the art with a specific question as to why there was such a dearth of English poetry, a question which he felt was central to questions of national identity and value.

I want to suggest that this constitutive crisis has reached a new stage, and that in many ways we have to go back to the Renaissance, to Sidney and his immediate aftermath, to realise how profound are the problems we are currently confronting. It is not simply that our national identity has been transformed, but our cultural identity as well. For Sidney, to be English was to be white, Anglo-Saxon and Protestant, and, if not male, than at least totally defined by one's legal relationships to masculine relatives. It may be that this notion of the English was always fictional, but it was a fiction which remained plausible as recently as the end of the Second World War. Indeed, much of the heat and anger generated by the current debates is that for many, any attempt to question this identity is deeply resented.

But the matter is further complicated by a change which may be as fundamental. There is no doubt that, for Sidney, to be cultured is to be lettered – a definition which covers not simply our functional notion of literacy but a familiarity with classical literature. The dominance of the written, obvious already in Sidney, is accentuated in the period after his death as printing makes more and more books available to more and more readers. However, this dominance of the printed word, which continues right up to this century with the growth of mass circulation newspapers, is also challenged in this century by the extraordinary growth of film, radio, television and recorded music. For 400 years in the West, writing was the fundamental medium for both information and entertainment. If film and radio challenged this dominance, television displaced it.

English thus finds itself confronting two challenges. On the one hand, it must re-define its content to address the fact that insofar as it is concerned with the transmission of the national culture, the nation of today is not the same as the nation of the past. At the same time, the very means of transmission have been altered. It is my argument that in the long run these questions cannot be divorced and that it is impossible to solve the questions of national identity without widening the reference to cultural forms.

When the British Minister for Education reforms the English curriculum so as to give more weight to traditional literature, he justifies his decision with the comment that a good English curriculum, 'can provide pupils from whatever background with a key to an extensive and exciting range of literature which challenges the imagination far beyond anything' – he should perhaps have a lesson with Roger! – 'offered by television, films and video'. He thus automatically opposes literature to the moving image in a way which simply ignores the history of twentieth-century culture in which there is a constant interchange between the two.

From James Joyce's opening of the first cinema in Dublin in 1912 to Salman Rushdie's meditation on the forms of media in *The Satanic Verses,* the history of literature in the 20th century is inseparable from the history of the mass media. Even if one were to allow a certain imaginative primacy to literature (which in fact I would do, but that is a much longer argument) that is no justification for suggesting curricula which sponsor the study of literature independently of the study of the other media. Indeed it is my argument that literature now must be studied with those other media in order to realise its full potential, and that it is these media which are an essential element in any real attempt to make the classic literary heritage available within our education system.

The simple fact is that most of the literary tradition is simply unavailable to most children. The knowledge of Christianity in the Authorised Version assumed by most literature up to D. H. Lawrence, and the familiarity with classical myth which is essential to reading pre-Romantic literature, are esoteric knowledge for the vast majority of contemporary children. Even more serious, however, is the fact that the language of even nineteenth-century literature is fantastically difficult for most contemporary speakers of English. The development in radio, television and recorded sound of what Walter J. Ong called 'secondary orality' has led to a simplification of sentence structure which means that any kind of periodic sentence presents difficulties of comprehension. If we look in some detail at past education history, we will find that the numbers who achieved a real engagement with the literary tradition were always small. However, it is now infinitesimal.

At this point, one can turn to the contemporary media as part of the solution, rather than as part of the problem. This solution consists of two very different elements and two very different arguments which should not be confused, although both lead to the conclusion that literature should now be taught in the context of media studies.

The first argument is that the media can provide the general concepts with which children can approach the literary tradition which is now close to unreadable in its own terms. In collaboration with a large number of pupils and teachers, the British Film Institute has produced a *Primary Media Education Curriculum Statement*[1]. It expects all children aged eleven to be able to understand the following categories: media agencies – who is communicating and why; media categories – what type of text is this; media languages – how do we know what it means; media audiences – who receives it and what sense do they make of it; and media representation – what is the relation between text and reality. These concepts are reasonably graspable by children from their own vast knowledge of film and television. They provide a series of questions that children can ask of any literary text and begin to place it within a comprehensible context.

Second (and this is a very separate argument), the media can provide the first access to the literary text in the form of an adaptation. Anyone who has taught an undergraduate introductory Renaissance course including *Edward II* and *Henry IV, Parts I and II*, and then taught the same course using Derek Jarman's film of the Marlowe play, Gus Van Sant's *My Own Private Idaho* and Orson Welles' *Chimes at Midnight*, will know that the experience is transformative. It is not simply that the films stimulate an interest in the texts which the texts by themselves cannot, but they also allow the class to regard the texts as material that can be worked on rather than as cultural monuments unapproachable in their seamless and incomprehensible unity.

We have been asked as witnesses to address the question of whether English can unite a fractured society. I doubt whether any academic subject can promise such wholesale social engineering. I do think, however, that the study of English in schools and universities must be the crucial space in which we forge a connection with our cultural past. The technological and social changes of this last century make any simple repetition of the past as impossible as it is undesirable. It is, however, crucial that we continue to seek what is valuable in our cultural heritage. This search is not simple. Shakespeare has, as always, been mentioned today in terms of glowing approval. Yet Shakespeare's theatre was located just along the river from here, next to the Bear Pit and just outside the gates on which the bleeding bodies of heretics were regularly displayed as witness to the piety of Elizabethan England. I do not suggest for a moment that Shakespeare is thus to be dismissed. I worship him this side of idolatry as I do Ben Jonson. But one of the questions we have to ask of his texts is how the violence of that society is inscribed in them so that we may understand how it is still inscribed in us.

There is no possibility of an optimistic view of a developing future culture which is in active relation with the past. English is the crucial institutional site of this relation. It is for that reason that debates about it are so bitter, and why agreement will always be provisional.

Alan Howarth   You told us that the concept of nation-hood, as typically held in this country up to the Second World War is no longer valid, and that insularity is no longer an option. Is it not something of an irony, when just at this moment, as more and more of us are recognising this, we introduce something called a National Curriculum? What is this National Curriculum? Is it an exercise in nostalgia? Is it a fertilisation of the ground for a more unpleasant nationalism of the kind that we see threatening us in Europe? Or is it simply a product of inertia and idleness on the part of the English Establishment which is having difficulty in adapting itself to modern necessities? Does it make sense to have a National Curriculum in the new world that you have described to us, a world in which we can no longer think of ourselves as compartmentalised in an especially privileged English culture? And is it not a curiosity that in this world in which the media are changing the technology of our culture as radically as print did in that first Renaissance that you mentioned, that we should introduce a National Curriculum that contains such a very small element of media studies?

Colin MacCabe   You have asked me many questions, but let me try and answer them in some sort of order. I think that there is no doubt that the reason that we have a National Curriculum now, and a reason why a National Curriculum has been suggested at this moment, is exactly because the ending of that automatic sense of what England was as a nation is now very fully realised. But that then leaves the National Curriculum very wide open for a variety of possibilities. One would be simply as a method of ensuring that that identity which was felt to be threatened in various ways would simply be re-asserted within that curriculum, and that we would simply define Englishness in a traditional way through that curriculum.

Another way of looking at the National Curriculum would be exactly as a continuously provisional area in which the relation to past definitions of Englishness and future ones were to be, as it were, thought out, debated and discussed. It is my belief that it is that second sense that one is talking about, though it has to be said that if one is talking in those terms, one must realise what one is assenting to. Norman Tebbit made some very unpleasant, nasty and small-minded remarks some years ago about the problem with all these new immigrants being that they did not cheer England in the cricket matches and therefore were not properly English. Apart from the kind of phenomenal ignorance which ignores the extent which, for most Scottish, Welsh and Northern Irish people, the defeat of England at any sporting event is one of the great pleasures of life, it seems to me that behind that very small-minded and inaccurate description was the articulation of something which, in accepting a National Curriculum, one is accepting quite strongly; and that is that there is some way in which there is a central set of knowledges, skills and beliefs to which one must have some relation in order to really count as a full member of the society. In that sense, I think that the debate

59

about the National Curriculum is one of the crucial debates that we are engaged in as a society at the moment.

Then if I could come to your final point about media studies on the National Curriculum, it is for that reason that it seems to me so alarming that the media had such a small part within the National Curriculum as first set out and why it is so distressing that even that small part is, according to certain statements, to be reduced even further. Because it seems to me that if we look at the National Curriculum as one of the central areas in which we will define our communality, if it does not include the media, then the other element of our communality which might exactly be examined there has been left out of the equation.

Alan Howarth   Culture certainly is evolving strikingly fast. Some would say that your concept of a continuously provisional culture is itself a contradiction in terms, and at all events, at a rather practical level, that is indeed what it has been, and it has been a very difficult thing for teachers to handle.

Colin MacCabe   When I say it is continuously provisional, I do not mean by that that one wants to be changing the specific contents of it at every moment. Certainly in relation to English (I am not talking necessarily in relation to other subjects, though it would apply to some) what one wants to frame, it seems to me, is a subject in which exactly this debate with the past can be most usefully, properly and fruitfully articulated. That is the sense in which I mean 'provisional'. I do not mean you are changing the regulations every year, though it seems to me evident that every generation, let us say, may well choose to take a substantial look at such details. But what I am saying is that the curriculum itself should be designed to harness and locate these kinds of arguments and relations.

Marilyn Butler   You have given us an alternative model, in effect, to the curriculum in the Cox report and in its modified version since, which would obviously represent a very strong shift in the direction of media. As I understand it, you are suggesting that literature should preferably be approached or framed by media, through representations, say, in the media, and that language should take as its basic model – and I think this is the most radical thing I heard you say – the secondary orality of the spoken word in radio or television speech which gives a very simplified sentence structure. That is obviously a very radical proposition in general, and I wonder whether you think that anything would be lost if, in fact, the elaborations or complications of the written language for certain purposes were no longer a staple part of the education system?

Colin MacCabe   Yes, you have actually mistaken me. I am wanting to correct Cox but only in relation to the rather small part given to literature. If you look at what it says about language, what you have is a rather radical and well-informed version of nationalism in which there is an argument for variety but there is an argument for a standard very strongly put. I think why there is so little said about literature in the Cox report is that you cannot make the same argument about literature, because if you make it all the way through, you end up defining what everybody would have as a national standard at an impossibly high level. It becomes very clear that the vast majority of the population will not have this access to literature.

So I am making a very radical supplement to the Cox report on literature, but I am not actually disagreeing with it upon language. What I am saying about secondary orality is not to say that that is how we should base the teaching of reading and writing in our schools. What I am saying is that one of the problems we have to face up to is that the audiovisual media are now the dominant mode of the reproduction of speech and writing outside the schools, and that the schools are, in a sense, having to address a new linguistic situation in which giving to students the kind of power and command over language which Roger Scruton indicated is ever more necessary, but actually is probably considerably more difficult than it was.

Anthony Smith   It seems that there are two separate operations at work in what you are is saying. There is the stuff about the debate with the past, the reconstruction and notions of nationality (or of our nationality in particular), and then there is the material connected with the secondary orality. I do not think you have proved the link between the necessary mutual dependence of those two operations. It seems to me, that given that secondary orality is a dominant within our culture at the present time, or certainly among young people, we have to find some way of working through that material in order to get back to the texts, which provide the material for the debate with the past.

Colin MacCabe   Yes.

Anthony Smith   Now there is an obvious difficulty in doing that. Presumably what we used to get, perhaps in a mythical golden age, was that we absorbed from texts all the echoes that gave us a sense of our national identity. The echoes come very easily to our consciousness from the new media. They are planted there all the time. We have a vast area of common illusion, very effectively delivered.

Colin MacCabe   Yes.

Anthony Smith   I think that in order to achieve what you really want to achieve, you need, to some extent, to use the opposite means. You are saying that we have somehow got to get back to the texts, renew them, enrich student's understanding of them, and simply use the secondary orality as a starting point for doing that.

Colin MacCabe   I think that is what I am trying to argue. You are right in saying there is a kind of hole in the two parts of my argument. On the one hand, there is the essential relation to the past, and on the other hand, the new technology. It is through the technology that, for the first time, the vast majority of the population can be offered a way back to texts which at no point in the golden past were ever the property of the majority of the population. So one might actually be able to have a situation in which it was not unreasonable to think that the whole of the population had some relation to this past. But that would exactly be a move through media texts. I was talking previously on the radio with a teacher in Leeds who was discussing how her class were reading *Jane Eyre* and using various other film and BBC television adaptations, and of course what her pupils were coming back to was how many more possibilities and richnesses there were within the literary texts than in any of the particular visual representations or adaptations that have been worked on it. Now that seems to me to be the central kind of activity which I would like to think was going on in classrooms up and down the country, and that is where I would try and join the two things together. It is exactly that the path back to the text and the differences in the texts may be, paradoxically for the first time, easier through these popular forms that the new technologies have delivered. I am not certain about this, and I cannot pretend that there is enough evidence or practice or knowledge for me to say this is true, but it seems to me that this is something which we should learn and know a lot more about.

Robin Alexander   Perhaps I could start with an observation. I noted with interest your reference to primary education. It seems to me that that is the first attempt we have had so far in this Commission to break away from a kind of monolithic and generalised view of the English curriculum which I suspect is pitched somewhere at thirteen to sixteen-year-olds. I cannot necessarily ask you a direct question about that, but I hope that the audience will pick up that issue during our time here. We are inquiring into the education of children between rising five and sixteen at this Commission.

My question is to refer you back to the question of the session's title: can English unite a fractured society? I wonder whether English in schools sometimes takes too much to itself. We recall – it is a bit of a caricature – the saying: 'Never mind life, read a nineteenth-century novel'. Is there not a question begged by this session? Is uniting a fractured society really the task of English in a school curriculum – or only of English?

Colin MacCabe   I responded to that question when I said that I doubt whether any academic study can propose such wholesale social engineering, so in that sense, I think the question is a bit over-ambitious. At the same time, without promising to unite a fractured society, one can say that one of the things a society needs to be called such, is to have not a unified relation to a past but some kind of commonality about what the past is. It is very difficult, it seems to me, to talk about any notion of identity without a notion of memory, and if you think institutionally, within formal institutions, English as a subject is exactly the place that marks that process of memory and identity.

Robin Alexander   The observation I made and the question I asked are actually in a way not disconnected. What I am getting at is that sooner or later in this Commission we are going to have to talk in more detail about the translation of a generalised view of English into the specific stages in compulsory education, and also, of course, the relationship of English to other subjects and we have done neither of those things so far.

Mary Warnock   Our third witness in this session is John Hickman. He is Head of English at Forest Gate Community School in London, and he is Chairman of the Language and Learning Committee within that school.

John Hickman   I suppose I am the performing classroom teacher this afternoon, so those of you in the audience who know what I am going to say will have to bear with me if it seems fairly self-evident. Questions like 'Whose English?' tend to relate, as has been explicit so far, to two very general areas. One is language, with particular issues relating to standard English. The other is literature, with its links to culture, heritage, national identity.

To echo something that a couple of speakers have said, over the past few years the parameters of the debate seem to have been set by people who have very little knowledge of what I understand to be the real schools. Indeed, the educational establishment, whatever that might mean (and I suppose I am part of it), has been deliberately excluded from much educational policy-making. That was outlined very well by the speakers here.

So what has been ignored over the last ten years? I think the nature of real schools has been ignored. I think the diversity of our school population has, on the whole, been ignored. There have been some token gestures towards an acknowledgment, but on the whole, I feel it has been ignored. And perhaps fundamentally, something that is very rarely approached in the higher echelons of the education debate, is the issue of how learning takes place most effectively. If we are looking at a real school – take mine as an example; you will have your own images of it – my idea of a real school could be summarised by a piece of paper – my school's language survey of last year. If you were to look at that, you would see that in my school there are fifty languages that are understood. You would see that out of 871 students, 628 are bilingual or multilingual; 102 students have almost no English; 156 students have a certain amount of English, though not really enough for total access to the curriculum; 289 students have access to the curriculum but still are in need of help and support with their English. To help those 600-odd students, we have three and a half members of staff in an explicit ESL (English as a Second Language) capacity. After the Section 11 cuts that John Richmond mentioned, it may well be that we are reduced to two and a half teachers, and if the reductions in the budget occur as a result of shifting finances from the inner cities to the shires, then it may well be that we have no support at all for those 600 students.

That is one aspect of the school. Another aspect of the school is its diversity, as I have said. It appears that certain people who are in a position to affect the lives of teachers and school students believe that classrooms are made up of homogeneous groups of students who sit in rows, are at the same developmental stage of learning and have similar backgrounds and interests and expectations. All the classroom teachers sitting in front of me will realise that the reality is very different.

Let me offer you a thumb-nail sketch of my last year's, year 11 class (ages

63

fifteen to sixteen). Ten languages were spoken. Five boys who had been in the country for about six months at the start of year 11 had almost no English. There were four others with a limited amount of English. Three of the girls had enormous domestic responsibilities: cooking, cleaning and washing for large families when they got home in the evening. One girl had come to school with no English five years previously. She worked for two hours after school, three times a week, because she could not go home because of the responsibilities there, and she eventually achieved a B grade at GCSE. One boy was arrested half-way through the year for stealing cars and was never seen again. One boy was transferred from another school half-way through the year because of violent behaviour. One girl whose sister had just won a scholarship to Oxford (and totally coincidentally that was the girl you saw earlier on today on the screen) was suffering in comparison to the sister. One girl was preparing to go to Pakistan at the end of the year to marry a person she had never met. One boy wandered around listening to Mozart on his personal stereo, reading E M Forster and proclaiming that he was going to be the next Labour prime minister of England.

I have only offered you a thumb-nail sketch of eighteen of them. There are twelve others that I could offer, but time does not allow. We followed a 100 per cent course work exam and the future prime minister boy gained an AA. The five boys who came with no English gained a GG each and most of you in the audience will recognise that the GGs were far more of an achievement than the AA. The fact is that in the present system those boys would not be entered for an exam.

What we have, as with so many of your classes and so many of the classes in British schools and certainly the inner cities, is a group that is linguistically and culturally diverse. It encompasses a vast range of behaviour, a large spectrum of concerns and interests and an array of different talents. That diversity is often overlooked. In that context, the question of 'Whose English?' becomes rather more problematic. How is it best to approach the issue of standard English and cultural heritage? I think that here we lead naturally into the question of how learning takes place most effectively. Again, I am reading things into the minds of certain people who have made decisions that have affected us all over the last years, but I think that the model of the learner that many people in positions of political power seem to have is that the learner is an empty vessel that the teacher fills with knowledge and understanding. So I suppose, to take that to its extreme, you would fill up both legs with standard English, fill up the torso with Shakespeare, fill up the arms with some pre-twentieth-century poetry, top it up with Austen and Hardy, put the lid on and the learners go off into the world to become – what? Advisers, I suppose.

That view of learning has an assumption that learning is linear; it is like climbing a ladder. Most of us understand that learning is rather more like climbing a tree. You may go up one branch and explore that, and then you may have to go back up to the middle to reach to another bit. You may leap from one branch to another. But it is rather more complex than climbing a ladder. That view of learning also presumes that learners are passive, compliant and of similar backgrounds and interests and abilities. Going back to my thumb-nail sketch of my year 11 class, I think that is patently not the case.

Of course English teachers are concerned about issues related to standard English and to the canon of English literature. To deny the importance of both or either would be limiting and patronising. But the key to exploration and understanding is very complex and does not reside in the systematic correction of playground grammar or in examining fourteen-year-olds on Shakespeare texts. To suggest that my year 11 students came to my class as empty vessels would be an insult to their experience and their different types of expertise.

We have to be aware that in all learning contexts, the teacher has to begin at the place where the students are. That is a fundamental tenet of education. Their language and interests are the foundation upon which all development and all new understandings are built. Their language and culture has to be validated in order that the proper trust can be established, so that horizons can be broadened. No one would ever suggest that we leave kids where they are. We are in the business of broadening horizons, but we have to make certain that their lives are validated before we move on.

So in the typical English classroom, many of the tasks are individually negotiated with parameters set by the teacher. In my year 11 class, we were concerned with a wide range of texts in a wide variety of forms. I wanted them to have access to the great traditions of literature. I also wanted them to examine film texts, to analyse the language and imagery of adverts, and there was also a scheme of work which had at its core accent, dialect and standard English.

Throughout the course it was established that in their formal writing standard English was a primary consideration, although it was made clear that things like drafting and note taking could take different forms. With regard to talk, it is self-evident that form and style are dependent on purpose, context and audience. With sensitive handling, students develop a finely-tuned understanding of appropriateness and are skilled in moving between a variety of registers according to where they are and who they are with. I do not speak like this when I am in the bar with my friends and I think kids actually quite understand that. For different audiences, you might perform differently.

In conclusion, if we want our students to understand the complexities of our society and to engage in a constructive dialogue about the world in which they live, we cannot ask them to leave their language, their experience and their culture on the doorsteps of our schools. That was a phrase first coined by the Bullock Report in 1975-76. If we allow the ignorant pronouncements of government advisers to go unchallenged, we are in danger of producing a generation of young people whose own language has been devalued, whose self-esteem has been damaged and whose learning has been positively impeded – if something can indeed be positively impeded. If we attempt to funnel the richness and diversity of our classrooms into an inflexible, mono-cultural curriculum framed in a rigid adherence to standard English at all times and for all purposes, we deny everything we know about the way people learn and we should at best marginalise and at worst destroy the voices of our students. Those voices demand attention both in our classrooms and here today. I would hope that in discussing the question, 'Whose English?' this Commission is the beginning of a process that will ensure that these voices finally get heard.

Alan Howarth   Mr Hickman, I suspect that you were caricaturing the debate, no doubt deliberately. I do not recognise this polarised situation that you were presenting to us. It is suggested, on the one hand, that there are proper teachers like yourself and your colleagues in your school who are engaged in enabling children from an immense diversity of backgrounds to have access to the opportunities they need to realise their full personal potential both as individuals and as members of society. On the other hand, you posit an attempt by Mephistophelian government advisers to impose an entirely different model of teaching on the schools – a model that was satirised by Dickens in *Hard Times* with his little pitchers – the image of children who are simply there as receptacles to receive the information and the learning that their elders and a rather oppressive society think appropriate for them. I simply do not see things that way. Are you seriously saying to us that the National Curriculum, as we have it, or even as it has been proposed that it should be modified, would require you and your colleagues to abandon what you really think are proper teaching practices and go over to treating your pupils as empty vessels?

John Hickman   I think that the way in which I have characterised this is an honest appraisal of what teachers perceive to have happened, not from the point of view of what has happened with the National Curriculum, but what is being generated by those very government advisers that you just talked about. I think that John Richmond did a much better job than I can do of outlining what has happened over the years and the sort of headlines that have been grabbed by people who I think would quite like us to move back into that form of teaching. However, you may suggest that I am misrepresenting that, I think that over the years teachers have come to that conclusion. I think that what has happened is that with Brian Cox's Working Party and the National Curriculum as it stood, English teachers got together with other people, for instance like Brian Cox, and worked out the best possible way forward using that as a very positive framework. What is likely to happen, if we are not very careful, given the demise of 100 per cent course work, given the new curriculum, is that we are danger of moving away from the good practice that was established with the help of the Cox report, with the help of the National Curriculum as it stood, and with the help of people like John Richmond and the LINC project.

Marilyn Butler   I would have asked the same question, in fact, and I suppose a follow-up could be, if it is not 100 per cent course work, is there a compromise that you think could be worked that would save course work? I assume that to go back to 100 per cent course work is politically impossible but can you imagine some sort of negotiated settlement?

John Hickman   I think again John Richmond outlined a very positive model this morning. I think also that people who have made pronouncements about 100 per cent course work, Mr Major included, have not been fully aware of what course work really is and the various processes that are gone through. There have been headlines about teachers being able to cheat or students being able to cheat, which is just not possible with properly moderated teacher course work. I would suggest that given the National Curriculum as it stands at the moment, given the old 100 per cent course work syllabuses which outlined the sort of requirements and the entitlements of students, we could still work towards a system whereby there was a large proportion of course work with, as often happened in the past, certain times during the year when controlled pieces were undertaken. With proper levels of moderation, that can happen. I could just spend a bit of time outlining, to people who do not know, what a properly moderated course work exam would look like. What happens at my school and in a number of other schools is that as a head of department, I would look at all the scripts of a fifth year – every single folder – after they have been looked at by their classroom teacher. So there would have been the classroom teacher looking at the scripts, then I would have looked at them, then my second in department would have looked at them. If there had been any worry about agreement, we would have offered them to a fourth person. With the Northern Examining Association (NEA) regulations, those scripts may have gone to a fourth person in Leeds. They would all have gone to another person or two people on the panel in Manchester. So by the time a grade was offered, it could well have been that eight people would have moderated each course work folder. Then included in every folder there would have been at least one piece of controlled work, carried out in class, as a moderating factor. I see nothing wrong with that, and I have not yet given up on the fact that we could return to 100 per cent course work, because that is by far the best possible and most effective and most efficient and most fair form of moderation, and one which we cannot abandon now because of the political climate.

Robin Alexander   I would like to ask a practical question. You have argued that if we want our students to understand the complexities of our society we cannot ask them to leave their language, their experience and their culture on the doorsteps of our schools, and it seems to me that that is something which could be argued for the whole of education and not just for English. However, my question is this. How, as a matter of practical classroom strategy, do you use this diversity of experiences and languages in your teaching?

John Hickman   To go back to the unit of work that we did last year on language, accent, dialect and standard English, obviously we watched a number of videos which were generated by the LINC project dealing with those issues. We discussed language histories. One of the options at the end of the piece of work was a language history where students were asked to outline how their languages had developed, if they were bi or multilingual. We also look at the way language may well differ according to different circumstances. For instance, the bilingual students were asked to discuss with each other the different ways in which they used different languages in different contexts; what languages they use at home, with their grandmother, their brothers, their sisters. Ultimately, we would have brought in the experiences in the language of each child to discuss the variables related to language and language use, which would then lead to a piece of course work at the end. It was a six-week module.

Anthony Smith I thought Mr Hickman's account of the multi-ethnic classroom was so alarming that it made me wonder whether English was, after all, the appropriate vehicle for resolving some of those problems. All sorts of other actions clearly need to be taken and resources and facilities made available way beyond our topic of today. Clearly what he is saying is irreconcilable with the Roger Scruton set of priorities. I am wondering what it is he feels his classroom actually needs to solve the problems that he described. It is clearly not the National Curriculum – or certainly not on day one. But what is it? What is the nature of the resource that can cope with the problems of a forty-language classroom?

John Hickman I think there is a danger of being superficial if one immediately resorts to talking about resources when that sort of question is asked. But the fact is, more resources in terms of staff and books are essential. As I say, I feel very fortunate in my school at the moment if there is a support teacher in the classroom with me, and that is what is essential, for another member of staff to be helping us.

I think another layer which we are very bad at getting hold of is the classroom teacher who is himself or herself bilingual or multilingual. We do not have enough people who speak Gujurati, Punjabi, Bengali in the classrooms to help with translations and with pushing students on. I think we also need many more texts in other languages, and certainly I would think people from other curriculum areas would be saying that louder than perhaps English teachers. We need staff, and – to push it even further – we need much smaller classes, which is another cry from a number of bodies.

Alan Howarth May I just come in here? So you are not really talking about the teaching of English. You are talking about a completely different set of social and pedagogical problems?

John Hickman Everything I have just said relates to the teaching of English in my classroom. If I had more support teachers, more resources, more works of literature in other languages as a beginning for some of those students, if I had more dual language texts available, my life would be easier, yes.

Mary Warnock Our last witness is Professor Stuart Hall. He is Professor of Sociology at the Open University, and a very well-known writer and academic whose speciality is cultural studies. He writes and broadcasts on all kinds of issues of ethnic and cultural identity.

Stuart Hall Many of the points that I would want to make have already been touched on, and I suspect have been touched on already when I was not able to be present, so I will try to be as brief as I can and go on to the questioning.

It seems to me, just to pick up Anthony Smith's last question, that one of the reasons why these issues come to rest so definitively in the area of English is because they are centrally related to aspects of language and literature. Although, of course, the problems that were just identified spill out across the curriculum as a whole, I think it is not just by chance that it is where language and literature are taught that these deep questions of cultural identity and of identification and of competence in the cultural languages in which people are placed arise and have to be dealt with.

In some ways English literature and language teaching over the last decade has been the repository for collecting together from one decade to another all sorts of problems that belong to the curriculum in general but seem to come to rest somewhere around language. After all, the introduction of film and television and media studies generally into the curriculum at all first happened only in classes formally declared to be about language and literature. I think there are good reasons why that should be so, and I certainly think that the teaching of English language and literature is, as has been established in many contributions so far, absolutely central to questions of cultural identity and cultural belongingness and cultural authority. It is impossible to divorce them from it. That was certainly the case with the National Curriculum.

I do not want to ascribe motives of one kind or another to the people who have been involved in establishing the parameters within which the National Curriculum for English teaching has evolved. However, I certainly think that the reason why the teaching of language and literature, like the teaching of history, provided a kind of key fulcrum to the debates around the National Curriculum, and why this was the moment historically in which the National Curriculum was put on the educational agenda, does have something to do with a particular crisis around the question of who is British, who is English, what does 'Englishness' mean, how are the traditions of English cultural belongingness carried and transmitted in the classroom? What does students' increased access to speaking and writing in the varieties of English and their acquaintance with the varieties of English literary texts have to do with shifting and negotiating problems of cultural identity now?

Once you link the teaching of language and the teaching of literature to the questions of cultural authority, you are inevitably confronted with problems about cultural power. Power is a nasty word in the classroom and a nasty word in educational debates. But there are questions given to teachers in classrooms right around the country at this moment, which are inevitably questions about cultural authority. These are questions about how one can, as it were, produce Englishness in the 21st century, and how the varieties of people who are now occupying school places in this society can come to feel some kind of connectedness or belongingness to the culture.

We sometimes confront the situation that has just been eloquently described, which I think must be very familiar to many teachers who are here, as if it is a passing phenomenon. I want to make the case that there are very good reasons, which I cannot go into in detail at this point, why it seems to me that we are talking about the end of a whole epoch. Globalisation is a nasty term, but it is a simple way of gathering together under one horrible word all the forces which make it impossible now for national cultures to produce and reproduce themselves in a key way through a variety of cultural institutions of which the school must be one of the primary ones. It is impossible for those cultures to insulate themselves from the play and influences and presences deep in the heart of other cultures. That is partly because we have simply moved into a phase of cultural, economic, political and social interdependence which does not permit cultures any longer to establish their authority around a homogeneous conception of who they are, what they are and who belongs to them.

English is a world language in which vast numbers of transactions of one kind or another are being made around the globe by people who do not have an organic, natural or genetic connection to Englishness. But it is also – to introduce another nasty term – the language of empire. Because it has been the language of empire, great varieties of experiences across the globe are now inevitably condensed into English. Partly because the spread of English as a language of empire had the effect of subjugating some varieties of other languages, inevitably now the experiences of negotiating forms of life will be conducted in English, in relation to English, in relation to the varieties and displacements that go on in English. On the one hand, that is confronting teachers with an enormous problem. On the other hand, it is, in my view, what continues to make English as a world language the most vigorous and creative medium in which expression is taking place.

Of course I recognise all the difficulties and problems that that presents for designing an effective mode of teaching, strategy and curriculum. Nevertheless I want to say what an enormous opportunity it provides. The negotiations of past and future and present for varieties of peoples who do not have a kind of natural indigenous historical belongingness to something called Englishness, is nevertheless going to happen in English, in some variety of English, and it is going to happen in some relationship to texts which are written in English and the English literature tradition itself. It may be that that relationship is often one of contestation, of decentering, of displacement, and the varieties of experience are going to be harshly expressed. But nevertheless that is what maintains English and its promise as a massively creative medium of expression and writing and speaking.

One of the tasks which the National Curriculum did not address is how to communicate to students at all levels within our education system the possibilities of literary and linguistic pluralism as a stake or a wager for people in the future. What I mean by that is, of course, not to deny the access which children must have to standard English; I did not hear the previous discussion, but if that is the conclusion that seemed to arise, I would certainly agree with it, but perhaps for a

70

rather different reason. It is not for the reason that this is, as it were, the standard to which they ought to adhere, but partly because this is the language in which the key negotiations that affect their lives are going to be conducted. They have an instrumental relation to the demand to have access to standard English in terms of the power which those who have such access have upon their own lives. In order for them to negotiate their way through those situations, they need access to standard English. That is the first reason.

Secondly, of course it opens the range of texts and experiences to which they can have access. But just as access to standard versions of the language and indeed of the classic literary tradition is one of the rights of children in education, so it seems to me that we ought to establish a second right at this moment, and that is precisely an access to some understanding of the varieties of English that are likely to be spoken and written, of a valorisation of the experiences which will appear outside of the traditional literary canon, of the different varieties of media in which those expressions are likely to take place. This is as important an access to, as it were, a cultural resource for the future of young people as the access to the literary texts which have formed and shaped us.

That is to say, I make the claim for cultural relativism and for a kind of literary pluralism, not as the best that we can do in bad circumstances but as a positive thing. I make it here not as it is usually made in the name of multi-culturalism – of my own kids and kids like me, of the large numbers of people whose whole history has been formed in the imperial shadow of English as a spoken and written language and of literary tradition, whose future belongs in this society – I make it not in the name of what those people need to survive. I make it in the name of what I think little English boys and girls need to survive. I think they are the people who need to know the varieties of non-English experience which are now being written about and spoken about in varieties of English. I think they need to know that English is a decentred world language. They will hear things in English which do not flow naturally out of their indigenous culture, that will reflect varieties of different experiences. That encounter with difference in language, in English, is as valid and important a task for English to perform as the transmission of an inherited literary culture. If you ask what cultural lesson they might learn from it, it seems to me the most important lesson which young English boys and girls can learn at the beginning of the 21st century is that eating people is wrong!

Alan Howarth Professor Hall, we saw in the video that opened the session a wonderful class taking place, I think under the aegis of the English National Curriculum – at least I assume so – and, if I am not mistaken, taking place in John Hickman's school at Forest Gate. I want to say how impressed I was and I thought it was an exciting experience watching other people enjoying that exciting experience. There they were, all using English in common, engaged in an impassioned enquiry into social norms and a quest to find norms that they could all share, though they perhaps had a long way to go. Arranged marriage in the story they were discussing was associated with a slap in the face, but I suspect that it would be another metaphorical slap in the face if they were to proceed very far in attempting to assimilate and arrive at the kind of common cultural identity and cultural belonging of which you spoke, because after all, we have no norms in modern Britain, and that is seen very poignantly in the institution of marriage. In short, is not this quest of which you spoke, and I think you held this up as being very much a central virtue of what English teaching and English learning was about, this quest to find a shared cultural identity of belonging, in fact a pursuit of a chimera? Could you help us, at any rate, to balance your twin advocacies of authority and pluralism?

Stuart Hall To take the first part of the question first, which is the question about whether I think that English can provide the arena in which a set of norms are defined which could unite a fractured society, to use that expression, that was not what I was suggesting. What I was suggesting was when people try to negotiate common forms of life without letting go of variety and difference, that is precisely the terrain which has to be negotiated. It seems to me that no society can hold together as a politically and socially-functioning entity without some negotiation of what is to be respected and reflected in common. But the arena of what that is and how widely it is to be interpreted is, it seems to me, inevitably now a result of a long and probably almost certainly unfinished process of negotiation. Now all that I am saying is that it is that process of negotiation which seems to me to be the task especially, on the one hand, of language and literature, and secondly of history. I know history is not our topic but I happen to think that the debates that have gone on in and around the National Curriculum in relation to history are very closely related to those which have gone on in relation to English, and fortunately the same opening up of the agenda has been achieved in both areas.

I was not arguing in favour of using the site of language and literature teaching as a place to define cultural authority. What I have suggested is that literary texts and the question of standard English have been too long caught up with the attempt to enforce a rather homogenous set of norms and with the exercise of cultural authority. It is precisely divesting the involvement in language and literature from the imposition of that notion of cultural authority that makes it a living space. We ought to welcome the possibilities, while recognising all the difficulties of conducting it. But I think the class we saw on the video shows it can be done. In vernaculars which are not, of course, standard, in varieties in which already you can clearly hear the varieties of other spoken languages inflecting, you can nevertheless see as the unfinished business of these negotiations the seriousness with which questions of norms, questions of relationship, questions of family authority are being spoken to in that classroom. The issue is whether cultural authority can be secured through the curriculum which is exactly that linkage which I am trying to open up and to review.

Anthony Smith Surely the question of the negotiations of cultural difference are first confronted in the area of religion and in forms of family authority and always have been. Right through generations of imperial life in this country, that has always been the case and it has always produced a double community membership. After all, Isaiah Berlin speaks English as a second language. You find it in every area of British life going back for generations. I think the difference today seems to be obviously at one level with the extent of it, but at another level with the fact that it is being confronted in a different way. There is a suggestion that because we are living with this intense experience of multi-culturalism, particularly among the young, we should somehow abandon notions of centrality. I know Stuart Hall is not saying that, but I think he is burying the answer in this concept of permanent negotiation of the status of each child and each community. After all, Roger Scruton began the afternoon with a very strident statement with which some of us felt uncomfortable but we also perhaps felt there was a lot of truth in it that we had to confront. There is actually only one way in linking with this society and coping with its problems, which is to learn standard English in a pretty sophisticated way, which does impose on teachers and pupils a lot of problems. But it would seem that what for the Isaiah Berlin generation was the answer to the problem, you are suggesting – or perhaps I am wrong in interpreting you as suggesting – is simply a continuation of the problem.

Stuart Hall   If what you mean by centrality is that there is only one way of negotiating with the culture, then I have to say I do not agree with that. I do not think it actually describes the situation. I do not think any of us only negotiates with this culture, as it were, symbolically in our standard English. We all negotiate with it in a variety of ways already. I gave the concession to you about the indispensability of standard English, not because it is the norm but because it is the arena in which the norms are negotiated so you need to know it. You need to have access to the language that power speaks when you are negotiating with power. So I want my children to be able to do that, not because they are going to find the only forms of life which are of any value but because when they need to do certain things in society they had better know how to write and speak like that. I am putting it negatively. There are many other positive things they get out of that, but if they got nothing else they would need access.

But I am trying to argue the second case which is that standard English alone is no longer sufficient to negotiate culturally in this society. It is all right for some places but all of us always negotiate all the other spaces which are not set in that way, and if we think about that as negotiation for something which is central, then I think you get back to a very homogenous conception of whose English it is, a very unified and monolithic conception of what Englishness is and a very non-diverse conception of the variety of cultural worlds, and consequently languages which we all occupy, and which everybody occupies. I am pointing to a world which is irrevocably in translation, in which all of its negotiations are going in part to be in languages which are not, if I can use the metaphor, their first languages, not mother languages, but second, third and fourth languages, and these are as key to the negotiations that we have with the society as the ones which are conducted through, as it were, standard English.

73

Marilyn Butler I think the implications of what you are saying are really that Cox would never quite allow this decentred world language and literature to be achieved within the curriculum. I think that you have already gone beyond Cox because although his report stressed variety, it also acknowledged a central uniformity and a standard language is at the core of that. I think you are saying that your emphasis would be truly decentred and would presumably involve not exactly coercion or regulation but it would involve positively nominating non-English, English generated texts, would it not?

Stuart Hall Yes.

Marilyn Butler It would actually involve another list of a completely different kind. I do not mean that crudely, but you would have to introduce a sense of curriculum that was truly decentred on the literature side as well?

Stuart Hall On the literature side I think what one would want to do is have a mix. I have two purposes. If you are in a culture that is centred, you had better know about the centre, and if that centred culture is wrong in imagining that its forms of life and language are the only ones that exist, you also need other texts. So without prescribing a canon and its alternative, I would certainly want to insist that over the experience of the acquaintance with literary texts, some would be precisely those which had been the bearers of the central definitions of Englishness which anybody alive in the 20th century had better know about, whether they want to adopt it as their norm or not, because it is there. You climb Everest and you know about the English because they are inside us all, so you had better know about that culture and the texts that have so powerfully defined them. But at the same time, I would want to see, and I want to think, that the curriculum is not sufficiently established until there are some texts there – I will not tell them which texts to use – that are the bearers of a quite different cultural experience, written in a variety of English, because that, I think, is to begin to reflect in the classroom what English actually is now as a language and as a literary language.

Robin Alexander Just a short point of clarification on which I am genuinely not clear. It is about the National Curriculum. How far is the view which you are advancing, which has a lot to do with inter-cultural negotiation, compatible with the notion of a National Curriculum centrally determined by a government enjoying a parliamentary but not a popular majority?

Stuart Hall I think it is negotiable within the National Curriculum, put on the agenda by a government such as you describe, which fortunately has been obliged to shift its ground by other people getting their fingers in the pie. If what I would call the narrow purpose of the National Curriculum had been institutionalised without the intervention of teachers in the much wider debate, I think the conception of Englishness and of cultural belongingness which would have come out of that would have been extremely narrow, would have been mono-glottal and mono-lingual. It would have been a very homogeneous conception. It would have been an attempt to precisely reverse the movement towards cultural difference which I have been trying to describe and to restore the kind of centrality which I was discussing earlier. I think that was what putting the National Curriculum on the agenda was about. It is not what it is about now, but we all know what has happened to it.

COMMENTS AND QUESTIONS FROM THE FLOOR

Alan Newland (Lecturer in Primary Education, University of North London) Firstly, if John Hickman's school was largely peopled with speakers of French, German, Spanish and Italian rather than speakers of Bengali, Urdu and Punjabi, I doubt if Anthony Smith would have characterised this as a problem, as he did three times. Secondly, I take seriously what Professor Scruton says about an incipient theory of human thought expressed through grammar, but I would like to know what he would have to say about the incipient theory of human thought expressed by the sentence: 'We are a grandmother'. Need I ask whose English is this?

Bob Davis (Lecturer in Language and Literature, St Andrew's College, Glasgow University)   I have a sympathy of almost melancholic proportions for Roger Scruton's point about Latin, and I have heard him speak about that before, as we fight tenaciously in Scotland to hold on to the teaching of Latin in our secondary schools in the face of the Scottish Office injunctions to retrain our class 6 teachers as computer specialists. Nevertheless, I find much more questionable the point he made arising out of that about the relationship between a knowledge of Latinate and generative grammar and competence in standard English. We have agreed, I think almost unanimously here, that competence in the spoken and written forms of standard English was a central responsibility of the teacher of English. That is incontestable. But Latinate grammar does not map onto the complexities of standard English in either its modern or historic forms with anything like the fluency that proponents of this approach pretend. Nor does competence in or understanding of these grammatical forms necessarily lead to competence in standard English. It is a tired old phrase but surely one that is borne out by decades of research that children learn language, standard English included, by using it.

A final cultural point which I must get off my chest: where I come from, we have a dialect spoken and written by substantial numbers of my countrymen: Scots English. I would appeal to Professor Scruton in terms which I would hope he will recognise. In Scots English, in the writings of Henryson and Dunbar, we have the full flowering of the Ubi Sunt tradition. In Gavin Douglas we have the first English translation of the Aeneid, and in Robert Burns we have quite possibly the most linguistically competent poet that these islands produced in the 18th century. This language is still spoken, recognised and appreciated by my countrymen. Is it not central to our understanding of ourselves as English speakers?

Jon Davison (Senior Lecturer, Canterbury Christ Church College)   I would like to endorse what John Hickman said about the purposes of teaching, and refer

75

Alan Howarth to the central metaphor of the National Curriculum, which is about 'delivery' and 'delivering the National Curriculum'. While that might not involve empty pots, it certainly characterises the teacher as a sort of educational Postman Pat.

If I could turn to Roger Scruton, who talked about deviant usage and unsuccessful transactions equating with ignorance, I would like him to refer to the discussions that we saw between those students on the video, with which we were all impressed, who patently were not speaking in standard English. I would also refer him to the deviant usage of John Patten in his recently published lecture, 'Literacy and the Opportunity Society'.

That brings me round to Colin MacCabe's point about contemporary media as a part of the solution and not part of the problem, and on to what John Richmond and Stuart Hall said about people shifting their ground. Well, in fact I do not think they have. I think we are sitting here with a rosy view of things. In the same lecture Mr Patten says: 'It is no wonder that children struggle at school when they are allowed by their parents to spend more time in front of the television than they do in front of the blackboard'. That is what the majority of five to seven-year-olds, I am told, now do. I would like your comments on the mismatch between your view of the shift of ground and what seems to be the same old problem.

Anthony Adams (Senior Lecturer in Education, University of Cambridge) I would like to address my remarks primarily to Roger Scruton because he seems to represent a very powerful voice which is somewhat under-represented on the panel this afternoon, and indeed for most of the Inquiry. But I think the Roger Scrutons of this world are the people who are influencing policy to a very large extent at the present time. What worries me is the dichotomy between the rational voice of the philosopher that makes a perfectly valid distinction between the practical use of grammar in one's everyday life and a theoretical understanding of grammar, and the way that the rhetoric then shifts into something else and denies the rational statement being made so that we have phrases like 'those who have no grammar' coming into play. It seems extraordinary that anybody could have no grammar and still be a sentient and speaking human being.

Alongside that we get the phrase 'deviance' being used, which has a perfectly legitimate linguistic non-pejorative use. But when it gets shifted into a phrase such as 'the dialects and the language of the streets' it reminds me very much of a phrase in the Newbolt Report of the 1920s about evil habits of speech being contracted in the home and the street, and no sooner do you get the word 'contracted' in the context of the 1920s than you begin to think about disease and tuberculosis, and what you have immediately is a set of moral overtones which become associated with the idea of standard English. That is a phrase frequently assumed to be synonymous with 'proper English', with its overtones of cleanness and morality and all the middle class values that I think the whole notion of standard English effectively embodies. Indeed, Roger Scruton went on to say that we were talking primarily about Britain and the people who live in it. Immediately afterwards, hearing John Hickman's snapshots of his own classroom, I realised exactly who the people who live in Britain are and it seems to me that what Roger Scruton had to say had very little reference to that indeed. The trouble is that deviance very often becomes deviant if you accept the kind of analysis with which Professor Scruton has provided us. That seems to me to be very dangerous indeed.

Finally, I had my breath taken away completely by the reference to our Latinate grammar and the idea that grammar is better learnt in relation to a dead language. In particular, it is a very quaint idea that in English we ought not to split infinitives. Obviously the Latin 'amare' cannot be split; 'to love' in English is split very frequently. The notion that somehow a non-split infinitive sounds better or conveys more accurate information seems to me again an extraordinary one to come from a philosopher. I remind Roger Scruton of Burke's phrase 'to nobly stem tyrannic pride' and ask him where he might place the word 'nobly' in that phrase to improve Burke's rhetoric.

Roger Scruton I will try to answer all four speakers because I think a lot of important things have been said. Mr Newland asked me to say what I thought was the incipient theory of human thought contained in 'We are a grandmother', Mrs Thatcher's remark, and what I would say that it is not a theory of human thought but an expression using a well-known feature of standard English, namely the Royal plural. It is knowing that feature of standard English which enables people to identify precisely the moral nature of the person speaking. So I think it rather bears out my point.

The gentleman from Scotland, who expressed, unlike the last questioner, some sympathy for my views on Latin, made the perhaps very good point that Latinate grammar does not map onto the grammar of modern English in any easily intelligible way, but I perhaps should return here to the question raised by Mr Adams, who was apparently aghast at my suggestion that theoretical grammar is better taught through a dead language than a living one. I would adhere to that view, though as I said when I put it forward, it is a difficult one to sustain in a short time. I would adhere to it precisely for the reason that Mr Davis was suggesting, that it keeps the practical knowledge of language, the knowledge that should be that of the competent speaker, properly separate from the theoretical knowledge of language structure, which is a completely different matter, although valuable in itself, and for that reason I think it is much better to get people to meditate on language by meditating on a language which they could not use, as Matthew Arnold says, to fight the battles of life with the waiters in foreign hotels.

Let me say one more thing on the split infinitive. Sometimes it is of course properly split, but Burke, although a great rhetorician, was given to sentimentality, which spoiled his style and spoils his style precisely in this sentence by putting the world 'nobly' between 'to' and 'stem.' 'To nobly stem tyrannic pride,' because it is trying to inflate a sentiment which, if properly expressed, would make it quite clear that people do not, in the face of tyrannic pride, stand up nobly as a rule. There is always what Stuart Hall would call a negotiation going on, and I think this attempt to produce a posture which is that of the Burkean ideal is precisely what blights his conservatism: a rhetoric of sentimentality which is revealed in syntax.

Let me go back to Jon Davison, who reproached me, as did Anthony Adams, for my use of the concept of deviance and the implied criticism of deviance as a form of ignorance. I agree that this was a provocative part of what I said. I did not want to say that deviance was an evil habit, as it is in other areas – or as it could be. But I would like to adhere to my original definition. If deviance means anything, it is, in this context, ignorance rather than the speaking of another dialect.

That brings me again to Mr Davis. Of course Scots English is a wonderful language, and I completely back up his admiration for Burns, a much underrated writer in the modern world, and for Henryson and Dunbar. But that is a dialect of English (and perhaps one which you might want to say is sufficiently established in English literature to be a separate branch of the language) and not deviant usage. Deviant usage, I would like to say, is that usage which expresses some form of ignorance, either about the meanings of words or about the grammatical structures into which they are incorporated when one tries to think clearly.

Colin MacCabe   There are three points I would like to make. One is about the theoretical understanding of grammar. I share with Roger Scruton, as I taught it for five years, the belief that one enormously enfranchises and enables any students to whom one gives that theoretical understanding of grammar. On the other hand, I do not think there is any possibility, from long experience of teaching this, to teach it to the whole of the population. The degree of intellectual sophistication needed in getting a theoretical understanding of grammar is just not on in terms of the whole population. At the same time, we can produce for the whole of the population writing which gives them at least one of the great advantages which theoretical understanding historically within education gave, which is actually, when they have written a sentence, to realise that there are three, four, or five different ways to write it. It seems to me that what we have to do is think about ways in which exercises which can give that kind of ability which will exactly, in using the language, teach people about it, are not necessarily tied up with the theoretical understanding of grammar, which, although I do think is good, I just do not think can be taught universally.

Secondly, and really this is a question to Stuart Hall, what I wondered in the end was how he would describe Englishness in the 21st century, because it does not seem to me that one can simply be talking about a kind of globalisation in which we all become similarly hybrid, and yet I am not at all clear – it is a genuine question – in what sense one might talk about Englishness in the 21st century.

Thirdly, and in relation to what John Patten said contrasting the television and the blackboard, which you can find actually at the end of Edward Said's book *Culture and Imperialism* with exactly the same sentiments in almost the same phrase, those sentiments are out of date. They are not out of power, but the whole aim today is to have some small step in moving the situation forward. That simple opposition between cinema in the beginning of the century, and television now, and education, is just not sustainable in the long run, and one just has to hope that one can contribute a little bit to getting beyond what is a useless dichotomy. That is not say that a lot of television is not trivial but it is just to say that that particular trope which is produced again and again is very unhelpful.

Finally, seeing as we are on the split infinitive, it strikes me, Roger, that the history of the split infinitive, as you must know, is that nobody ever thought in English that you had to unsplit an infinitive until the 18th century. It is the one bit of English, I would say, which is entirely modelled on Latinate construction, and it seems to me that although you do not like Burke's 'to nobly stem' (and presumably you do not like the USS Enterprise's 'to boldly go' either) when you actually put the adverb there you do get – and that is the point – even in your analysis a slightly different sense of the verb. You actually have a different relationship between the adverb and the verb. I think you can say that you do not like the particular usage, but you cannot say that it is simply grammatical to keep the infinitive unsplit in English.

John Hickman   Just to pick up on two points, one was from Roy Davis who, I think rightly, said that children learn language by using it. Obviously the job of the teacher in that is to provide contexts for learning and then to encourage students to reflect upon what they have done during the course of the activity.

The second point is from Jon Davison who spoke about shifting grounds in the same old problems. I think it is very important that we hold on to that during the course of this Commission. The fact that there has been some shift, both from the point of view of the initial draft of the Dearing Report and the withdrawal on Key Stage 3 tests in 1992, has meant that some people are in danger of feeling fairly complaisant about where we are. I think there are still some very basic and fundamental principles that have to be negotiated, one of which is something that Malcolm Thornton raised, and that is teacher ownership of the curriculum, which he signalled loudly and clearly. Another is the negotiated curriculum with students within the framework of the National Curriculum. Another one, at the risk of labouring the point, is 100 per cent course work, and I would just make the point here that Mike Lloyd in Birmingham, who is organising the Save English Course Work campaign, has received more than 3,000 replies from secondary schools across the country, ninety-eight per cent of which have been wholly in support of 100 per cent course work. It is perhaps time that certain people started to listen to that sort of message.

Stuart Hall   If I could just make two or three points briefly, first of all I recognised the argument that Roger Scruton was making about Latin. You might not believe it, but as the product of a good colonial English education I was, of course, hauled backwards through Latin for more years than I can tell you, and I never found a use for it until, after six years at university, in my first teaching job – this is all entirely antediluvian! – in what was called at that time a secondary modern school. In attempting to introduce my students to standard English, I reached for Latin grammar. What struck me afterwards was that Latin, as an approach through a dead language to grammatical structure, is very useful, not at all for the pupils who learnt absolutely nothing from my attempts, but for the teachers. It is a kind of short hand crutch for the teachers. If only it was still available to us, it might enable some quick contacts to be made, but unfortunately I had to give it up because of the point that was made at the back: it is only and absolutely through the continuing practice of a language, and working with students through their practice of the language, that anything like that can be taught. I made absolutely no headway with an attempt to induce them into a formally Latin-based grammatical consciousness.

To pick up the point that was made about 'deviance' and 'deviant', it is key to the argument that I was making about an instrumental approach to standard English, and then all the connotations that it carries. That was exactly what I meant by cultural authority. To describe as 'deviance' simply the numbers of ways in which one deviates from a standard norm is a purely descriptive term and is perfectly acceptable. The point is that it is almost impossible to separate that usage from its cultural authority. I think that is true right across the whole field that we are talking about. Thus I would have Shakespeare deeply entrenched in my literary canon because of what Shakespeare does and enables you to do in the classroom, but it is very difficult to separate that Shakespeare from Shakespeare as a figure of cultural authority and the institutionalisation of Shakespeare as a bearer of wider cultural values. That is exactly how an instrumental and functional approach to competencies in language, for example, carries these feelings of cultural authority, without anybody being able to distinguish the one from the other. I think that with 'deviance' and 'deviant' that slide is a very common one, and not only in that area, though that was a very good example of it.

Finally let me just address Colin MacCabe's question about what Englishness might be in the 21st century. I think that lying behind that is the notion of how we might want to describe what I think is inevitably the premise of what I said, namely the relative decline and the impossibility of restoring a closed notion of a national culture from what often is then taken to be its implication, namely that everybody will be completely hybridised, synchronised, homogenised, and so on, and I think neither of those things are possibilities. The traces of the specific national and other cultural traditions on which people are drawing are going to continue to figure, and, as it were, people's identifications are going to continue to be composed of the different ways in which they draw on those resources and repertoires which have formed them. Those will always be to some degree inscribed. Consequently, children born in this society, if they are to take your question about negotiating with the past seriously, will of course be in some relation, however that relationship is negotiated, with what we call Englishness. It is not going to disappear over the horizon. The question is what it is and how established its authority is. With what else does it have to occupy the space? That seems to me to be how we have to think about it, and not in terms of something which has lost all its specificity. That seems to me to be what negotiation is really about.

Richard Hudson (Professor of Linguistics, University College, London)   Can I make two brief comments. One is on the support that Latinate grammar has had. Surely the only attraction of Latinate grammar is that for those people there is no alternative grammar. If they had a decent prescriptive grammar of English, that would do them even better.

The second point is to do with Colin MacCabe's comment that he really does not believe that it is possible to teach grammatical analysis across the board. There is a lot of evidence that that is not so. There was a very interesting piece of research, which you may have heard of, in the late 1970s, very thoroughly done in a New Zealand school, which produced non-academic fifteen-year-olds who could do very sophisticated transformation analyses. There is another question about whether there was any point in it, but it was possible and was demonstrated.

The other piece of evidence is that the rest of the world seems to be able to manage to do precisely that. I have the impression that all of our Continental neighbours teach grammar of their native language non-prescriptively across the board in secondary schools.

Bethan Marshall (Member of Executive, National Association for Teaching of English)   I have listened with great interest to the debate of the four panellists, and particularly to the contribution of Roger Scruton. He is obviously somebody who is really interested in English and I cannot help but admire the kind of linguistic versatility which he shows, and also his analysis of language which is part and parcel of the craft of English teaching. But it seems to me that what he demonstrates is an over-simplistic view of what the debate is all about, and that far from being imaginative in his approach, which is what he claimed he wanted people to be, that he is being literal-minded in the way in which he approaches grammar and the teaching of grammar. If you listen carefully to the arguments of people like John Hickman and Stuart Hall, you will see that the debate is considerably more complicated than that. I am not sure what applications Roger Scruton's model has for John Hickman's classroom, for example, and if we are thinking about knowledge about language, these are the issues that have to be addressed. I do not agree with Colin MacCabe when he says that you cannot teach sophisticated linguistic models to children, because I think you are in danger then of being elitist, which I am sure he does not want to be. It seems to me that that is a problem. What John Hickman was amply doing when he demonstrated how he taught a 'Knowledge about Language' module is that you can give children an incredibly sophisticated knowledge and understanding of the way in which language works, of register, of the influence of dialect and all these kind of things, and enter into the kind of debate that Stuart Hall is hoping to open out; Roger Scruton's analysis just does not touch that kind of diversity and that

81

kind of debate. It is just too simple and too naïve to describe what is going on – while being quite interesting.

Andrew Hart (Lecturer in Media Studies, University of Southampton)   Since Stuart Hall raised a question about how well equipped teachers might be to teach about grammar in the context of standard English, I would like to raise another question, and a simple one, for any of the witnesses who care to express a view. How best can we prepare and develop English teachers in training to teach about media texts, to teach knowledge about language, to teach drama, to teach multi-cultural English, as well as the traditional forms of English that we have been discussing today? It simply cannot be done by dictat. How can we actually do that?

Colin MacCabe   I would be very interested in the research that Richard Hudson mentioned on New Zealand, and I do not think I was actually saying there was some kind of total inability by people to learn theoretical grammar, if given enough incentive, or indeed probably if threatened with enough punishment. But I think that the particular pleasures and difficulties of it (and this is my experience of teaching across a wide range) are just not likely to make it something which is appropriate to universal education. This is not to disagree at all that there is not a great deal of knowledge about language which can be taught. It is absolutely central that we continue to give people the possibility of writing in English with as much fluency and complexity as possible. Simply to hang oneself on questions of grammatical teaching in relation to that is rather unwise.

John Hickman   I would have thought that the answer to the point being made about the question relating to teacher training is, sitting here now, to use the Language in the National Curriculum (LINC) material. Although the Government has banned it – or not allowed it to be published in its final form – there are numbers of editions of it around, and I would suggest that teachers in training would find that very useful in terms of the context, purpose and audience relating to the teaching of grammar. I suppose a rather more pessimistic point is that teacher trainers may well not have a job in the near future because everybody will be shifting their training into schools.

Roger Scruton   I probably ought to reply to Bethan Marshall's assault on my naiveté. I think that this language is motivated by something that also motivated Mr Adams earlier, namely the completely erroneous belief that because I am a conservative, I have some influence on the Conservative Party. On the contrary, I am regarded with as great a disfavour by them as by most of the people in this room. I have never been a government advisor or sat on a committee or anything like that because I have this unfortunate philosopher's habit of saying what I think to be true rather than what is convenient. This is really why Ms Marshall thinks of me as naïve.

I agree with her entirely that the issue to be addressed by teachers in the modern world is how you cope with a classroom such as that of John Hickman. I do not actually see this as a great problem, not because those classrooms are a minority of classrooms when considered in the context of the country as a whole (although they are) but because I believe that human beings of whatever race and cultural background are all of them rational, interested in life and usually interested in learning things. My own classes in America are as multi-cultural as any that Mr Hickman has to deal with. Of course, they are eighteen-year-olds, but nevertheless, they come from as many linguistic and cultural backgrounds as any that you could meet here, and I find it quite easy to deal with the situation; namely, I teach them what I know. What I know, of course, is philosophy, English literature, music and my own language, and they want to learn all those things. They especially want to learn my language and how it is spoken by somebody who knows how to write it. So I teach them that.

Note

1. Cary Bazalgette, ed., *Primary Media Education: A Curriculum Statement* (London: BFI 1989).

Day Two: 27 November 1993
Session Three

Changing the Subject: Can English Remain a Separate Subject?

Mary Warnock What struck me particularly about most of sessions one and two was that there was among the witnesses, and certainly in the audience, a diversity of views and experience that was being shared, but there was also a considerable degree of consensus. I found it surprising that the polarisation of issues: tradition on the one hand and great concentration on the new, the contemporary, the immediately available on the other, was nothing like such a polarisation as one would expect from reading some newspapers and listening to some members of government.

Exactly the same was true when we were discussing language and the need for access to standard English. The polarisation here, and in general, is far less extreme than we are sometimes, and I suspect quite deliberately, led to believe. Therefore, in practice, achieving balance within the curriculum, though it will always be difficult and a matter of juggling, seems to me to be not impossible. So I was left with an optimistic feeling that things were not quite so fragmented and difficult as I had perhaps supposed.

Professor Robin Alexander will be the lead Commissioner for this third session, which is entitled 'Changing the Subject'. We need to address ourselves to the question of whether English is a separate subject and what can legitimately be included in it.

The session began with a five-minute compilation of extracts from programmes made by BBC Education, showing children of different ages reading their own stories to a variety of audiences.

Mary Warnock I would like now to call our first witness, Margaret Hubbard. She teaches English and media in Scotland. She is the editor of the Scottish media teachers' magazine called *Media Education Journal*. We are often

84

told, I think with great justice, that the Scottish education system is an example we South of the Border ought to think about more frequently. The National Commission on Education has recently made this observation yet again, so it will be interesting to hear how her work compares with what teachers do here.

Margaret Hubbard   William Shakespeare – no words in literature are more loaded. Shakespeare trails across a classroom a pedigree larded with accolades which often lose sight of the fact that he was primarily a businessman who knew what would sell in the professional theatre. He worked in the visual medium of his time. His scripts resonate with sound and light and action. They come alive in the visual and in the aural. If he were working now, he would be very comfortable in film.

Shakespeare himself was educated in the classics. Contemporary English drama was not erudite enough for the curriculum of the time. The debate of literature versus contemporary media has moved not a whit from the 16th century. There is still what is perceived as high culture, and there is still the rest. The absurdity of this split has nowhere more clarity than when one considers how Shakespeare's own work has been shifted from one end of the cultural spectrum to the other.

The word 'English' is not neutral. To those living near football stadia in European cities, it carries dread. To geographers, it the designation of an area of land. To us here today, it is to do with language. The context, then, as well as the politics, history and economics and culture construct the meaning of the word.

English teachers are in the business of facilitating pupils in grasping the meaning of a text. A close study of the value of words and the context of a piece of writing is the way to do so. Pictures are often a part of how meaning is made. One has only to think of adverts, diagrams, and film to realise that this is so. Pupils have to be taught how to read pictures as well as words, if they are to make inroads into meanings.

A text is anything which makes meaning – Shakespeare, a T-shirt, a film, a poem. The media are the most pervasive way that people have of making sense of their world. A study of the media, then, is the *sine qua non* of teaching children how to make sense of the world that they are living in. If we deny children access to understanding how meaning is manufactured, we stand accused of betraying the ideals of education. To lead children to this understanding, we must study how language is used in its context, the political and cultural values which words carry in their context and how they all integrate with pictures to make meaning. The most effective way of doing so, in my experience, is a combination of analysis and creative work.

So what have we in Scotland done to change the subject? The entire structure of the Scottish curriculum has, in the last fifteen years, undergone a thorough transformation. Media studies is now firmly in place from Primary 1 through to 6th year level across a broad sweep of the curriculum. As far as English is concerned, it does not stand in opposition to literature but rather alongside it. Media also has its place in other subjects in the Scottish curriculum where it is appropriate.

I am an English teacher who genuinely loves teaching Shakespeare. For all teachers, watching children reach the moment of understanding or of realisation or of expression is always exciting. When I teach the media section of the syllabus these moments occur most frequently when children are able to make connections between what is broadcast to them and the world that they are living in.

For children, media studies is not an easy option. It is intellectually challenging, and it can be emotionally hard as they experience the fictions of the adult world stripped bare. It takes energy to teach media studies and to support children realising that all is not solid with the adult world. It amazes them when they discover that the images they watch on television are the choices of editors and are not necessarily precisely how events took place.

Studying the media and supporting children through it is a hugely rewarding experience – every bit as rewarding as coming to grips with the great themes of literature.

I will give you a simple example. When we study a poem in the traditional Leavis way, and lead children into a situation where they have to re-structure the narrative of the poem into the narratives of other genres, that provides a learning situation for a wealth of activities in an English classroom. They have to come to grips with language awareness, writing skills, discussion, genre awareness of both the literary and the media tradition. Far from damaging literacy, media works develop the understanding of literature, enrich the creative spirit, as well as providing a discipline in their own right. From writing newspaper articles for the local community newspaper, to participating in the local radio station's live broadcasts through to writing mini-screen plays, the work is demanding.

You are not the first to hear this speech. I tried it out on, among others, my seniors, who have come up on traditional literature and the media. I explained the context of today and invited constructive criticism. 'They might not like it', one of them said, 'it's not in jargon'. 'Do you think they will take you seriously when they hear your accent?' was another comment. And the third comment was the most telling of all: 'Is anyone really saying media studies is bad for us?' Then we got down to the planned work of the day, the rhythmic patterns of *Romeo and Juliet*.

Media studies enhances literacy, sharpens critical awareness, is a spur to creativity, raises pupils' confidence in their own judgment and makes them more able to make sense of the world, thereby aiding them to take their place as confident, caring and capable adults. This is not bookish theory. This is from experience of over twelve years of teaching English and media in three separate Edinburgh schools.

Sometimes I am asked, what place is there in an English classroom for making films? My answer is that in the same way as children derive immense pleasure and success, as well as engaging in real learning about literature, from writing

86

creatively, so they engage in real learning about meaning from making films. No random home movies for them. With animated discussion on which camera angle is most appropriate to the meaning, which words or music should accompany which shot and which shots should be edited together, the medium becomes de-mystified. Its construction of reality becomes explicit. The children become critical consumers of what is broadcast to them, and are thereby able to use the media more selectively. In just the same way, making speeches is all very well, but nothing can replace direct experience of standing in a classroom with children, watching them learn.

So I shall simply end by inviting the Commissioners and any other interested persons into my classroom to see precisely how media education, far from operating as some kind of fifth column, is in many ways the touchstone of good English teaching today.

Robin Alexander Thank you. The session as a whole today is concerned with boundaries – the boundaries between English and other subjects, and the scope of English. What you have chosen to concentrate on, very helpfully, is the boundaries between English as traditionally defined and media studies, and I think it would be useful to explore that, though we actually spent a bit of time on that in previous sessions.

I wonder if you would consider whether English is indeed the proper, or at least the sole home, of media studies. There has been, I think, a tacit acceptance that it is, over this Commission. But it seems to me that since media studies is necessarily concerned with visual images, one could suggest that art might play some kind of role in the teaching of media, and indeed the more you think about media studies – which of course we have not really defined – the more you might consider the role of media studies in the context of history and social studies and so on. You touched on that when you talked about media studies across the curriculum, and I would very much welcome a development of that particular point because the more we talk about the relationship between English and other areas of the curriculum, the more we need to raise questions about the nature of the rest of the curriculum. I have a feeling, which I voiced in the previous sessions, that the problem of boundaries is much more acute in respect of secondary education than primary, because it has a lot to do with departmentalisation. But if I would compose a particular question, it is very much this one of media studies in the context of the curriculum beyond English.

Margaret Hubbard We have changes in Scotland in the sense that media studies does appear right across the curriculum in quite a number of subjects. I'll put it historically into context in Scotland. Media studies came from English teachers, so it found itself in there to begin with, but it has moved out because, increasingly in Scotland, we have become aware of the fact that it is not the prerogative of English teachers. My concern is that English teachers are not in the business of words. We are in the business of meaning. We are living in a world where meaning is constructed to a great extent by the visual media, or through it. Therefore it was teachers who were in the meanings business who got into it first.

Clearly, to an art teacher a painting has meaning, a statue or a sculpture has meaning and therefore art teachers are very competent to teach media education if they have undertaken the essential difference in the critical skills of analysis.

Media teaching in Scotland is about skills of analysis, of what meaning a product is making, what meaning a film is delivering. It is not a qualitative hierarchy or Leavisite interpretation of the fact that a particular film is better than another film. We are trying to teach children skills of analysis in order that they themselves can make these discriminating judgments. Therefore, anybody who is choosing to learn these skills of analysis as a separate subject from the way they were trained in the Scottish universities at the time my generation were trained in it, could undertake the same form of analysis. I am not an art teacher, but I would assume that most art teachers were trained in the same way as I was trained as an English graduate, in that we studied literature in the traditional way. I have had to learn other skills of analysis to apply to the media, which in turn has spun off in teaching English. I would reckon that most art teachers are in the same business and therefore, if they learn the skills of analysis, of course it has a place in art too.

Equally it has a place in history and science because history programmes construct history as fact and ignore the fact that there are selective ideologies operating behind that, and there is selection of which particular piece of information is going to be broadcast. In science as well, there is little questioning in science programmes about the ideology of science. It is taken as good – well, there have been times when it has not been taken as that, but the morality of how science programmes are constructed is something that is seldom discussed.

My point is that if children are taught the analytical skills in the media right from the beginning, and a whole generation of children come up with that, then the media will find their place right across the curriculum, which is increasingly what is happening in Scotland from the bottom up, and in the external exams in Scotland now there is a media question in art and in music, as well as in English. That is also true in modern studies and there is a media question in economics as well.

Robin Alexander   Nonetheless, it seems to me that a tension is now clearly emerging in respect of this thing called media studies. It has been presented for the first time during this Commission as essentially multi-disciplinary, and yet what we have heard is a number of statements which suggest that its proper or sole home is English. I think that we have a problem there which needs unpicking, not necessarily by you, but more generally.

Alan Howarth   You have told us that a text is anything which makes meaning, but is there a hierarchy of meanings? Are some things so important that they should have priority and other things give way to them?

Margaret Hubbard   I am not equating Shakespeare and *Eldorado*. I am not saying they have the same quality. I am saying they are equally valid for study for different reasons and to different ends, and that media education is in the business of looking at how meaning is made. Therefore, I personally would say that there is more value in Shakespeare than there is in *Eldorado*. But I am not

88

trying to tell children that. I am trying to teach children how to discriminate so that they themselves can come to that understanding. Certainly how I was taught English in Scotland at school and to an extent at university is that I was probably more than half-way through university before I began to understand that I could discriminate for myself. The name Leavis was never mentioned to us. Somehow we were supposed to know that *Paradise Lost* was essentially better than *Coronation Street,* but nobody explained the tools by which we reached that realisation. I think that what English teachers should be doing is teaching children the various methods of analysis, and Leavis's is one of them. So is the pedagogy of media studies. We should be teaching children these different methods of analysis so that they themselves can become discriminating and so that they can reach a point whereby they say, 'Yes, I think Shakespeare is better than *Eldorado,* and I can explain why'. Significant numbers of children come through the educational system, knowing that they are meant to know that Shakespeare is better than *Eldorado* but not being able to explain why.

Alan Howarth Would you, with Colin MacCabe, accord an imaginative primacy to literature? I do not know whether he meant, for example, that a work of literature is the product of a single consciousness, whereas the media are the product of syndicated or co-operative activity that perhaps entails a dilution of the creative imagination. When you say that Shakespeare is superior to *Eldorado,* does that make a case for according more time within the curriculum to the study of literature than to the study of media?

Margaret Hubbard Every educational document I have ever read will tell me that you start where the children are at. Of course *Hamlet* is of value. Even for me to say to you: 'Of course *Hamlet* is of value' means we are making a shared assumption that *Hamlet* is of value. But one thing I think we would probably agree on. *Hamlet* is not of value to Primary 3. The children come in very aware of the media, and one has to start where they are at. One then leads them through the spiralling curriculum to what perhaps we could consider to have more quality. Equally, I could argue that Fellini has as much quality in his own right as Shakespeare has. So what I am saying is that we should be teaching children from where they are at and leading them to where we would like them to go, much in the same process as bringing children up. As one does that, it is not a case of saying: 'Don't do it, this is what you ought to be doing'. It is like suggesting to children that they should not eat sweets and expecting them to leap out of their beds the next morning and say: 'Lead me to an apple.' That is not going to happen. You work from where they are, and I choose to lead them to what I consider to be of more value. But the essential point is that I am asking them to learn the methods of analysis, and I really feel I have made it when I reach a point where a child will take me on on the issue of whether or not Shakespeare has quality.

Alan Howarth It could seriously be argued that Verdi's *Otello* is a greater work of art than Shakespeare's *Othello,* which takes us back to Professor Alexander's concern with boundaries. Are you happy with the compartmentalisation of your subject, considering that you have been making a claim, with which I am very sympathetic, that it is a broad-ranging and diffuse and protean subject?

Margaret Hubbard   I realise that is not the way it is perceived in England, but I argue from the wisdom of the way things are done in Scotland. I have been involved in media education from the beginning, and we went through this debate in Scotland about ten years ago as to where in the curriculum it should be. We have reached the conclusion, for the reasons that I have pointed out, that it should be diffuse because it draws on different disciplines. That also means it is co-operatively taught. When I am dealing with a still image, I am better with words because that is my discipline. The art teachers are better with pictures, and I have, not in the school I am in now but in both the other schools I was in, taught co-operatively with the art department, who brought to it their own particular knowledge, as I brought to it my own particular knowledge, and tied it to the pedagogy of media education, creating the teaching experience that we were creating for the children.

Alan Howarth   Whatever the categories in which we conceive teaching and learning, we still have to organise in practice and there still has to be selection. You have argued attractively that children ought to learn how to film and edit, but that implies very difficult choices about resources, in terms both of time and money. How much space would you give in the overall time available, and what sort of monetary resources do you think ought to be given to film?

Margaret Hubbard   Would you like me to answer from how I actually organise it in my own curriculum as the head of my own department? From first year through to fourth year, the children are taught in blocks of work, and they do fiction, novel; fiction, short story; drama; poetry; non-fiction; and media. That forms six blocks in each year. Within each of these blocks, they do a balance of analytical work and creative work, so when they are doing poetry, they are doing lit crit answers and also writing poetry and so on. When they come to do the media section, again we work with analysis of the texts, and then they do a written answer.

When I began teaching media, I did not have access to a video camera and I did not know how to work one, so we worked with stills in order to look at how pictures make meaning. We acquired a video camera through a great deal of pressure, and I had to learn how to use it and then teach the children how to use it. So within the media block there will be time spent on that, perhaps about a third of that block in the year. Separate from that, the children can opt to do a media studies module, separate from the Scottish Certificate of Education exams. They can opt to do a module on film, which involves more analysis and more practical work.

I take the point that significant numbers of teachers have to learn to do this, and within my own department, we are all English graduates but I am the only one who has gone on to get some certification in media education. But the others have all started learning it, and we collaborate with other schools, with a newsletter that goes out. We have a double page spread in the local community newspaper and if the teacher chooses to do the print section rather than the film section, then the teacher can take the double page spread on that so that their classes produce all the non-fiction once a month. So it works in that way.

In terms of the actual amount of time, sometimes when they want to do the film section I will use my own time to work with the children if they actually want to film, and sometimes it is the senior pupils, whom I have taught in media education, and who then go and work with the teacher with the smaller ones to help with film-making. But it is a huge logistical problem. I am aware of that. All I know is, you can teach children the film section without using the machines. You can teach them to story-board, and you can get them to visualise what it would be like. You can take a poem, and say: 'Suppose you were filming this, how would you do it?' And the children can do that. But they are desperate to do it, and they actually only learn their mistakes by getting their hands on the camera and having it wobbling all over the place and upside-down. You can actually do it in a very small way, in that you can say to them: 'I want you to make ten shots and in these ten shots there is to be absolutely no speaking at all, but you have to create a certain effect. How would you open this door, how would you take ten shots to open this door?'

Mary Warnock   Our second witness is Phillippa Giles, who is a BBC drama producer. She has produced a number of well-known television drama series including the Barbara Vine adaptations on BBC 1.

Phillippa Giles   As someone who graduated with a First Class degree in English Literature, I think it is clear that I have a very strong commitment to English as a literary tradition. I also, however, believe in the ability to translate literature into accessible and important television drama. During my career at the BBC, I graduated from directing *Jackanory* to script editing Sunday teatime classics such as *The Diary of Anne Frank* and *Vanity Fair* to producing *Oranges Are Not the Only Fruit*, and at the beginning of November 1993, I was made Executive Producer Drama Series for Adaptations.

As an executive producer for drama at the BBC, I feel I have a very strong stake in, and responsibility for, the future of the national culture in Britain.

My job is to trawl all the best writing, directing and performing talent and get it on the screen. The reason the best talents in theatre and film want to work in television is to participate in the work we do and reach the very wide audience that we reach. As a result of the recent Broadcasting Act, we will see, over the next four years, a marked shift towards increasing commercialism from ITV drama. In the area of script development, we are already seeing that impact. The broad range of work the BBC does from performance, theatre plays like *Suddenly Last Summer* and *Hedda Gabler*, to adaptations like *The Buddha of Suburbia*, to original TV writing like *Screen One*, reaches more people than any other cultural phenomenon.

The broadcast drama that I am talking about represents the cream of these traditions. For many people it is the only chance they get to come into contact with writers like Stendhal and actors like Maggie Smith. What I want the next generation of television viewers to be able to do is not just watch and enjoy these dramas but also be able to analyse and appreciate them at a more critical level. I do not think children should necessarily be able to shoot and edit themselves but they should be able to discuss the choices that go into making this editing decision or that camera angle in the finished product in the same way I learned to critically appraise works of literature. Children need educating about the techniques of scriptwriting, performance and direction in order to gain even more out of their experience of watching television drama.

Television drama is unique in its ability to open up metaphorically whole new worlds of experience and imagination. Children need to develop critical tools to analyse this experience beyond the ephemeral. Drama is the most complex of all the television disciplines. Traditionally, within a production house like the BBC, it commands the best designers, the best directors, the best writers and the best camera people. The level of intellectual rigour that enters even the simplest decision such as how to dramatise a character's motivation at a particular point is of the highest order.

The historical research that goes into designing costumes of the 1970s, let alone the 1870s, is exhaustive. The specialism of skills to do with casting and performance is acute. All these and many more factors contribute to bringing a drama off the page and to the screen. It seems to me quite straightforward that children can be set projects or participate in workshops that take them beyond the finished product to a detailed consideration of the meaning of a particular camera angle or cutting point or design look. It is also imperative to note that television drama is often the only form of live drama that children encounter. The study of writing in a literary tradition is one thing, but drama can best be studied off the page rather than on. Even drama of a popular genre like soaps or detective series can widen a child's perspective when related to drama as a text. The video camera is now just as much a tool for expression as are pen and paper. *Video Diaries,* the innovative BBC 2 series, has led the way in showing how people can harness video techniques for themselves.

But drama is far too sophisticated to allow that kind of access. However, in order to equip people to get the most out of television drama's cultural wealth, the tools of sharp critical analysis is the key. I am proud of the work I have done and continue to do in television and I feel very strongly that it will stand alongside other art forms when we come to look back on the 20th century. Education can help to enhance television's standing as an important element of the national culture, not diminish it.

Robin Alexander   You are dealing centrally with the relationship between the printed word and the visual image, and you have talked of, among other things, bringing literary works to the screen and creating something that stands as a work of art in its own right. In that sense, the title of this session is doubly apt, and I think it is important that we spend a little time thinking about the transformation that you are discussing, as to whether it enhances or diminishes the original, or at least changes it to excess.

So there seem to be two quite separate issues. One is the case that you have very powerfully made for the rigorous study and exploration of television drama as part of the curriculum, and for the sake of the argument, as part of the English curriculum. But the second one which I would like you to develop is the notion of reconstruction as television drama of something from another genre – not the general defence of that which we often hear, but the educational implications of that in the context of children's growing understanding of literary works. Would you like to consider whether there is a sense in which that transformation might actually do damage to the originating form?

Phillippa Giles   So, say, when we adapted originals for the screen, was it a diminished version of the book?

Robin Alexander   Yes, and particularly in the context of schools. We are familiar with the arguments more generally about this, but we are talking about the school curriculum.

Phillippa Giles   To be honest, I think it depends on the quality of the work, and you can get bad adaptations and bad television drama. You need the tools to appraise whether it is good or not, and that is what I am arguing for in the same way as the first speaker argued for it, for the audience to be able to differentiate for themselves, so that we are not actually dictating whether *Middlemarch* is better than *The Buddha of Suburbia* as a television experience, but they can watch both and decide which they think is the superior dramatisation. In actual fact, the dramatisation that I have been involved with, and a lot of the ones that I have seen recently on ITV as well as the BBC, have been of an incredibly high order, and actually I think often add to the original experience of reading the text, but it is a very different experience. I would never argue that you should only have the one. The two are different forms.

Marilyn Butler   If I could follow that up, it seems to me that if we are talking about a literary curriculum, and basically we are coming from a literary curriculum as part of this Commission, you might well say that the fascination of the televised version could really be seen as a seduction, a taking of interest away, particularly when technically the medium is so interesting. There are so many new terms to learn. Does it not seem to you, particularly in your specialism (and you obviously specialise in complex works and a complex style such as that of Thackeray) is an additional challenge to you, and can you really say it is towards the literary text and the literary methodology that your expertise would be pointing students.

Phillippa Giles   No, I am not saying that, and you make an interesting point about it being seductive. I would say that not everybody who watches a television adaptation is ever going to read the original novel. One acknowledges that, and it would be foolish to think that people were going to go away and read

93

Vanity Fair. It is just very daunting as a novel. They are more likely to read Jeanette Winterson, because her books are shorter. But I do not think that that in any way devalues either form; as I am saying, it will actually encourage some people to go and read the novel, but I do not think that the seduction needs necessarily to replace or in any way completely devalue the literary text. For me, yes, the literary text is always going to have something; particularly the internalisation of novel writing. You know, you can do things in a novel which you could never do dramatically. But then, dramatically you can do things which you can never do in a novel. So all I am asking for is the tools to analyse those differences and to send people off in directions where perhaps they would not have gone before. But, no, I am not arguing for replacing the original.

Anthony Smith   Can I just ask you the same question again? Are you saying that children should enjoy and learn to criticise the television version and then read the original? You see, a lot of people would say – I do not agree with this myself – that television lives off literature, that it sucks the blood out of literature – and particularly your branch of television. I think one could argue there is something in that view. Look at what has happened to *Pride and Prejudice*. It has gone through twenty different radio and television adaptations, some of them not very good, and some of them wonderful. And there are going to be another twenty of them . . . .

Phillippa Giles   There is another one coming up next year, I think.

Anthony Smith   Yes, there are going to be lots more. Which of them gives the experience or the essence of the experience? I suppose, any of them. My bottom line question really is, does television not, at the end of the century, have to say that in the case of adaptation, the literary version is the primary experience and everything else is trying to lead you to it?

Phillippa Giles   I do not believe that it sucks the blood. That is a very interesting remark which I have heard in different contexts, but not quite so strongly as you put it. To say that everything that I am working for sucks the blood from literary work is something that I would be very shocked by and would completely reject. I think the work I do with writers – and let us talk about the writing rather than the other sophisticated things that come into drama because those are other layers – the writing is absolutely the primary thing. Unless you get that right, none of the other things get brought to bear because the script does not make it as far as I am concerned. Obviously different people have different editorial judgments about that, but to say that a dramatisation of a novel can suck the blood from the original is almost to demote the original, to think that that could happen, because the original is still there to be read for the people who want to read it. All I am saying is that I think television is a different experience. It is a very broad experience and something that we should not ignore and we should prompt it alongside the other art forms.

Anthony Smith   Yes, but let me ask my question again very briefly. Do you say to the child in the classroom: 'There is, next week, the twenty-first adaptation of

Pride and Prejudice. Watch it, tell me what you think of it'. Do you then say: 'Now go and read the book because that is where you get the real experience', or do you not?

Phillippa Giles   I would, yes.

Anthony Smith   Thank you.

Alan Howarth   I must say that I was disappointed by the last response. Surely the film or televised version of *Pride and Prejudice* is a wholly distinct creation. It happens to draw some raw material from the novel of the same name, but they must stand apart from each other, must they not, with separate validities?

It may well happen that the child or the adult may be prompted to go and look at the book and perhaps even better to read the book, and we note that the sales of novels with the same title as films do rise rather dramatically. Who was buying Galsworthy before *The Forsyte Saga* was made? I hope very much that a lot more people will read *Middlemarch* because of the BBC adaptation, but it does not seem to me that there is a necessary connection. We must hope that there is a useful prompting and associations are made. But surely we have to defend each genre and each medium distinctively in terms of the validity of works of art. I accept, with you, that the common benefit in teaching young people these texts is that they learn, in your own phrase, to critically appraise – and congratulations on the split infinitive!

Phillippa Giles   Can I say that when I said I would recommend going and reading the book, I mean that definitely the book can never be replaced but I am saying the same thing you are saying. I was not saying, to read the book instead, but yes, of course, go and read the book.

Mary Warnock   I suspect that if I allowed it, an altercation might break out between the Commissioners, so I think in order to forestall that I will thank Phillippa Giles very much. I move on to call our next witness, Margaret Maden. She had a very distinguished career as a headmistress working in the Inner London Education Authority, and is now Director of Education in Warwickshire. She is a member of the National Commission for Education whose report came out in November 1993.

Margaret Maden   I would like to say a few words first about the National Commission for Education. This is the report, *Learning to Succeed,* which I show you because I gather you cannot get hold of copies![1] That was the product of two years' work by a core of sixteen Commissioners, drawn from industry, from Academe, from the law and from schools.

Much of what I have to say to you is based on an enormous range of evidence presented to that Commission from all parts of Britain, and the work of the Commission was also informed and assisted by a good deal of enquiry and visiting of educational establishments in other parts of Europe and in the United States.

The Commission was really quite overwhelmed by the evidence coming to it relating to English in what I think in the trade is called its transactional form. The

Commission was much impressed by the calls for more attention, not only but especially in the early years of primary education, on basic skills, and was persuaded that basic skills was a fundamental part of learning before which nothing else could be done.

So for many parents and employers, English is, or they believe, should be concerned mainly with its transactional functions: how to write and read letters, memos or reports, how to speak clearly, how to listen to others with a degree of accurate recall. I think this contrasts strongly with the academic or perhaps humanities-oriented view, which as far as I can understand it sees the study of English literature and indeed what we have been listening to for the last hour or so – media studies – as the real, palpitating heart of English.

It is this latter view which has tended to dominate recent debate, and not least what sometimes seems to an interested outsider as a struggle for mastery over social and cultural values. These values underpin and inform consideration of what it is to be human, because considerations of what it is to be human lie very much at the heart of good education and certainly, in terms of children in their teens in secondary schools, which is what I know most about, it is very much their primary concern. That is why there is a struggle over them.

On this model, English teaching operates certainly on the commanding heights of education in the humanities, and it is not surprising if English teachers and their associates in media, drama and theatre studies colonise this territory as their particular domain. But meanwhile, I would wish to draw the Commission's attention to the fact that there is, of course, a growing range of courses, modules, units, going under the name of 'communications', especially within pre-vocational and vocational education and training. This body of work relates to the purposes of English outlined in my introductory words, but not, perhaps, to the English literature notion of English. I think there is something of, if not two cultures, certainly a very divided concept of the range and purposes of English, therefore, between the specialists, and the many people who are not specialists – in other words, many people who are not sitting here today, but whom I am trying to describe and represent.

I think it is interesting just to ask questions about communications which seems to me a veritable industry these days. Who is teaching all these communications courses? Does it matter who is teaching them? The connections between the concerns that you are discussing here and what is meanwhile going on very dynamically and actively and busily in communications courses needs to be considered. I should just add at this stage that many of the industrialists, not only on the Commission but with whom we had discussions, believe that it is through the communications courses that the faults implicitly of the school system will be corrected.

There is also a significant number of young people, certainly in secondary schools, variously described by some as functionally illiterate and by certain industrialists and others we spoke to – not necessarily in the business – as remedial.

We took evidence from the Adult Literacy and Basic Skills Unit and they had a great deal to tell us about their particular definition. I think this is the real problem: what do we mean by 'illiteracy' or 'functionally illiterate'? They persuaded the Commission that forty per cent of young people on various kinds of courses and activities post-sixteen required quite specific additional help to reach craft level, or what is now called National Vocational Qualification level 2. I am sure you all know what that is. There are also, of course, many young people with specific learning difficulties, sometimes called dyslexia, and also other linguistic block-ages to their learning, and these can be quite crippling. Access to *Middlemarch* or anything else becomes a very academic issue for such young people.

So I would want to know, is English meant to address or include this raft of very pressing needs, because certainly for those interested in genuine access and participation, these language problems are absolutely crucial. Such evidence as we have collated on teachers and teaching suggests that in so-called remedial or special educational needs work in secondary schools and in Further Education colleges, the teachers first of all are few and far between. Very frequently, in the analyses we have received, they are teachers of other specialisms who are filling up the timetable, rather like games used to be in public schools, I am told. Sec-ondly, they are not connected, certainly, with English departments nor with the agenda and purposes of English departments, certainly in secondary schools.

In conclusion, English seems to have a vast, even inchoate range of responsi-bilities and purposes, but it may also be that there is an unwillingness to take on board some of those more transactional aspects of English, or perhaps to assume, as I have found in my own fairly recent experience at the chalk face, so-called, that there sometimes is an assumption that I think needs testing very thoroughly that through a full engagement with literature these transactional 'bugs' in the system will be sorted out.

Perhaps all schools and colleges do need an English consultant or adviser, and indeed I think in some of the best primary schools one sees that particular kind of role developed very effectively; in other words, a permanent adviser of a profes-sional kind to the other staff within the establishment, an adviser or a consultant who works across the curriculum and ensures that the diverse purposes and needs are fully addressed by colleagues and not simply in English lessons. That would then lead to some quite interesting and important questions about what would happen in proper 'English lessons'. There would need to be, I would imagine, a much clearer definition of what is the core purpose of English in the sense it is being discussed here at this Commission.

Robin Alexander   You have raised a lot of questions, and I suppose the really interesting, but slightly mean thing would now be to ask you to answer all the questions you have raised. There seem to be two issues. You have rightly reminded us that the matter of boundaries between English and other subjects, which we have spent a bit of time on already, is only one aspect of a larger argu-ment about English, and there is a vital question of balance within English, particularly between what you call the transactional aspects and the study of literature and the media. I wonder first if I can direct this question to you: what do you think that balance should be? Have we got it wrong?

Margaret Maden I am not clear what most English teachers now believe are the responsibilities and the purposes that they are trying to fulfil. Therefore, the question of balance is really impossible for me to address. I am clear that what I think English needs to be concerned about in schools, certainly, is so extensive and so all-permeating that it is probably unreasonable and impracticable to expect, certainly in the context of a secondary school, an English department to satisfactorily address all of those purposes and needs.

Robin Alexander Although it has to be said that there did seem to be a more than tacit suggestion that the basic skills may have been neglected, and that would imply something about balance, yet the matter of English in relation to the curriculum as a whole is a very important one. Perhaps we can come to that next. It seems to me that the community of professional discourse in the secondary school is the subject; in the primary school it is the whole curriculum. There are obvious reasons for that in terms of professional structure and backgrounds of those two kinds of institution. That means that in the former, the secondary school, there is a danger that the whole-curriculum dimension of the subject may be neglected, and this is particularly critical in relation to English. In the primary school, it seems to me there is a danger of neglecting to explore the distinctiveness of the contribution which each subject can make to the child's general education, and I wonder if you could reflect on that, and particularly, perhaps, given the concern you have just voiced, suggest how the Bullock Report's notion of Language Across the Curriculum now ought to be updated?

Margaret Maden I think there is a very difficult pedagogic issue that is not restricted to English, about the notion of basic skills. I have reported to you what was incessantly put to the National Commission because I think that is of interest. The people who presented evidence, whether it was parents or industrialists or others not directly concerned with teaching as such, see basic skills as quite discrete and as sequential. If that is not the case, and I am persuaded it is not the case, then it is for this Commission and for people here to explain more clearly to the wider world of interested people – largely of goodwill – why that is not the case.

For example, an analogy perhaps is the row that occasionally erupts on design and technology, where there is a view that unless children have acquired and been taught – and, it is sometimes suggested, drilled – in the basic craft skills, they cannot possibly move on to a higher level of reflection and design and problem solving. We kept coming across this notion absolutely fixed among others who are not in the business of teaching English or necessarily working in schools or colleges, and I have to say shared by many academics, that unless the fundamentals of literacy are (though perhaps not expressed this way necessarily) drilled into children, nothing else of any real value in the curriculum can actually develop.

On the question of balance within primary and/or secondary schools and how the Bullock notion of Language Across the Curriculum could be implemented, there were, in the mid 70s and beyond, some quite good practices emerging. There are resource implications as usual (although maybe not vast) where English departments were empowered in secondary schools to advise staff generally on issues to do with language development, whether that language development was occurring in history or science or geography or wherever. It is very important that this is understood in terms of the whole curriculum in secondary schools.

I think also there are questions about some kind of theoretical framework within which special educational needs language work is going on in most schools. Indeed, what are the linkages with the learning of other languages, French or German, within secondary schools, and what are or should be the linkages with English as a second language? These are all very important questions to do with language that I believe in most secondary schools are not treated and dealt with or managed in any kind of integrated or coherent way, and I think, therefore, before one gets into the heart of considering text or media – text in the sense of literature or indeed choice of other texts – these questions and policies to do with the more integrated approach really need to be developed and set in train.

Marilyn Butler   I think this is a very important point, and yesterday we addressed it when there was a strong sense, for instance, that language is indeed logically at the heart of the curriculum and that the initial justification of literature, certainly in Cox, is that it enriches and develops and gives people further experience of language used in a variety of more sophisticated ways. Fundamentally, it follows on from the core of language, and I think your point about this is really important, obviously, for the question of the media.

As we have started on media in this session, one has the sense that the two elements are pulling apart, the cultural studies or 'to be a human being' element is pulling right away from the language, and I think it could be argued by an opponent or critic or sceptic about media studies that it is fundamentally a little specious to be smuggling media studies into an already quite full programme to do with language, when already literature is only half-way through the door because it is obviously a refinement. It is not at the basic core of the language study. You were very judicious in the way you set out the breadth of English, but did you feel that you were in fact producing a kind of covert warning against media studies as making the whole thing further complicated and more dispersed?

Margaret Maden   No, I did not mean that. What I am trying to say is that there are so many important tasks to be undertaken by everybody on the staff of a school if we are to be effective for the whole range of children, that I think it is quite unreasonable to expect English teachers to do all that I think in many cases they are trying to do and perhaps not doing very successfully. This is not simply because it is the usual problem of an overcrowded syllabus or curriculum or scheme of work in the case of English, but because I do not believe that the proper language development that is so critical in terms of full access to education and learning in every sense can be undertaken just by one department. Other staff have responsibilities to understand what good practice represents in a realistic sense without everyone trying to be English teachers. These are very important issues about boundaries. What can you expect a reasonably good, hard-working science teacher to take on board in terms of language so that English teachers can, I would hope, undertake the kind of work, including media studies, that we have been hearing about?

For many young people, and some of those I have been most concerned with in my time in schools, opening doors to an imaginative response to their own world and to the world around them can often occur through media studies and not necessarily through a direct engagement with text. It may lead to a direct engagement with text, but that may not be the way in which that particular learning is opened up.

I have often been very bothered – to give a couple of practical examples – that some of the texts that history or geography or science teachers are using are very poor quality texts. I would expect somebody who is acting as an English consultant in a school to advise in that sense as well as helping other teachers to adopt reasonably consistent practices in terms of what is still a central form of learning and teaching, which is writing and reading.

Alan Howarth   I am very pleased indeed that you have raised this question of learning difficulties and special educational needs. I think you are the first person in these proceedings to do so and I congratulate you on it. But I would like to press you further on the practicalities. What, in practical terms, do you as a county education officer consider is the appropriate balance of attention and resources to be given to this? What should we most appropriately do? For example, do you want to see more time spent in training to enable not only English teachers but teachers of other disciplines to be competent to help children with what we are learning to call the basics? Do you want to see more money channelled in this direction? Do you think that the syllabus should be stripped down to enable more attention to be given to this set of needs? What do you think should be done and what practical means do you, in today's circumstances, as a county education officer, have at your disposal to advance that programme?

Margaret Maden   On the latter question, I have virtually no resources or means to advance this, expect in the sense that should not be underestimated, perhaps, of having access to a wide range of schools and heads and governing bodies and teachers. One must identify as closely and accurately as one can, not only what is actually happening, which is changing very rapidly for all the reasons we know about, but also what is possible from the point of view of resources, and not least with co-operative activity between schools through means such as local management of schools and greater budgets being in the hands of schools and relating to in-service training. The National Commission recommended that in initial teacher training there should be more attention paid to special educational needs and also to Language Across the Curriculum, which sounded slightly old-fashioned because that is now seen as an idea past its time. But we had reason to believe it is still tremendously important for all teachers to have, in their initial teacher training, but also subsequently through in-service training, far more awareness of some of the techniques and the skills that now exist among English teachers, some of which can be adopted by teachers of other subjects, just as we are seeing in primary schools. But I think there is still a core of English – an essence of English – that must be left for English teachers to deal with. It is the defining of that core or essence which, as I understand it, is not being done, and that is partly from my vantage point of being a county education officer and being in at least one school every week, albeit rather superficially, and also such evidence as is collected by the inspectors we manage to retain.

Alan Howarth   Can I ask just one other thing? This is really a yes or no kind of question. You heard Margaret Hubbard describing very interestingly how she uses moving image technology to teach communicative skills in Scotland where these practices are, we are told, very firmly established. Do you think that that area of teaching will support or displace the teaching of the transactional functions of English that you began telling us about?

Margaret Maden   I would think it could or would strengthen the transactional. I am against a harsh divide between transactional and the other purposes of English, which I suspect are at the heart of your discussions here, but I am, in a sense, rather rudely bringing in some quite basic issues that I suspect may not be very much on your agenda otherwise.

Mary Warnock   Our next witness, Jennifer Chew, is a teacher of English with responsibility for special needs at Strode's sixth form college in Egham. She's played a considerable role in recent education debate, and she's also written a pamphlet on spelling, published by the Campaign for Real Education.

Jennifer Chew   I'd like to start poetically, with apologies to Messrs Marlowe, Raleigh and Marvell, and I think this actually follows on quite well from the previous speaker:

> If all could read and write when young,
> And spell with ease the English tongue,
> Then media studies might be moved
> To live with them, if not quite love.
> But time is short and standards fall;
> Some children cannot read at all.
> Young adults lacking business basic skills
> Contribute to our country's ills.
> Had we but world enough and time,
> Then broadening English were no crime;
> But first we need to concentrate
> On getting children literate.

English teachers, like lovers, have to be realistic, and what might be possible and desirable in an ideal world may not be possible in the world as it is. I have been an English teacher in real classrooms for most of the past thirty years. As recently as yesterday, I was being an English teacher in a real classroom. My aim is, and always has been, broadly two-fold: to teach children the skills in speaking, reading and writing which are essential to their future and to take them into realms of language and literature where most would not venture on their own. Most children, as I know from my own experience as a mother of three, venture very willingly into the realms of films, television and advertising, and they are biologically predisposed – some would say programmed – to communicate orally. They need no encouragement to watch soaps on television or to talk informally among themselves. The same is not true of reading and writing, which are highly artificial activities requiring careful teaching and much practice before even basic competence is reached.

One of the BFI's concerns is to ensure that children acquire a good critical understanding of the audiovisual media. Desirable though this is, teaching everyone to read and write well must come first, as the Cox English order itself implies. Far from sanctioning a golden age of media studies, according to my count it mentions the media only from level 5 upwards and only in six out of 159 statements of attainment, which is about three per cent.

Study of the media has never formed a major part of the English curriculum, and it should not, in my view, do so now, although I must say that even rabid traditionalists, so-called, such as myself, have always made occasional use of newspaper articles and advertisements to make certain points about the way in which English can be used. I believe that reading and writing are supremely important and that they should remain so. They cater for communication from the mundane – the note to the milkman – to the highly imaginative – poems and novels. They also make it possible for people to absorb and express ideas which may be too complex for spontaneous oral communication. Indeed it seems to me that the decision to publish a printed version of the views expressed at this conference is a recognition that the printed word has a special status.

Proficiency in reading and writing is uniquely mind-expanding. Lack of proficiency is mind-impoverishing. If we are not teaching reading and writing very well (and there is growing evidence that this is the case) we are almost certainly impoverishing young minds. I find that unacceptable. I believe that this should be remedied before we think about broadening the study of English. I am not against broadening; it is just a matter of priorities. I believe that we need to spend more time on the nuts and bolts of language, not as an end in themselves but as the foundation for more elaborate structures.

English teaching has, for too long, been dominated by the erroneous idea that children's growth as readers and writers is stunted by attention to the mechanics of language. Phonic decoding, for example, is still too often presented as highly unreliable and antithetical to reading for meaning. I have actually heard these views expressed by lecturers twice recently, so no one can say that they are no longer current views. They are views which contradict research.

Eric Bolton said during the debate here that HMI had found teachers to be using a mixture of methods for the teaching of reading, and this is often said, but many signs point to its being a mixture in which the limitations of phonics are too often grossly caricatured. The truth is that in both reading and writing, the mechanics of language are inseparable from its more creative uses. There has been some research done in Wigan on children who have been taught grammar in ways that have long been frowned on in English teaching circles. The children improved markedly on objective measurements of reading and writing, and perhaps even more significantly, the number gaining five or more GCSEs at grades A to C rocketed over just a three-year period from twenty-eight per cent to fifty-six per cent. In other words, more attention to the nuts and bolts of language improved their performance across the curriculum. This is not to be scoffed at.

I would also plead for a much more systematic teaching of vocabulary. The key items in written texts are words, normally used with more care and precision than in speech. Reading and writing are an excellent way of enriching children's vocabulary and teaching them to think with clarity and discrimination, not only about the message but also about the medium in which it is conveyed. The two really cannot be separated.

Children need to be stretched far beyond the words and expressions that they pick up in their everyday lives, whether from one another or from *Neighbours.* They need to acquire a more and more extensive vocabulary, together with paraphrase skills and other modes of extending their ability in speech and writing. One reason for my own enthusiasm for spelling is that I think that teaching it properly is a wonderful way of teaching vocabulary and also of developing children's sense of the structures of words and the links between them. So many children now think of every word as a one-off, unrelated to other words.

I also believe in teaching rather than in leaving children to find out for themselves, as the latter is bound to put children from poorer homes at a disadvantage. I think this is one way of closing up the gap that we heard about here – the gap between the educational haves and have nots. I have to confess that I am baffled when I hear the argument that more attention to the nuts and bolts of language will restrict children's linguistic and literary horizons. The reverse is surely true. Too many children at present are heavily dependent on teachers for help with reading and writing. We are producing students who cannot cope with their maths because they cannot read well enough, or, as one sixteen-year-old put it to me, they 'can't do all them sums with lots of words' I believe that children would be much freer to think and express themselves independently if the nuts and bolts of language were more securely in place.

Robin Alexander   Let us go straight to nuts and bolts then. I wonder whether your anxiety that the nuts and bolts of English have been neglected perhaps needs a bit of examination. You suggest that phonics are widely scorned. I wonder if actually it is not the case that phonics are widely used but what is scorned is the claim that phonics are the sole way to teach reading. Certainly all the research that

I am aware of, particularly the surveys of HMI, suggests that although the teaching of reading seems to be a bit of an ideological fixation for politicians and the press, it is one of the areas in primary education where actually teachers tend to adopt a very pragmatic approach. Obviously there are some exceptions, but overall that is the evidence of HMI research studies, so the question is this. You argue for more emphasis on nuts and bolts, but by whom, at what stages of education and by what means? I also wonder whether it is a question of priorities or more fundamentally a question of pedagogy. Put another way, are there really that many teachers who argue that basic language skills are unimportant, or is the more important question how the so-called basic skills should be taught?

Jennifer Chew   I agree that probably teachers would never put their hands on their hearts and say that the nuts and bolts are not important. I have to say that, of course, I cannot go into primary schools and see from the inside what is happening there. I do try to read a great deal of the sort of publication that we get from teacher trainers, and the impression given by many of them is of a rather dismissive attitude towards the nuts and bolts. Whether that is reflected in real primary classrooms or not, I do not know.

I think that the proper time for attention to nuts and bolts is in the primary school. I do not think that this means that primary education has to be a matter of endless drilling and very dreary classroom scenes, because I think that even the basics, so-called, can be taught in a very stimulating and interesting way, and in a way in which children love. I do not know whether that answers the question.

Robin Alexander   References to teacher training are very much in the news and again I have to say that you may have seen some prospectuses, but the Council for the Accreditation of Teacher Education (CATE) – a body on which I sit for as long as it survives – was asked by the Secretary of State a couple of years ago to look at the matter of training teachers to teach reading. It commissioned an independent study by the National Foundation for Educational Research (NFER) which showed that that kind of dismissiveness of phonics was not the case. There were other problems, but by and large, courses now, as indeed they have been required to do by the Government's own stringent criteria, do not neglect this area. So I am very concerned, I think, about the extent to which politicisation of this area has actually obscured the truth.

Jennifer Chew   I clearly do not have the over-view that you have, Professor Alexander, or that CATE would have. This may sound anecdotal, but a friend of mine who is on a teacher training course at the moment told me of a lecture that she had had on the teaching of reading which had started with the George Bernard Shaw example of G-H-O-T-I, which could spell fish, with the G-H as the G-H at the end of enough, the O pronounced as the O in women, and the T-I pronounced as in station. The lecture went on from there to present a very negative view of phonics.

Now that example of the spelling of fish is a ridiculous example because G-H

104

never says F at the beginning of a word; women is about the only word I can think of which has an O pronounced in that way; and the T-I pronunciation as in station only ever comes in the middle of words and never at the end, so that the position of the letters makes that pronunciation absolutely impossible.

As I say, the sort of things that I have read also, often will present this negative kind of view, but I accept that I do not have the over-view that you have on this.

Alan Howarth   I would like you to elaborate, if you will, your reasons for your enthusiasm for spelling. You started by giving us a very enjoyable parody of Sir Walter Raleigh, one of the most successful practitioners of the English language, and he observed that he spelt like a gentlemen and not like a pedant. Why do you attach such importance to it?

Jennifer Chew   For one thing, Sir Walter Raleigh lived before spelling became standardised. We live in an era when spelling is standardised. I feel that I can, if I teach spelling properly, teach almost everything that I want to teach about the English language. For example, I regularly give my students three or four words to spell, one of which is the word 'conscience', as in 'guilty conscience', and I am lucky if one out of twenty spells that correctly. Later on in this short three or four word test, I will give them the word 'science', and usually nineteen out of twenty spell that correctly. I can then show them how science and conscience are linked, not only in spelling but also in meaning. I can go into the roots of words, so that I can teach them a great deal about meaning as well as just about spelling and help them to see relationships between words.

Also very often I can help them to see the reasons for some of the illog- icalities or apparent illogicalities of English spelling. For example, a word like K-N-I-G-H-T which now has several silent letters in it, in Chaucer's time would have been pronounced 'K-nicht', and that gives them a historical dimension back- wards in language to realise that pronunciation and spellings have changed over time. I think that is very important knowledge about language for children.

Anthony Smith   Our project today is really to solve the question of balance be- tween different aspects of the teaching of English, and I know that your presenta- tion, having been a very interesting one, has concentrated on one part of it, but you have heard what some of the other witnesses said, and I wonder whether you would entirely reject the notion that media teaching has been relevant to what you feel English is about or whether you feel it can play some useful part. If so, where would you place it on the curriculum?

Jennifer Chew   Since I started teaching in the 1960s, I have never totally neglected media in my own teaching, because as I said in my paper, I have always made some use of newspapers, magazines, advertisements, but the print media are what I have always considered to be appropriate for my own teaching. I do not find that I have the time to venture into other areas of the media, and particularly pictorial media; and at the moment I would not really feel myself ca- pable and competent to deal with that. That is pressure of time. I use television adaptations. I have shown my A Level English class within the last week the

BBC version of *Emma,* which is one of their set books, when we had finished reading the book. They enjoy it and I enjoy it. But I use the media, I think, to further the teaching of English rather than for their own sake.

COMMENTS AND QUESTIONS FROM THE FLOOR

John Keen (English teacher, Glasgow) I want to ask a practical question of Margaret Hubbard which may afford an opportunity to assuage some of Jennifer Chew's anxiety. Margaret Hubbard juxtaposed references to Shakespeare with mention of the optional media studies question at Scottish Certificate level examinations and I wonder if she could provide a concrete example for English and Welsh classroom teachers which would convince them that senior secondary pupils would derive from a media course something similar to what Jennifer Chew called mind-expanding interests comparable to those that are assumed to derive from the study of Shakespeare or Marlowe or Malory.

Anthony Adams (Lecturer in Education, University of Cambridge) My remarks are addressed to our first two witnesses, but have some context also in the context of what Jennifer Chew had to say to us. I wonder whether, in considering the boundaries, we ought to consider not only the influence of the media on English teaching but also the influence of media upon literature today. It seems to me the difference between *Middlemarch* and *The Buddha of Suburbia,* to deal with two texts that have been quoted to us, is that the latter is itself very much a product of the media age, and the author is clearly influenced by this experience in media and cinema in particular. Similarly with someone like Malcolm Bradbury, who is equally at home in both worlds, it seems to me that his later novels in particular are very much influenced by his work in television.

It has already been pointed out to us that Shakespeare was working in the popular media of his time. I would want to argue that the novel in a pure form is very much a product of the 19th century. Before that, writers like Defoe or Sterne were writing in a much more diffuse set of forms and we see this also in the postmodernistic novel and in the new texts being generated from the media and the new technologies today.

In other words, print literacy, with an emphasis upon production of texts by individual writers, has had a very short life and it must not be allowed to dominate English classrooms today. Language is indeed the very core of English, but the language of the media is also the core of language experience today.

Laurie Smith (Graded Assessment Unit, King's College, London) I am struck by the dichotomy between the speakers, the first two and the latter two, and I wonder if, between the emphasis on media and on transactional and related matters, literature has been a bit squeezed. I follow Marilyn Butler's comment about smuggling in media studies when literature is only half-way through the door.

My question really is for Margaret Hubbard and Phillippa Giles. I am interested in this value-free analysis of techniques that they promote in schools, but I would like them to consider the question of whether the moral qualities of the visual media are in fact flattened and very crude. I have always been struck with the fact that most films have to have music to make their emotional points. They cannot do it through language, for example. To take a topical example, to compare *King Lear* with the film *Child's Play III*, of which I have seen part, the effect of seeing the blinding of Gloucester is very different from seeing a humanoid doll destroying a human being, and I wonder why. I think I would ask them to consider the moral implications and worthwhileness of having media studies and the resources that that needs, rather than concentrating on other matters.

Margaret Hubbard   I do not know if I am relieved or delighted to hear an accent similar to my own! Fortunately, it is a question I am quite comfortable with. Perhaps I should answer the question, instead of in theoretical terms, in terms of what my own fifth year, who are going to sit their exams at the end of the year, are actually going to write an answer on.

At the end of fifth year in Scotland, the children sit the exam which will provide them with entrance to the institutions of higher education, and when they sit Higher English, they do so as a combination of interpretation work, free writing, creative writing, non-fiction writing and the literature paper. The literature paper is divided into four sections: the novel, drama, poetry and the mass media. The gentleman who asked the question will know all this but I am putting it in context for everybody else in the room.

My kids actually answer on three pieces of literature. But in the exam they answer on two, although they are going in prepared for four. They are going in with *Romeo and Juliet;* with the poetry of Ian Creighton Smith, who is a Scottish poet; *The Great Gatsby*; and on the mass media section, they are going in with *The Untouchables.*

Now rather than me go through the value of all these pieces of work, I think that perhaps for the sake of this discussion I will concentrate on *The Untouchables* and *Romeo and Juliet*, because you can take it that my comments on *Romeo and Juliet* would be the same comments I would make on Ian Creighton Smith and on *The Great Gatsby*. When I am teaching *Romeo and Juliet,* they will be taught the language of Shakespeare, the imagery, the rhythm patterns, the dramatic structure, the characterisation, how the text changes, how the themes are set up at the beginning, how it changes after the murders of Tybalt and Mercutio and what Shakespeare is saying· at the end. Within the terms of the themes, I would go into the question of love, hate, prejudice and all the other issues that are part and parcel of *Romeo and Juliet*.

Now when it comes to these things, clearly the children understand. These things are relevant to the children's world. As well as getting them through the exam, they engage and they can make sense of these issues of love because it is so relevant to the situation that teenagers find themselves in in emotional terms, albeit not in practical situations because they are not in Verona X number of years ago. They then are able to make sense of the text by understanding how the language patterns and the construction of the characters have dramatic effects.

When it comes to *The Untouchables,* they are engaging in the same things. They are engaging in what the film is saying about racism, in terms of the language that is used. There are references in *The Untouchables* to dagoes and wops and Irish pigs, and these words come out of the mouths of the heroes, in some cases, and later on in the film, it is handed to the villain to say it and we get into how that meaning is changed in just the way that Romeo echoes Mercutio's lines.

In the same way, we will be looking at the imagery of *Romeo and Juliet* and how that shifts as the play becomes morally dark, and so we look at how the language patterns change within the screenplay that David Mamet wrote. We would also be looking at the issues in the text – that is, the question of law and order in America, whether or not the American legal system is able to handle the problems that it has, because those are the issues that the text is raising. We look at the whole position of women as it is constructed within the text, and the whole position of the men as it is constructed within the text, and in the same way as we look at language handling and rhythmic patterns to see how these issues are raised in *Romeo and Juliet,* we look at it in terms of how the music makes the meaning, how the editing makes the meaning, how the action, how the camera angles, how all these various things contribute to make the meaning of that text. So they have to understand the means by which the text is made in order for them to understand the meaning of the texts, in exactly the same way as they have to understand the means by which Shakespeare made his points.

So the children are then understanding, apart from the grammar – the literary analysis – that in *Romeo and Juliet,* they are also engaging with real issues that are relevant in our society now, because *Romeo and Juliet* is as relevant now as it was then, and so is *The Untouchables.* The issues that *The Untouchables* is raising are as relevant now as they were at the time of Capone.

Apart from that, a little bit of the answer to Anthony Adams' question is also this point about cross-over. The methods of analysis in media studies – you can go back and analyse the literary text in the same way, and you can look at it in the same form. Much of David Mamet's writing – and I think David Mamet is a very, very skilled writer – much of his theatre writing is influenced by his career in film. When I came down from Scotland the night before this Commission, I made my way to see *Oleanna* and I was aware of some of the filmic techniques that are operating in the writing there, albeit it was written for the stage. There is a real cross-over point there: so many modern writers are working from their own knowledge of film, because they have grown up in a visual age.

So it is possible, then, in the teaching of media studies, to engage with traditional literature through the same sort of skills of analysis. And on Jennifer Chew's point as well, I would agree that reading and writing is vital to children. Without it you are in a lost world, but the stimulus in order to get them to read and write – it matters not to me if it is *Romeo and Juliet* or *The Untouchables,* insofar as I am concerned that they learn to read and to write and to spell accurately, because spelling accurately is the passport to exams and to jobs, and I am concerned also that they engage with the meaning that is operating in great works of literature and in the world they are living in. So in all these counts, that is why I am prepared to send my kids into exams at the end of the year armed with *Romeo and Juliet* and armed with *The Untouchables* and would argue they are both of benefit to the children in terms of passing exams and in terms of engaging with real issues that they have to deal with in the world.

Phillippa Giles If I can just first pick up on Anthony Adams, who I thought made a brilliant contribution. I cannot add a lot to that. Perhaps I can place my own earlier statement in a bit more context, because I felt we got very sidelined in talking about adaptation. It just happens that that is my particular specialism. Actually I think we should talk about television drama much more widely, and obviously adaptation is often a poor brother to original television drama. If you look at Hanif Kureishi's works, actually what is much more important is *My Beautiful Laundrette* and arguably not *Sammy and Rosie Get Laid,* and *The Buddha of Surbubia* we would need to discuss further – but I think your point was very important and I would like to set my statement in that context.

Laurie Smith made several points, a lot of them very ignorant, I felt. I do not know what he teaches but of course I was not advocating value-free education of any sort. All these things – when you are talking, you are talking thematically, I think – but some of the things that Margaret Maden has said have been enormously stimulating for me to hear. That is exactly how we should be teaching. That informs every level and to assume that film is flat seems to me curious. To assume that we use music to try and add to the image because there is a paucity or lack of language, a lack of thought or depth. Often in drama we do not use music. You can contrast *Talking Heads,* the Alan Bennett piece which had very little music, with something which had a lot of music, and talk about why that might be. But to actually denigrate film seems to me a very curious notion and I really did not know where you were coming from at all, I am afraid.

Jennifer Chew I have been very intrigued by what Margaret Hubbard has said. I lived in Scotland for seven years and my eldest child started school there and in fact was in school for three and a half years before we moved to England. My impression was that Scottish primary schools were doing a much better job than English primary schools on the nuts and bolts of language and I just wonder whether the freedom to branch into the media in secondary schools in Scotland, and the success of that, is partly dependent on the good job that Scottish primary schools have done before the children get into secondary school.

On the other two points, I totally accept that writers like Bradbury have been influenced by the media, but it is a two-way process with people like that. One last small point is on the question of print literacy, and whether it is to be allowed to dominate classrooms or not. When I think of media and whatever I do to educate my students in the media (and I have to say that I spent a GCSE lesson yesterday with a GCSE resit group analysing six different newspaper accounts of the Bulger affair, which was fresh news), I see my job in educating them in the media as being as much to equip them to read the editorials in *The Independent* and *The Guardian* and the *Sun* and the *Daily Mail*, as to watch films and videos intelligently.

Hilary Lloyd (Lecturer in English and Education, University of Wales)   When I was a PGCE student myself, I remember the head of English where I was doing my teaching practice in Winchester saying to me: 'Hilary, be very serious about what you do, but for goodness sake, don't take yourself too seriously'. So in that spirit let me give a humorous postscript to the contribution of my friend and colleague, Tony Adams, who is also a Celt. The postscript will tell you that I am very much in sympathy with his view of the place of media studies in English teaching.

During November and December when people are beginning their Christmas shopping you will find the trains from the South Wales valleys to Cardiff very full on Thursdays because Thursday is known and has been for 50 years as 'Valleys Day' in Cardiff. So let me take you on the train from Merthyr Tydfil down to Cardiff and back again on the Thursday evening after shopping and we have Gwyneth and Idwyl sitting next to one another, worried to death because they have not finished their shopping, you see. And Gwyneth says to Idwyl: 'I don't know what to buy our little girl for Christmas' and Idwyl says: 'Ay, it's awful difficult when they get to that age, isn't it'. They both ruminate on this and then Idwyl has a brilliant idea and says: 'I know, why don't you buy her a book,' and Gwyneth says: 'She has got a book'.

Mike Clarke (Curricular Adviser for Media Education, Essex)   I would just like to ask all the witnesses to respond to one of the points made previously by Sir Malcolm Thornton, the Chair of the Parliamentary Select Committee on Education. He said that he felt that media studies and the use of media methods were especially valuable to children in their early years of schooling because of the connections that were made with children's experience before coming to school, and I would like to ask for the witnesses' responses to that thought.

Robert Beverige (Robert Gordon University, Aberdeen, and Chief Examiner for A Level Communication Studies)   My question relates to my experiences in England and not Scotland. The question is about progression. Is it possible or desirable to define a body of knowledge or skills in media education? I understand from colleagues in further education in England that there are substantial progression issues. In higher education as well we are finding students coming in with substantially variable levels of knowledge and understanding, and there is currently a proliferation of certificates and courses in media studies in the post-sixteen area, and I understand there is a problem also from GCSE into post-sixteen. That question is particularly to Margaret Maden.

Michael Gordon   I earn a living from mathematics and computing and in my spare time I am the secretary of The Queen's English Society. I both read user manuals and write them in the course of my work. What I notice with our young graduates is that they seem unable to use an index and unable to use a table of contents. Printed knowledge with an index is organised knowledge and accessible knowledge and is therefore worthwhile knowledge. My question is, do the witnesses agree for these reasons that there is a primacy to be afforded to the printed media and to the knowledge of how to use them in an effective and organised way?

Tim Leadbeater (Lecturer in English and Education, Trinity and All Saints College, Leeds)   To what extent do the panel think that an introduction to the principles of media education should be a compulsory part of initial teacher training? Is it good enough that only those English teachers who are interested in media develop their interest after they have become teachers? Jennifer Chew identified three per cent of the National Curriculum specifically mentioning media. I think a lot of people would say there is a lot more than that if you know where to look.

Jon Davison (Lecturer, Canterbury Christ Church College)   I think part of the worry here is still based on the perception of the quality of television or new media as compared to the printed text, and the assumption that somehow there is dilution of quality in the new media. I have seen numerous productions of *Othello* and one in particular at Stratford-upon-Avon with Donald Sinden as Othello which did nothing for the play but diminish it.

Jennifer Chew said that she finds no problem with using highly imaginative novels in the classroom. If we go back to the Board of Education Circular 753 in 1910, when English was just emerging, I quote from paragraph 34 which says that novels are rarely suitable for reading in school. Perhaps part of the worry is also linked to the terminology that has been used this morning: that of English and media studies. For me, media studies over the last twenty years has actually referred to a discrete subject on the curriculum. Should we not be talking in terms of media literacy and literacy in general, and actually seeing that as central to any pursuit in the classroom that concerns itself with literacy? If we are not actually addressing media literacy now, we are in fact mis-educating children for the next century.

Margaret Hubbard   Media education is particularly valuable for the early years. In the early years, children are watching television and they are aware of such things as pictures on the covers of books which are the advertisement for the book itself and carry all the values that are in the books. Children come into school aware of these things and I think they should be taught it from primary 1. That does not make it invalid later on. It becomes more difficult and complex later on. That does not mean to say that something that is valid in primary 3 does not have a value later on in a much more complex form.

I think children should be getting media literacy in nursery school. Indeed, there is a joke around in Scotland that we should be writing media studies modules for the womb. We think they should be getting it from the very beginning; in Scotland we now have it firmly in place from Primary 1 through to 6th year level. At the beginning, because it came from English teachers in Scotland initially, we were working in our own schools teaching it to our own kids and it moved up to the universities and down to the primary schools. Now we have children coming into secondary schools who have done media work in primary school and it is a bit of a muddle at the moment insofar as it is all happening at different stages. But we are moving to a curriculum where it is set down that by the end of Primary 2 they should be able to do this and so on, all the way through, leading to entrance to university level. There is a progression beginning to happen in Scotland at a national level, laid down in documents produced and agreed by the Scottish Office.

Should there be compulsory teacher training for media education? Yes, there should be, because I think it should be compulsory to living. The media affect our perceptions of the world in fundamental ways, and in a democratic society we should understand how the media deliver our ideas and events to us. In Lothian where I work, we are in the business of trying to get the courses set up for teachers going back to retrain. I did my first piece of academic work in media education through the Open University and then did a certificate in a Scottish college in the evenings. The colleges are doing in-service courses for existing teachers who wish to retrain. Pre-service training is now happening in Scottish colleges; not as much as we would like, but for the body of media studies teachers in Scotland who are agitating for training, one of the biggest areas of agitation is for pre-service training, and we are in negotiation with the Scottish Office on that. The Secretary of State for Scotland does not appear to be averse to it at all. He signed all the documents to say that media education should be in schools, so he has to set up the funding in the colleagues to allow it to be taught.

I agree with Jon Davison's point about media literacy. In response to Michael Gordon's question about printed texts, the answer is no, I do not think the printed text should have primacy. I think it should stand side by side with visual texts because they have such a significant effect on how we understand the world. I did say that one of the things we do is non-fiction work. Within that children study non-fiction pieces of prose and they are also taught how to look up indexes, tables of contents and Teletext.

Phillippa Giles Whether media education is especially valuable to children in earlier years; obviously it is very important as a stimulus, but for me, it is later in the real development of critical analysis and those skills, that the emphasis should lie. Teacher training in it should be compulsory, but there is a balance to be found between the perception of quality in the new media such as television, and in printed texts. What has really excited me about this debate has been the idea of integrating media studies across science, art, history, because for me that has to be the way forward.

Margaret Maden Perhaps I can just address the point about graduates – or undergraduates – not being able to use an index and contents. I do not know what the nature of the evidence is on that. I have to say that the academics on the National Commission, not least Sir Claus Moser, had a regular grumble about illiterate undergraduates not being able to write essays or have a sufficiently extensive vocabulary, or being able to spell, though as far as I am concerned that has always been the case. I am not being unnecessarily complacent but some of the most creative minds in the world have not been able to spell. I would be interested to know what evidence there is of a substantial kind. Certainly such research facilities as we had on the Commission could not nail this one at all. People have very passionately held beliefs about the problem, but that is not quite the same as secure evidence.

I do not think I can add much on the media studies matter, expect the wry observation that I have every sympathy for those people on the National Curriculum Council, or now SCAA, trying to make sense of very passionately and well argued claims for more and more to be included in the standard curriculum of children working through our schools. I am interested in media studies, certainly, as I understand it, and when it is properly taught and understood. It opens up a range of skills that certainly have a clear linkage as another form of language in terms of the kind of normal sense of language we are talking about here, and therefore I would have thought the multiplier effect would be quite powerful. But how much a school, or certainly in primary school, a given teacher can deal with satisfactorily I think is a real problem.

Jennifer Chew   I would like to reinforce the point that Phillippa Giles made on the question of whether media education should be paramount in primary. I also feel that its real place is at secondary level. I think there are more important things we ought to be doing, which is not to say that I do not think we can use television and videos as a way in for primary children, but so much is a question of balance. How much time are you going to spend each day on these things? I think that the setting place of reading and writing and arithmetic must be the first priority at primary level. On the question of whether media studies should be compulsory as a part of teacher training, I would prefer not. I would like to see it more specialised than that. If people have a commitment to media education and want to specialise in that, then it should be possible for them to do so. Surely learning how to, if you like, read a film or something on television is a legitimate claim in terms of everybody's learning. I am being thrown a bit by media studies claiming, as I understand it, its own stand alone position as a subject with content and skills and concept, whereas I would have thought as a form of 'reading' in the wider sense of language, it would have a perfectly legitimate claim in terms of what it means to be an educated and fulfilled person.

Notes

1. Report of the National Commission on Education, *Learning to Succeed: A Radical Look at Education Today and a Strategy for the Future* (London: Heinemann, 1993).

Day Two: 27 November 1993
Session Four

Future Visions: English 1998 – 2011

Mary Warnock   A child who is born today will enter school around 1998. I hope, as a matter of fact, that she will enter school a good two years earlier than that, because I hope in future school will start at three. But on current form, this child whose birthday is today will enter school compulsorily in 1998. Her school career will go on until at least 2011. So we are going to be putting our minds to what is likely to change and what is likely to happen to that child whose birthday is today and to her literary and media education within those years. What kind of cultural education do we think she should have?

The session began with a screening of a ten-minute video made by children of ten and eleven years old at Ysgol Bro Eirwg near Cardiff, made in association with the Media Education Centre at Cardiff in 1987. It is an animated production about the past, present and future of the city of Cardiff.

Mary Warnock   There is vision for you! Our first witness is Elspeth Howe. She was, at one time, a member of the Inner London Education Authority, and she is now Chair of the Broadcasting Standards Council.

Elspeth Howe   The terms of reference of the Broadcasting Standards Council are narrow. They are concerned with the portrayal of violence, sexual conduct, and matters of taste and decency which tend to concentrate on obscenities and Christian holy names. It has a relatively narrow remit, then, and is not, except in the negative sense, a guardian of language standards. The word 'standards' has a much broader meaning in relation to the national culture, to the preservation, where appropriate, of its past forms, and its continuing evolution as the eventual inheritance of future generations.

We confront a future in which the television screen will play a major part in the lives of both children and adults, but the passivity (and I think it is fair to call it that) which has marked television viewing until recently – the couch potato perception, if you like – has now been partly replaced by the interactivity that we are seeing, which will mean fundamental differences in the experiences of children born today in their use of the screen to those of children born fifteen years earlier as they pass from being viewers to users. I myself have grand-children aged fifteen and four, and I have seen a tremendous amount of difference, purely on an anecdotal level.

Lord Reith spoke approvingly of the brute force of monopoly as an agent for maintaining quality. It was clearly easier for him to promote quality than for us to try to hold back the use of four letter words. However, in the absence of that monopoly, other means must be found to ensure the effective transmission of the cultural heritage. Competition for money will put pressure on funds available for those programmes traditionally protected within the schedule, primarily programmes for minorities.

The role of regulator in broadcasting has already changed, with an increasing emphasis in the commercial sector on policing licences; a more negative role, once again, than in the past, and one for which quality and range of outputs are more elusive goals. It is important, therefore, to equip the new generation of screen users with an understanding of the nature of what they are seeing.

You have been talking about media studies, and it certainly has tended to be spoken of in some circles, with scorn, as a soft option. But that should not deflect us from attempts to teach, at all levels of education, the grammar of the media and, in particular, an understanding of visual literacy. At the same time, it is important to try to ensure that fragmentation of the use of the screen does not influence for the worse the use of language. The preservation of standards of literacy, to which certainly the media contribute, should therefore be one of the major objectives of policy in the coming years.

However, I wish to end by saying that I am not worried about the survival of the English language. That language and its culture already has an international head start. It is a main international language. We can use it, for instance, at con-ferences and use humour to make our point in a way that perhaps the French and Germans are not as easily able to do. In the broadcasting media world, it is cer-tainly other cultures who are worried by the take-over by our culture, and admit-tedly the American culture as well. Although we are the main recipients of American culture, I think we still have managed to survive, though we should obviously be wary and guard our own culture.

Another matter is the fact that the sale of cultural products is increasingly the same world-wide, and a need for instant intelligibility – the global village – works better with a single communications crutch. It was certainly easier when missionaries were selling the gospel; now, if you are landing a 747 at Tokyo Airport, it is vital that the language used is the same and intelligible, and that language is English.

All of that makes it entirely probable that our oral tradition is increasingly, as it was initially through print, going to be secured by all the other interesting forms – tapes, disks, videos and so on. It is also encouraging that Dean Acheson, appropriately the Rupert Murdoch Professor of English, has assured us of the robustness of the English language to take on board new concepts, new current cultural relevances, and throw them out or keep them permanently.

The last point I wish to make goes back to my educational and indeed my juvenile court work. We have been bombarded by the horrors of the James Bulger case, and truancy and other matters have been much discussed. I must say that it was very much my experience in court that children who offended had long truancy records. It used to make me cross; if I had to go to school, why shouldn't everybody else? Now I am by no means so sure. If there is so much out there to attract our attention, then the whole world of education has to be that much slicker and that much more able to communicate in a way that keeps our cultural heritage going. That is a challenge. I am sorry to be controversial, but I would think that such things as the Open University have done rather better for that generation than we have yet done so far as schools are concerned.

Anthony Smith I suppose that one should really link what Lady Howe has said to some of the things that have been said in the first two sessions. We were arguing about how to give all the people who live in this society the sense of having a stake in the language and therefore in the media. Are not some of the problems of language with which she has to deal and about which she is concerned, really, in a sense, the price you pay for trying to have a television system that gives everyone the sense of having a stake in it, in that everyone can see their ethnic community or the kind of family they come from, to ensure that they all see, at some point, a reflection of their own lives in it? Is it not important to judge between different ways of using that language? I am now speaking to you more as the head of the British Broadcasting Standards Council, which tries to deal in a creative way with such questions, but is having to fence with people who have a very particular view of how language should be used and what roles those four letter words or Christian holy names may or may not have in television programmes.

Is it not important, if we are looking at the education of a child ten to twenty years from now, that we retain and develop a television system that gives that child, wherever in the society he or she is located, a sense of being reflected in the medium, and is that not the best way to give that person a stake in the language and therefore a path to all the rest of our culture?

Elspeth Howe One of the things that I have seen over recent years is just that diversity and the fact that regional interests have been much more diverse. As we fragment into this amazing new world, there certainly is a case for some form of public service broadcasting. I would like to see that as not just the monopoly of the BBC. I would like to see quite a specific amount of time put aside for other channels as well.

What we try to do (and it is a difficult job) is to base our decisions on the complaints that are made to us by looking at current research. For example, let us take the word 'bastard'. That word, in one part of the country is really a genuine term of endearment; in other parts of the country, it would be far from that. One has to take some account of the difference of regions, and that is one way in which it can be measured.

If I go on to another aspect of public service broadcasting, I think we are all concerned to see that, given that children as well as adults use the media quite considerably, there is enough on television that is of quality for children to see. I would be very worried indeed if that was left purely to the market. So again I am back on the need for such an element. We have a very narrow remit and the Broadcasting Complaints Commission looks at individual disadvantage, and indeed matters of privacy. I think there is a need for a rather wider forum independent of broadcasters in which some of the issues, such as the one you have just raised, can be discussed and more widely researched.

Alan Howarth I understand it is the case that 'bastard' is also a term of endearment in the Cabinet!

Elspeth Howe I had forgotten that one!

Alan Howarth You chair a body whose job it is to uphold certain decencies on behalf of our society – a difficult job, since there is no particular consensus as to what these decencies necessarily are. But is not an organisation such as yours approaching the end of its life? The rationale for regulating broadcasting hitherto has lain in the scarcity of spectrum, and we are approaching a world in which that will not be an issue. There will be perhaps 500 channels conveying entertainment and other material into large numbers of homes within a remarkably short timescale. We will be able to use interactive techniques to access a whole host of material of the kind that we choose to interest ourselves in. Material will be sourced instantly from all parts of the globe. Will it not, at that point, be widely seen and be accepted that it would be as absurd to ration, regulate and censor broadcast material as we now take it is absurd to licence plays or newspapers, or indeed books, as we did once upon a time? In short, there will be no option but to treat people as grown ups.

But if that is so, what about children? Will there not be a particular set of requirements in relation to children? Should society not still try to impose certain standards of decency where children are concerned? Many people will feel it is important to protect the innocence of childhood. Many more people will at least recognise that we should try to protect children from abuse and psychological trauma. Is a body such as your own, or a somewhat differently constituted body, going to be able to grapple with that problem? How would the responsibilities of an organisation such as yours interplay with the responsibilities of teachers?

Elspeth Howe Obviously there is going to be much more choice. That is a good thing, as far as I am concerned, but it will be in a more fragmented market. There will be a much higher element of paying for what you want to see. I could make a pretty good libertarian case for saying that there is no need for anything, let everybody be grown up and choose what they wish to choose. If you start from an American system, which started from the market, there does not seem to be any less clamour for some sort of upholding of standards. They seem to be stuck on the First Amendment, but the clamour is there. There are arguments about too much violence on television and video nasties. The clamour is for some form of regulation of something that comes into your home. Not all the things we are speaking about will necessarily come into your home; but as far as television is concerned, I think there is a strong case, and an increased case so far as children are concerned, for saying there should be some regulators.

We are an advisory body. It may be that there are too many now and we are going to be facing a period of change in the future. But I would argue that, if in the past, we entered into the commercial world from this very important monopoly, that was doing a pretty good job because we wanted more variety, and if you have the good balance with the channels we have, now we are to be even more fragmented and we have a considerable national concern in that some sixty-six per cent from our three-year surveys say that there is too much violence on television.

Alan Howarth   What are you going to do about it? How do you police 500 channels, particularly when you have satellite broadcasting?

Elspeth Howe   I do not think you can police in that sense, but you can lay down standards to some extent. You could even say that X per cent is given over to public service broadcasting within any of the channels. There are lots of ways to do that. For the moment, I rather like the phrase used by somebody from Germany at a conference, when he said that in this transitional period when we do not really know where we are going, it is very important that there are various 'heat shields' which may delay things a bit so that we can see how it all works out and what we really need.

But I have been increasingly conscious of two things in the short time I have been doing this job. The first is that clearly there are a lot of regulators, and perhaps that needs looking at. But there is nothing really, apart from our two limited areas, that looks at the whole of broadcasting and looks at it from a consumer viewpoint and not from the viewpoint only of the broadcasters.

Marilyn Butler   I am going to ask you to be philosophical and reflective. I realise you were not here when media studies were being talked about in a very eloquent way, but it does seem to me that part of the strong case for media studies in the curriculum has to do with the positive nature of a lot that has been seen on the media in Britain in the last couple of decades, and it is possible to say that this is the most important medium that children already know. If one imagines a situation ten years hence in which there are 500 channels, first of all, the experience of any one child is not going to be so common with all the others, but it also will be necessary to develop a completely different rhetoric about media studies and strategy within media studies, because presumably more severity of approach to the actual material will become necessary. Or do you think that the case is going to decline for having media studies?

118

Elspeth Howe   No, I think that media studies, apart from teaching you how films are made and a few things like that, can show how you understand and interpret pictures and so on, and possibly how you can work through what is being pushed at you in terms which may be at variance with the pictures you are being shown; in other words, to be critical and to analyse what you are seeing. I think already we are having a problem about this, because on one of our roadshows we came across an absolutely fascinating bunch of Welsh teachers, one of whom was in the media study world. However, she said that (a) she was not technically very good – that is a generational thing – and (b) she knew exactly what the children were watching but because she had not recorded it and nobody had thought to prepare a package (and what a gap there is in the market there) so that she had a teaching device to take the children through. So she felt herself at a disadvantage.

That sort of thing, which is happening now, is going to happen much more in the future. But I think we will work out very quickly, even if the viewing figures do go away from our terrestrial channels and right up into the heavens, what are the popular programmes and what people are watching. There again, that can be used much more effectively than it is now.

Marilyn Butler   But you might be wanting to teach them a completely different line on certain things they are watching.

Elspeth Howe   Absolutely.

Marilyn Butler   I am trying to imagine how the forms of teaching might have to be much more critical. In that case it might have to be for older children.

Elspeth Howe   I would have thought there would be different ways of doing that which will develop over time. I am just amazed that it has not developed as fast as it should have done. I come back to the point I made, that we have not caught up with just how clever we are going to have to be, as well as effective and relevant to children, if we are to compete with all the other ways in which they can spend their time rather than going to school.

Robin Alexander   You spoke of standards in broadcasting and suggested that currently they are too narrowly defined. During this Commission we have touched from time to time on the vexed issue of illiteracy, and I wonder if you would like to tell us how you define standards, perhaps in relation to literacy in general, but perhaps particularly in relation to visual literacy. What are these standards, what should they be and who should define them?

Elspeth Howe   In terms of standards generally, there is an interpretation that, almost by definition, one is thinking of the standards of the past, so there is that way of looking at it: that you are trying to preserve something from the past. We would have different concepts, but I think my conceptions of standards and quality are that it is something that is gripping, something in which you do not think you are being taken along in order to achieve a big audience, and something that is not exploiting violence that is unnecessary to the story-line, whatever it happens to be. I do not think I want to get into the business of a specific standards definition. We could all, no doubt, give our views on that, but into the future we will all know what it is because we will all be looking at things. For example, I would like to keep some of the minority areas which almost certainly will not attract the funding we are getting at the moment because of the public service area. Whether it is programmes on fishing or whatever, I cannot see a majority audience for that, when the whole thing is going to be funded from the market-place.

Quality in whatever you are doing would be my definition. It will be a somewhat floating definition in the sense of goodness only knows what forms of media and interesting things will come. But what I worry about at the bottom end of things is this. If you are looking at some of the areas that we are responsible for, there is a need for, if not a censor, because we have moved out of censorship, something which reflects very much the current views of what people feel is acceptable and what is not acceptable.

Robin Alexander   And because we are talking about the curriculum, what would be the guidance you would give for teachers? What would be the principle which you would offer to teachers who were dealing with the area of media and visual literacy?

Elspeth Howe   As far as curriculum is concerned, you would have the basics of the things that need to be taught in the curriculum, all of which I agree with, that are in the National Curriculum. I would certainly add to that media studies, so in that sense, yes, but quality in all of it.

Robin Alexander   Are we not going to have to make up our own minds about standards, and is that not going to mean acting responsibly towards our children, and is that not going to mean educating their critical capacity so we can all work our way towards a new culture, or continuously renew our culture?

Elspeth Howe   Yes. I think the fewer nannies we actually have, the better. I would agree on that. It is an education to be in this quite different world, even more aware and alert and critical and analytical in what we see. But I think ultimately, so long as you base it in the reality of what is happening in the here and now, relate it to the past, think about the future certainly, but you have still got to have some sort of central standard-setting body, however flexible it is. If one looks at the whole business of what it is that people think they want out of public service broadcasting, for example, what everybody seems to say is that it ought to be the preservation of their national identity, and you can define that in lots of ways. If that is so, and I am now looking at you, Alan, as a Member of Parliament, I simply cannot see you or indeed any government letting go of this central issue.

Mary Warnock   I now call our second witness for this session, Sally Tweddle, who works for the National Council for Educational Technology (NCET), having previously been an English and drama teacher who was then involved in the innovation of the Technical and Vocational Education Initiative (TVEI) and thus came to be interested in the technology of education.

Sally Tweddle   I am currently working with NCET on looking at what the future is going to hold for the curriculum under the influence of Information Technology (IT). One of the things that we did when we started on this work was to canvass the opinions and look at the visions and speculations of a whole range of people.

We were surprised – perhaps you will not be surprised when I read the list – at the degree of agreement that we found among employers and educationalists about the aims of education for the 21st century. They said that the education system should produce young people who are flexible and delight in change; who are literate and numerate; who communicate effectively; and who are autonomous, reflective and motivated learners. They all said that unless such aims underpinned the whole structure and organisation of education, as well as the configuration of curricula and courses, education will fail the young people who are born today. They believe that the current education system is the product of a society which pre-dates the current technological revolution.

Why is this? One of the reasons is the influence that Information Technology is having. It is changing ways of living and working. It is changing ways of teaching and learning, ways of thinking and even what is thought. We are getting an information-rich society, in which many people are going to have access to vastly greater quantities of information than they have ever had before; new technology support communication systems which are going to enable that information to be passed rapidly around the world, and are thus contributing to the development of a global culture.

Information Technology is also generating a collaborative writing culture with information, writing and ideas shared, borrowed, jointly constructed in a way that they have not been before. The concept of literacy is changing. We have been talking about visual literacy, but the nature of text, the writing and reading processes and the contexts and purposes for reading and writing are changing.

More specifically, as was identified in a seminar that NCET ran, what IT creates are intermediate possibilities which show that previous dichotomies are in fact points along a spectrum of possibilities. That is quite a mouthful, but it is a very important principle. Let me pause for a moment to consider the dichotomies. The dichotomies that dissolve include reading and writing; teacher and learner roles; the home, the school and the work-place as separate sites for learning; and English, media studies and communication studies as separate and institutionalised curriculum subjects. So if we carry on with the title of English and accept that that is the title of this debate, then I want to pick up three implications.

First, there will need to be a broader representation of reading than we have now, of the media for reading, the processes of reading and the texts that are studied. By 2011, books and electronic texts will complement each other. The current overlap between their functions will be gradually disappearing. Both will be valued but they will be used for different purposes. The book, for instance, will be valued for its permanence, as a means of preserving powerful messages and giving access to cultural and literary texts of the past. It will be the most appropriate medium for the novel. The book enables readers to re-visit a text on many occasions and find it unchanged. It is portable and requires no power source. Children will still need to learn what to expect of a book, how to find their way through it and how to read and interpret what it says.

Electronic texts will be valued for the amount and range of up-to-date information which they make accessible as and when needed. Electronic texts are multi-media, using combinations of still and moving images, word and sound. They allow the presentation of information in a different way, and with different types of information. They can also be interactive. They will replace books as sources of hard information.

The range of types of texts carried by the electronic media carried by the console in the living room which will replace the television will in fact be very wide, so children will be able to read or view arcade games and databases; documentaries and what are now being called 'edutainment' programmes, the mix of education and entertainment; plays in performance and scripted texts. Young people will have to be taught how to read them: non-linear texts combining words, image and sound; texts which do not appear the same on subsequent readings. They will have to understand the origin of the texts, the validity of the information they carry and who wrote them. They will have to be taught how to make appropriate choices between the different types of texts. For this to be possible, the reading curriculum will have to be constructed so that it develops literacy through the study of a comprehensive range of texts, rather than with the aim of ensuring a knowledge of certain specified texts.

Secondly, the writing curriculum will have to change with respect to the forms of writing that are taught and to the writing process. The child who is born today will be expected to know how to write using combinations of words, images and sound – perhaps we should say 'compose' instead of write. She will have access through a computer to the tools which will enable this to happen. She will have as her models both Hardy's poems and twenty-first century arcade games. She will have the technological capability to emulate both, and it will be important that her entitlement within education gives her the opportunity to do so.

The writers of tomorrow will also be collaborators, as well as individuals seeking to make and convey meaning. They will use computers and communications systems to write with others or to take their ideas and re-shape them. No important document emanating from government or commerce is likely even today to have been written by a single hand. Children will be able to write with their classmates or children from other countries and cultures, just as they are writing for real outside school. So the English curriculum will have to ensure that children are required to collaborate and are taught how to do so, and assessment mechanisms will have to be devised which enable the accreditation of achievement in collaborative as well as individual writing.

Thirdly, because of changes to the ways in which teaching and learning will be organised, the English curriculum will have to be specified in such a way that schools can construct their own courses and so that pupils can negotiate individual pathways through those courses. Developments in IT will mean more individually-based learning and an increase in distance learning. There will be a blurring of the present divide between home and school which currently supports the construction of school learning as separate from that which takes place outside school. There will be a spill over from one curriculum area into another, as pupils use the same ideas, information and processes in a number of different ways.

If English is to be relevant to the needs of young people and to meet the aims of educationalists and employers, the curriculum must be specified in terms of concepts and processes, skills and knowledge rather than content and methodology. Assessment structures will need to provide scope for flexibility in the organisation of pupil's learning. As I have already suggested, NCET is already working on how this is possible for English.

A working group has succeeded in establishing in outline some of the principles which should govern the teaching and assessment of literacy in the 21st century. Our work will continue and we regard this debate as a very important part of that.

Anthony Smith It is difficult to assemble my questions, because I think that is probably the best statement I have heard of the tendency of information technology and its likely ranges of impact on education. But there are areas of fuzziness (or at least they seem fuzzy to me) that I would like to put to you, where you talk about the changing concept of literacy. Can I ask one of my 'are you or are you not saying' questions? Are you saying that children will use this equipment to learn to read in the way in which we have traditionally understood the term, and therefore presumably the skill, once achieved, whether gained from the new electronic device or by some other means, is then transportable in the way that the skill to read has normally been thought to be a fully transportable skill? I think that is a question that is symptomatic and applies elsewhere. If you are talking about collaborative composition, are you saying that children will still be able to leave school and write interested and excited letters to their friends, or will they be dependent upon this collaborative composition?

Sally Tweddle I will start with the second question because I think it is more specific. What I hope I said, and I should have emphasised, is the fact that people need to be able to communicate and to write individually, just as they need to be able to write collaboratively. But the current curriculum is based on the assumption that we are teaching individuals to write as individuals for their own individual purposes, by and large. What is happening is that the technologies are making more possible what in fact has been realised by teachers as they have been working in classrooms over a long period; the realisation that writing collaboratively actually is a different act from writing individually.

What we are saying is that children are going to have to learn the difference in writing collaboratively. They are going to have to learn both skills, and they are going to emerge knowing when it is appropriate, as an individual, to write a letter to a friend, and to be able to do that with a pen and paper on a train; but also to know when it is appropriate to share a draft and draw other sources into their writing. It is for that second aspect of writing that we do not have structure and framework for teaching sufficiently at the moment in the current National Curriculum.

As regards the first question, there is some thinking that children could use computers to learn the basic skills of reading, as I think you characterise it, in the traditional way; in other words, learning the skills of reading which could then be transferred to reading print in books. I say there is some belief that that may be effective. I suspect that computers may be able to have some small role in supporting the approaches to the teaching of reading, but I suspect that that is all. Computers, however, will have a very important role in the teaching of reading as I would characterise it, which is the teaching of reading the whole range of texts that one is going to come across, which includes print-based texts and electronic texts, because they are part of the reading material that children come across every day in their lives outside school. So in other words, many children are actually confidently able to handle the structures, the organisation, the language that is presented to them on computers, and they are successful readers in that medium. They may not actually be successful readers or may not characterise themselves as such in a print medium. I believe that it is going to be very important for developing their basic literacy that they recognise themselves as being able to read in all the media which require reading.

Anthony Smith   When we see someone today who we think of as well-educated – someone who has come out of some school in some part of the country, and you meet, and somehow you feel that that person has been well educated – in 2011, when that young woman emerges from all these processes, let us say that she is tremendously successful. Will you be able to identify her as a well-educated woman, as you would today? Is the end product of that education the same?

Sally Tweddle   I really do not know how to tackle that question. I suspect that everybody in this room would regard a well-educated person as being something different. They would also have some characteristics that I would imagine would be the same. In terms of English and how I would regard them as emerging from a successful education through the subject of English, if we accept for the moment that that will continue to exist, I would say that they would be very similar in that they would have developed critical faculties. They would have developed the ability to be reflective about what they read. They would have developed the ability to be able to choose what to read, when to read and why, and the same with writing. They would have developed the ability to articulate what they believe about what they read, and one of the reasons I was surprised when we came up with the aims espoused by educationists and employers for the 21st century was that they were, in fact, very similar to the aims that lie at the heart of the English curriculum as most teachers teach it at the moment. We are talking about literate, reflective, autonomous communicators.

Robin Alexander   You probably accept that futurology is a fairly dodgy business, do you not?

Sally Tweddle   Yes.

Robin Alexander   I wonder whether your scenario presupposes adequate or indeed limitless resources, full employment and cultural unity and consensus, perhaps to an excessive degree. If we extrapolate our vision of 2011 from the down side rather than the up side of life now, would it be the same? Would your recommendations for the school curriculum be the same?

Sally Tweddle   My recommendations for the school curriculum would be the same, because I think we have to change radically the assumption that we have at the moment, which is that the curriculum teaches, and that what the curriculum teaches is what is important. The recommendations that we have been coming up with were in fact that our assessment systems – and in the end they have a very significant effect on what we value in terms of education – should allow us to accredit and validate all the learning that takes place - both inside and outside school, but particularly outside school.

Now, to come back to the idea of not having technology available to everyone: at the moment we have a great deal of experience in reading, for instance, that is going unacknowledged in terms of the English curriculum that is taught in schools. Children have access, even if they don't have computers in their own homes, they have access through society, through the generally-available computers in libraries; children are using libraries more than they used to, and they are using computer systems in order to access information there, they are reading and viewing the computer games in the arcade. We need to acknowledge that experience at the lowest level of technological provision across society. Those systems will continue to exist and there will be more of them, more widespread, more available in society, even if not in individual homes.

So what we have to do is reconstruct the curriculum in order that we can acknowledge and validate and build upon those experiences. We have to have a curriculum which also recognises the possibilities that there will be others who will have different experiences of reading and of writing, with the technologies that are in their homes. That is one of the key principles that we held to when we were working on this, that you cannot any longer specify the content of the English curriculum because individuals will have increasingly disparate experiences of reading and writing if one is acknowledging the whole of their experience of literacy rather than acknowledging the controlled experience of literacy that we've previously validated.

Marilyn Butler   Do you think that, in some ways, like a lot of technological revolutions, when they come they do not come very suddenly, they usually come more slowly and more gradually than people expect? So they are not shocked in that sense. But in another sense they are taken in people's strides so you do not actually feel quite such a revolutionary thing has happened, as one supposes in advance. Have we not already been on this drift from knowledge and content towards skills for really quite a long time?

I think one would designate a well-educated person of the really older generation now, the sort of retired generation, as somebody who quotes a lot and has read a lot of very well-known books in prestigious subject areas such as philosophy and not in other areas that were in some way demeaning or popular; whereas I think that as you go down the decades, people do not know those fixed things any more. Generation by generation they do not. That is partly what the older generation complains of. Do you not think that we are already half-way to the revolution that you are describing?

Sally Tweddle   I think that in some senses, yes, we are. One of the problems is that what has happened is that practice has advanced in the way that you are talking about, and certainly if you look at individual English classrooms, for instance, you will find people who are looking at the nature of text. You will find people who are working with IT texts, for instance, alongside the texts which are specified in the English curriculum. But that has become the problem. The problem has become one whereby we have a curriculum structure which actually lags behind the practices which are developing, and in order for those practices to develop speedily enough to be able to catch up with the technology we have to be able to anticipate not just the technology but the general changes that are taking place. Maybe IT is one of the catalysts for this. It is the point at which we say we have to break the current English National Curriculum because it does not work any longer as it is constituted to represent what is happening and what needs to happen, for those aims as characterised at the beginning to actually come about.

Alan Howarth   You seem to assume that because the technological possibilities will be there, we will necessarily wish to embrace them. I would certainly go along with you, I presume, in a view that we neglect modern possibilities at our peril, but it may also be that there will be people around – not least teachers – who attach renewed importance to the contemplative elements in life and that indeed they would wish to see the school, at least in an important part, almost as a haven, a place in which you can meditate and strengthen the spirit, a place in which you can fortify yourselves before you then engage anew with the modern world.

What I am really talking about is balance and how we relate your vision of the future to the traditional strengths of the educational process which many people, I think, feel are imperilled by virtue of the very rapid pace of change that events and policies have forced upon education.

Sally Tweddle   It is interesting, is it not, that when you talk about IT and technology, there is always a risk that the impression one gives is that one envisages people using IT and technology – whatever kind of technology – all the time. That is certainly not what I anticipate. You talk about being contemplative. Let us perhaps talk in terms of reflectiveness, which in fact IT can support. IT can support reflectiveness about learning, but essentially I suppose what I am saying is that we cannot ignore the technology; it has to be part of the process of education that we are involved in for the next century. That does not mean that that education will be determined and entirely characterised by what is possible with technology.

I suppose one of the key principles that we were looking at – we were this group of people brought together in a seminar to look at the future for English – was actually to begin to look at a meta-language which would provide a new way of characterising text and the text which will become the focus of study in a new English curriculum.

One of the characteristics of the framework that we were drawing up was that it enabled learners not to feel that they had to read all 8,000 texts that we calculated would be necessary if they were actually to be able to experience all the possibilities of types of texts, but to be able to say that actually by working with a small number of texts you can touch on and develop a conceptual understanding of the different types and functions of text without having to do everything. In other words, it might well be that your English curriculum might involve a reading of the same number of texts in print as texts in electronic form. It might mean that because of your particular interests and experiences it involves reading far more texts of the print in electronic form. So we are not talking about the technology taking over; we are talking about actually reflecting it in its rightful place as one of the aspects of what we need to educate children for.

Mary Warnock   Our third witness for this session is Farrukh Dhondy, who is a successful writer and also the Commissioning Editor for multi-cultural programming on Channel Four.

Farrukh Dhondy   Allow me to start my statement, conduct my argument, as it were, as a kind of chess game because I cannot, with such a vast subject, think in a linear fashion.

Let me start with the story of a person who became a film. I am not talking about Mahatma Gandhi; I am talking instead about a more recent film, that of the life story of Malcolm X. I read *The Autobiography of Malcolm X*. It was not written by him, so it was not written in the kind of rich language that he might have used himself; it was written in internationally intelligible English so that it could be printed up by, firstly, the American publisher, and then by Penguin, and disseminated around the world. Then, of course, he acquired a greater notoriety, a notoriety which a certain generation in Britain would not have been acquainted with had they not seen the film which reached the huge screen, sold a lot of caps and became the talk of market-places from John O'Groats to Brixton.

The story of Malcolm X I do not think was interpreted very correctly, in my terms, by Spike Lee, the black film-maker. I have conducted this very small experiment. When I asked children of a school-going age, or black acquaintances of mine who had a certain revolutionary fervour, what they got out of the story of Malcolm X, they said: 'Basically he was a black anti-racist.' The emphasis was on black, black, black, on race, and the other emphasis was, of course, on a certain sort of anti-message. It is characteristic of our times that we begin to identify ourselves by antagonisms, even though we do not intend to.

I am going to say soon that that is not the significance I see of the story of

Malcolm X, but before that, let me tell you another very short story. I am driving along with my two Indo-Brit daughters, who are not yet twelve, and they are listening to songs on their Walkmans. I say: 'What kind of songs are in the charts today?' because I have absolutely no idea, and they sing me snatches of two songs, one by Shabba Ranks, whose chief lyric is: 'I've got a wagon-load of women', and another one by Buju Banton in Jamaican patois, saying: 'Boom bye bye in a batty man head.' I asked Sian and Jan: 'Do you know what "boom bye bye in a batty man head" means?' They said: 'We have absolutely no idea. Why don't you shut up and let us listen to our Walkmans?'

At the time when I was at university, to know a bit of Jamaican patois was quite unusual. To be able to talk in a street-wise fashion – you could dine out at any Cambridge party for a long time if you had a few phrases of Jamaican patois. Today it has become a completely common phenomenon. Every eleven or twelve-year-old in the inner city, and I would say outside it now, is picking it up. Why? Because the media have somehow, in the very few years between my teen-age and now, changed the landscape.

The landscape is such that Buju Banton and Shabba Ranks are coming through on local radio stations, be they pirate or be they licensed. Through these local stations, they are beginning to reach the national charts. You can see Shabba Ranks on *Top of the Pops,* for God's sake! It used to be such a minority taste that you could only get the records of that sort in one shop in one district in one city – yes, Brixton. Sorry, no prizes for guessing which!

The third story concerns a trip I took to India recently. We were shooting a film for Channel Four, for whom I work, out in the remote villages, and there, stuck on a tree was a television set with the appropriate aerials. About 200 people were gathered, who did not understand English, watching it. What was playing one morning and again in the evening was something called *Santa Barbara.* It is a soap opera from America. In the evening they were watching something called *The Bold and the Beautiful,* again a soap opera from America. All this stuff comes through on something called Star Television from Hong Kong, owned by Rupert Murdoch, and millions and millions of villagers in India are watching this stuff.

I decided to conduct, in my characteristic fashion, a little experiment and I asked the people there, 'What are you getting out of this without sub-titles?'

They said, 'Well, it's a very clear story. I know what's going on there.' I said, 'Don't you find it disturbing?' They said, 'Why should we find it disturbing?' I said, 'All these people driving around in beautiful cars, wearing these things. Aren't they totally unlike you?' They said, 'Are you crazy? They're exactly like us. The people from *Santa Barbara* and *The Bold and the Beautiful,* I see absolutely no difference: two eyes, one face, two legs. What's the problem?' I tried to say: 'Well, there is disparity in development and culture, and what not.'

These anecdotes simply lead me to believe that there is an internationalisation in culture. I need not have told you those stories to put that point across, but I

128

think they get it across just a little better. What I am trying to say is that if one examines what the Buju Banton lyric was about, which I proceeded to do when the kids came back from school, 'Boom bye bye in a batty man head' means 'I want to shoot homosexuals'. I tried to tell them that was not right, but they had moved on to the next song before I could get the point across. There was no assessment inherent in their listening to Buju Banton.

Secondly, the story of Malcolm X for me (and this is very subjective) is that he is the quintessential American phenomenon of our day. Lenin, Trotsky, Keir Hardie were all sort of leaders of the working classes. They got themselves to that position, but they got themselves to that position from the education of the middle class or the advanced miners' working class, working people's institutions, and so forth. Malcolm X did not. Malcolm X was a pimp, a drug seller who did not know where he was sleeping the next night, who did not know what he was selling. He was a violent person. He had committed a lot of robberies. He had been to jail. Then, he turned himself into a leader. He was not an anti-racist leader. He was a person from the lower ranks of modern American society groping towards a vast social message, and it would not be too bold to say that he had picked up the elements of a Marxist description of what America was and should be and he was groping towards something more. That was the distinction of Malcolm X. The reason I understand that is because I have read some Marx. The reason the youth in Brixton do not understand that is because they have not, and no number of films by Spike Lee will tell them that. I have the conceit to believe that I am better educated and more appreciative of Malcolm X and his life.

Let me move another rather large piece on this chess board. While people say that this internationalisation of culture will soak us and completely submerge our values in those of *Santa Barbara* and *The Bold and the Beautiful,* I want to pose a piece of counter-evidence. We know that through print, through radio and through television, for nearly eighty years, the Soviet Union from Latvia to Vladivostok was bombarded with propaganda: the Soviet realist message, in its drama, in its news, in its documentary output, in its soap operas, in every news bulletin it transmitted. And nobody at all believed it. It remains a mystery to me. How did they get away from what they were being bombarded with if we, and me in my job, believe that television is all-important and influences people's minds?

I believe that products from that era of television, radio, even literature will become nothing more than a curiosity, nothing more than museum pieces. The era will disappear completely from the canons of European and even Russian literature and culture. It will be seen as an era of pure propaganda, which is what it was. Somehow generations of people saw through it even at the time, though more towards the end.

What I am trying to say simply is that we live in an internationalised culture. No doubt there are technical satellite and cable and interactive technologies which are going to be responsible for more and more of this phenomenon. But where does it leave us? I do not believe that the media themselves can educate. I believe they can

129

inform, I believe they can allure, I believe they have taken away some of the lustre that the written word had by telling their own stories, but I do not believe that any of those stories can substitute, especially in the internationalised form of *Santa Barbara* and *The Bold and the Beautiful* and Buju Banton, for a core set of values by which a society needs to live.

There is an additional dimension to this. I know that the internationalisation of culture need not only be one way. It need not only be that the American soap operas flow to the East; it can easily be that Eastern music, African creation, Indian religions (which have already done it) and other forms of Indian culture flow back. We saw the Mahabharata on Channel Four television. These things will come across and impose their significance on the West and be appreciated here. So there is that flow too, even though that is a small counter-culture because one nation – America – is more powerful and imposes a world cultural order which the other nations do not have at their disposal yet. Nevertheless, I am not pessimistic about that. I know that the flow will eventually be both ways.

Even if the flow is both ways, by what standards are we to judge this? My personal belief – and that is what I was asked to give you – is that one ought to judge it by the standards of the excellence that the Western scientific and critical tradition has evolved. Believe me, I have lived – still do in my mind – in more than one culture, and I am making the very bold, if unpopular, assertion that there are certain sets of values inherent in the criticism of *The Prelude* which one will not be able to pick up from even the best commentaries on certain kinds of Hinduism. There are certain values and possibilities of life inherent in Western novels and music which are not inherent in Maya Angelou or the Urdu Qawwali[1].

The internationalisation of culture will no doubt give us a vast amount of content to play with, but the central matter of the content, if one wants to know how to live – and that is the content of education – will have to remain in a sense the repository of values that has been generated by the best minds, the best creation – the canon, if you like – added to, expanded, reconsidered. That is, Western cultural values with the religions of the East added, with the creations of the East added. I believe that we live in a world in which this is technologically not only possible but inevitable.

Anthony Smith   Farrukh, you have given us this very eloquent account attempting, as it were, a cultural reassurance.

Farrukh Dhondy   I did not do it for that reason.

Anthony Smith   No, no. I know. But it is a shock to us because it is very different in tone from what we have heard over these two days.

Farrukh Dhondy   I try!

Anthony Smith   You seem to be offering us two internationalisms. There is the bad internationalism that your teenage daughters are subjected to, then there is a good internationalism which is based on Western values with other things added on, and someone is presumably somewhere working out a suitable canon of Oriental add-ons to Western culture. It seems to me, though I instinctively share your value system to a very great extent, that it is extremely difficult to achieve. The probability is that even though these things are maybe ephemeral and they fade away, young people are going to be subjected to more and more of the half-digested, half-understood international culture that came through the Walkman.

What is the best educational tool, either to help them avoid it altogether, or to help them through the first phase into the second phase that you suggest still lies almost inevitably beyond? I am speaking about educational tools within this culture, within Britain, because that is what we are talking about today. Is it necessary to go back to solid standard English as defined in the last ten, twenty or thirty years, however far back you want to go, to establish its boundaries? Is that the tool that saves them? Or is there something else that has to happen to our education system?

Farrukh Dhondy I think that the British education system has in fact picked up ways of transmitting cultural values. I would adduce in evidence a whole critical school that has grown up around English literature. Shall we say, it is one particular critical school. I recognise that. But it starts with, if you like, the novels of Jane Austen and finishes through the arguments of F. R. Leavis, with modern poetry being capable of being assessed in the same way. I am sure that that critical school will tell us that criticism is a 'Yes, but . . .' or a 'No, and . . .' phenomenon. You are able to talk about the artefact of writing and possibly the artefact of television also in a particular language, and that language is a language which has a moral subconscious. But the moral subconscious does not come to the fore. You do not discuss Dennis Potter as though you were having a Church of England debate, but you ask: what possibilities of existence, what possibilities of the use of human character or the story, to put across a particular aspect of life, is being made by Dennis Potter on the screen? So, yes. Media studies, to that extent, does come into it, and I am sure that we have, inherent already within the educational system, the method by which such a criticism can expand and be largely more inclusive.

I do believe, though, that one has to guard against certain fashions. I was talking to a graduate of a London University college who came for a job at Channel Four. I said, 'What are you studying?' She said, 'English literature.' I said, 'What poetry do you read?' She said, 'I don't read poetry. I read black American literature instead.' I said: 'That's a shame.'

Alan Howarth You have given us evidence of the advance of homogenised culture with the same literally meaningless lyrics and soaps, barren propaganda saturating people's minds across the world. You have said that the media cannot educate. So I just wonder how this core set of values to which you are attached and I am attached, the values expressed through Western rationality and high culture which we would both like to consider are indispensable, will actually survive against the experience of mindless mesmerisation? What is this principle? How will this, as it were, Darwinian survival of quality actually be able to take place?

Farrukh Dhondy Can I start the answer to that question by saying that I believe in relative absolutes! In other words, for our time I believe that what I am saying is absolutely correct. It is a pity that I cannot convince Ghengis Khan of it; he is dead. But I am sure that if he lived in our times what I am saying would be relevant to him too. When one talks about literature and the use of English, and one makes contentious statements about black literature or the canon of English poetry, one could argue on *The Late Show* about this forever.

But one can resort to a different argument within the same cultural value, and that is the argument about science. Lady Howe touched upon it when she mentioned the pilot who needs to land in Tokyo. I am not sure that they will be using English. They might be using symbols on a screen, but there is the idea that you do not crash planes, that you cannot let your wing tip lift too much or it will hit the runway. So about science there can be very few arguments. I know that in the realm of medicine there are vast arguments, but still, to cure, to heal, to prevent, are better than to do the opposite. So one knows those arguments and has absorbed them into the core of our culture, and those will get inter-nationalised willy-nilly whether or not there is a meaningless lyric from Jamaica being disseminated.

I do not know what one can do to fight against the hordes of that barbarism, but one conviction I have, through my Soviet example, is that if people did not listen to that relentless propaganda, then something else in their lives – and I do not think it was school because school put out the same stuff – taught them that school is hogwash and the television is not telling the truth. There are forces apart from school and the media, apart from organised education, that teach us things about very, very important dimensions of our lives. I am sure that those would prevail and I am sure those would be the subject of an inquiry not into English but into extra-curricular influences.

Mary Warnock Our final witness for this session, and indeed for the whole Commission, is Michael Armstrong. He is Head of Harwell Primary School in Didcot, Oxfordshire and is the author of a book entitled *Closely Observed Children*, which is a study of learning in a primary classroom.

Michael Armstrong I think the greatest need in education at the present time is to rediscover the imagination. If there is one thing which I would hope for chil-dren born today it is that they might be taught in schools which recognise in the power of children's imagination the chief condition of learning and the crucial test of a curriculum.

From infancy onwards, children struggle to make sense of the world through a creative engagement with the various forms of expression which define our cul-ture. Their earliest stories, poems and plays are evidence of that struggle and its outcome; the beginning of a critical practice that underlies and controls the entire history of learning. The business of education, as I understand it, is to excite, sus-tain and interpret that practice week in, week out throughout a school life.

132

Here is Holly, a pupil in my school at the age of six, pondering in narrative form what it means to destroy a habitat: 'Once upon a time there was a hedgehog. He had a friend called Mr Caterpillar. They went to Mr Hedgehog's house in the hedge. The farmer chopped up the hedge. At the bottom there was a pile of leaves. They fell down. They sat on the leaves. In the morning they were dead.'

Elementary syntax and a simple vocabulary do not constrain this young story-teller. They have become an opportunity, the appropriate means by which to express her unsparing vision. So it is with every young writer. Teaching means recognising the creative achievement and seeking to advance it.

I want to draw attention to three consequences of looking at education in this way, each of which has been neglected by the National Curriculum. The first is this. The development of technique in matters of punctuation or grammar, argument or style, is dependent upon each child developing imagination. 'The basic skills', a profoundly misleading term which has not been analysed at all in this Commission so far, are neither the prerequisite of a critical practice nor its complement. They are embedded in practice and advance by way of practice. Take punctuation, for example. Long before they master the standard forms, children become adept at their own punctuating devices, radiating lines around a word requiring special emphasis, huge letters denoting a shout, a single large stop, or the words 'The End' to signify closure. A more conventional fluency comes only as children see that their practice requires it if their intention is to be understood.

The second consequence is larger. Any curriculum is necessarily provisional. The shape of learning is determined by the interplay of authorised knowledge and naïve inquiry within the classroom. To prescribe what books are to be read, which writers are reputable, what language is correct, what forms are appropriate for which purposes, is to ignore the innovative aspect of education. Education is a process which redefines culture in the act of handing it on. We look at the way young children begin and end their stories, how large a space they leave for interpretation, how readily they incorporate visual elements into their writing, and our own sense of narrative possibility is changed. No subject matter is quite the same after teaching it. A good curriculum undermines itself.

The third consequence concerns assessment. The critical evaluation of children's learning depends upon documenting and interpreting their intellectual enterprise as displayed in their stories, poems, plays, mime, dance, conversation, argument and speculation. It is a matter of tracing the progress of their thought from year to year, identifying the themes, motives and concerns that govern their practice, observing how they incorporate new material and fresh experience into their composition, examining the ways in which they exploit a developing technique. Its appropriate form is the edited archive; a body of work selected, arranged and annotated by teachers in collaboration with their students as representative of present accomplishment and indicative of future learning. The archive is the antithesis of the test. It emphasises uniqueness and individuality. It resists standardisation. In the archive learning is made manifest as nowhere else.

So when I imagine a classroom at the turn of the century, I see it as a co-operative of writers and readers, dramatists and film-makers, exploring the imagination in as many forms as come to hand, anxious to share their work with each other and with their parents, their teachers and their local communities, guided and directed by teachers but always ready to challenge their preconceptions; a classroom in which the acquisition of knowledge is always in part a reconstruction of knowledge. In its present condition and under its present leadership our own society may not be capable of realising this vision, but I propose to go on working as if it were.

Alan Howarth While working as if it were, do you want to use a lot of Information Technology in your classroom, or would you prefer to carry on teaching as if it were not there?

Michael Armstrong I was very impressed with what Sally Tweddle said. I already use a fair bit of Information Technology in my classroom, and I would very much hope in the next few years to use a good deal more. It is an area where I think most teachers, certainly myself, are still quite largely ignorant. It is not, in a sense, part of our culture in the same way in which it is part of the culture of those whom we are teaching already. Therefore, it is in a sense a particularly fascinating area because in exploiting Information Technology one is always to some extent – to a larger extent than in perhaps other areas – learning from those one teaches since their facility with both the apparatus, and to some extent with the ideas that inform Information Technology, is often in advance of our own.

Alan Howarth What about the media material that is carried on that technology? During this Commission, we have been given the example of *Neighbours*, which constantly cropped up in the conversations. Would you find it helpful in the task of opening their imaginations to give your children lessons based on *Neighbours* or some other familiar television programme? Or would you want to keep them away from it?

Michael Armstrong No, no. Not at all. Even if I wanted to keep them away from it, as with my own children, my chances of doing so are virtually negligible. So it is not going to be worth my while trying. But in any case I would not wish to because I already know from the stories that my own children write that *Neighbours* has a very positive impact on their writing in all kinds of ways. Like other television soaps, it gives them material which they can transform in their own writing in ways which probably would never have occurred to the producers or makers of that particular programme.

I find that the extraordinary thing about working with young children is the way that they transform material that you regard as corrupt into a form that completely switches the way in which you regard it.

Marilyn Butler I am very fascinated by this because obviously it is no accident that your three points are all topical matters – in fact, the ones that we have discussed – but they are in the current arguments. They were arguments over punctuation and grammar, arguments over curriculum and arguments over texts.

So here you are describing the kind of various road-blocks that you encounter and that your children's imaginations so brilliantly drive round. You see it as if it were 'three to the children, and nil to the road-blocks'. So I was not sure how you mean this: as a sort of cry of protest about what you see as irrelevances really; or the wrong emphasis on what happens in the educational world; or whether you do in fact see it as a hopeful sign that in another decade or so the children will in fact negotiate.

Michael Armstrong   As with all futuristic talk, one is always poised between hope and expectation. My expectations are profoundly pessimistic at the present time. From its outset I have regarded the National Curriculum as a mistake; I still do. I am not persuaded that it is necessary, I am not persuaded that it is desirable, I am not persuaded that in the long-run, although it has had certain undoubted benefits, it will do anything to advance the learning of our children. I think there are better ways. That is the first point.

The second is that you are right; that each of those three points I mentioned, I mentioned precisely because they are areas in which I think the National Curriculum has got things wrong. Particularly we have heard here previously from all speakers about the problems of a curriculum that was to some extent assessment-driven. I think the urge to see everything in terms of statements of attainment which can be measured through standardised tests has a great deal to answer for. That is what in the end dished even Cox's version of the English curriculum, let alone the, to my mind, much narrower version that now appears to be coming out to replace it.

But in terms of curriculum as a whole, it is a point that Robin Alexander has been trying to get at once or twice. The trouble with the National Curriculum is that it was set up without discussion, without argument, without any intellectual consideration or defence of a position on the curriculum that is determined by ten separate subjects which were simply taken as given. So even now when you write to the members of SCAA protesting against the ten-subject curriculum as something which has been set up without discussion, without argument, you are dismissed. That seems to me, certainly at primary level – I would also wish to argue at secondary level – a profound mistake. So I do think that those three areas I have outlined show how the curriculum we have been given is actually hostile to learning rather than advancing the course of learning.

Robin Alexander   One of the reasons why your contribution is so important and perhaps unique in the Commission so far, is that it deals with the all-important question of the development of understanding and skill. We have tended, as I think I have observed on previous occasions at this Commission, to presume a static generalised model of English which makes no particular distinction between what is appropriate for six-year-olds, or sixteen-year-olds, nor indeed how progression is achieved. You have focused on that and that is a very necessary focus.

I wonder if I could just pick up one question about assessment. You argued that the archive is the antithesis of the test and you seem to be presenting assessment in terms of sort of Eisner-ish terms: responsive and descriptive, rather than preordinate or judgmental; having to do with flexible criteria rather than fixed norms. But are you saying that there really are no judgmental criteria of a general kind which can be applied to children's learning in English?

Michael Armstrong   No. I am not saying that. I think there are judgmental criteria. I do not think they can be expressed in terms of a position on a set of hierarchically arranged levels. I do not think they are adequately expressed in terms of marks in an examination or a test. I think they require a good deal more elaboration than either of those two particular instruments of judgment.

I do not wish to deny that there are judgments to be made. I make them all the time as I am teaching. When a child hands to me a piece of work and we talk about it together, my response is not always to say: 'That's lovely. Go away and write me the next piece.' Very often there may be criticisms, judgments, things that I think have not gone right, things that I think have gone particularly well which I want to say to the child and will then discuss with the child what she feels she has done and whether she agrees or disagrees with the judgments that I am making and why.

All the time I feel a vital aim in teaching is to make children more self-conscious about what it is they are doing. What I object to is the kind of judgments that are being forced upon us. Judgments which I think, certainly if my school is at all representative, most parents themselves do not actually wish for. They wish for something a good deal tougher, a good deal more rigorous and a good deal more imaginative than what they have been offered, and that is what we try to provide.

Robin Alexander   So would you agree that it is worth making some of these alternative criteria explicit?

Michael Armstrong   Yes. Absolutely.

Robin Alexander   Or do they remain in the head of the individual teacher?

Michael Armstrong   Yes. Certainly.

COMMENTS AND QUESTIONS FROM THE FLOOR

Brian Hustle (English teacher, North Liverpool)   I liked very much Sally Tweddle's vision of an English department developing its own curriculum, to meet the needs of pupils in the community. I would argue that when we had 100 per cent course work we were half-way to achieving that. Unfortunately, that has been taken away from us. I just wonder whether she would advocate the restoration of 100 per cent course work as a means of ensuring they are objective.

Do the witnesses think that there will ever be a clear way forward to a more balanced and coherent English curriculum, given the fact that so much of education is an open field for politicisation and for the internal market and the disruptions that go with it?

Bob Davis (Lecturer in Language and Literature, St Andrew's College, Glasgow University) I am a parent whose third child will go to school in 1998. I think Sally Tweddle's contribution would be what Professor Scruton would have characterised as the metaphysics of the future tense. However seductive its machine-tooled, bright-eyed rhetoric might be, I would urge the Commission to be resistant to it on several grounds. I will itemise just two of them for you. First of all, the value of using technology in the way in which Sally has suggested has not stood up to appraisal and scrutiny carried out in this country or on the other side of the Atlantic. Indeed, assessments of the impact of hyper-media, CD-ROM, and various other kinds of interactive learning on pupil language compectence particularly has shown it to be very largely marginal. It seems also to me that we have heard all this before. I can think of at least four occasions in the 20th century where technology has been infused with this rhetoric of salvation, this quasi-religious rhetoric. It is simply the obverse of technophobia, the belief that technology is to be our undoing. I feel that however noble Sally's intentions might be, another grave danger, given the particular cultural and social constructions in which this technology is embedded, is that it slides inexorably into the language of the 'technocracy', a tiny international elite in which are concentrated knowledge, power and information.

Finally, I would suggest to you that the people I find most sceptical of this vision of Information Technology are the children themselves. They have all seen *Terminator 2*.

Judith Garrahan (English and Media Studies teacher) I would first of all like to thank Michael Armstrong for trusting the kids that he teaches to make sense of what he teaches them and then to take on and do with it what they actually choose to do. I think it is an interesting point that it is the classroom teachers who are making these kind of comments and who have been making these comments during this Commission.

I would invite Alan Howarth, if he wants to spend some time in quiet contemplation and reflection, to come to an IT lesson in my school because that is the only time you are going to get it. The kids are so absorbed in what they are doing that they never open their mouths. They are just very, very busy and they are working very hard. So you can actually get all the contemplation that you need.

My second point is to do with the lyrics of the song that Farrukh Dhondy was talking about. I cannot remember who it was that referred to them as 'meaningless lyrics'. I would urge you to think twice about this. They are not meaningless lyrics at all. They are very, very powerful in their homophobic content and if media teachers are going to do anything, what we all need to do is to get our kids to be able to read and understand the meanings and the hidden meanings of lyrics in contemporary pop music and in all the other media. They must be able to look at these things critically and start asking questions about what we are putting down as 'trash', in the previous session in terms of soap opera and now pop music, which the kids actually embrace, perhaps at the moment without questioning.

The third question is: says who? We are talking in terms of regulating standards, of protecting people, of saying what is right and what is wrong. We need standards in the broadcasting media. We are talking in terms of Western culture. Farrukh is talking about Western culture as somehow being better than any other culture. Well, says who? Who says it is better? And whose culture is it? We have asked the question previously here: whose English? I would like to know who it is that makes these kind of decisions, because after all when we are talking about the canon of English literature and all that we hold good in terms of our own cultural heritage, we are also talking about our cultural imperialism. The reason that English is the most powerful language or the most used language is because of the imperialism of the past. The reason that we now have in small villages in the Indian sub-continent the broadcasting of *The Bold and the Beautiful* and *Santa Barbara* and programmes like these to people who cannot read or write or speak English is because English imperialism has been replaced by American imperialism. I would like to know why the American imperialism is somehow not as good as English imperialism. I happen to like *The Bold and the Beautiful.* I think it is great, and there is a lot that can be studied in it. Kids given access to study programmes like that are going to get as much into the actual analysis and criticism and questioning of programmes like *The Bold and the Beautiful* as they can from *Romeo and Juliet* or any of the other things which we hold so dear as part of our literary canon and heritage.

John Dixon (Retired teacher and lecturer)   I have two questions which are principally addressed to Sally Tweddle and Michael Armstrong but which are very much reflecting too on the panel and their thinking. We are faced here by a thing that says: 'Balancing literature, language and media'. In other words, the categories we have had in front of us are literature, language and media. I think Sally said at one point that Information Technology has helped us to dissolve some of the dichotomies. That is a very funny set of categories actually, I would have thought. To have taken those for granted, as we have done so far, has led us, it seems to me, into some pretty awkward scrapes.

The second thing, which is related to Michael Armstrong, is that I think he is the first person to have used the word 'imagination', which actually might appeal to Mary Warnock as well. She has written a book on it. But I want to say to you, Michael, how about imagination and practicality? It was theorised twenty years ago as transactional and poetic in writing research work. Imagination and practicality might help people like Margaret Maden when they are talking with employers.

Elspeth Howe   I am so fascinated by this whole business of technology. Yes, I belong to the generation that is not very good at it. I did a very late degree in my life and I am sad to say that, having finished the first year early, there was an election and I was called off to go and help my husband fight it. But at that moment, we were just beginning to learn how to work computers, as we were ahead of ourselves. I had just learned, as somebody who can type, to get to the point of pressing and saying the right things and out all this lot spewed out. That was the

138

most wonderful moment in my life. I have not really got beyond that. I wish I had. I am fascinated by it all. I agree with you, we owe it a tremendous amount. If I had been about, I like to tell myself, when we had some of these incredible programmes coming over like the ones put forward by David Attenborough, I would have been interested in biology instead of being bored rigid by it all through my life.

I think the whole of this Information Technology that we have got available, and the interactive side that is increasing, is incredibly hopeful for widening our knowledge and increasing our understanding of things. I am very much an enthusiast for it, and I think we will get through this phase. I think it will add to both our cultural identity long-term but also our co-operativeness. I like very much what has been said by two of our speakers, that we will be working more as teams. There is, anyhow in management, this philosophy these days. We are moving away from the individual to working as a group, the co-operative scenario. That is an enthusiasm as far as I am concerned. That is the way I think we ought to work. The competitive thing should be there, but it should be harnessed much more for the common good.

Sally Tweddle Having had the experience of teaching 100 per cent course work and having been involved in a team which devised an alternative syllabus which actually dealt with what was beginning to happen in terms of changes in children's practices in writing, in drafting, and so on, I would support wholeheartedly the retention of 100 per cent course work. I believe that it is possible to derive the sort of information that is needed about standards nationally from moderation and validation of course work. I believe that one can make it do that, if that is what one wants it to do. But actually I do not believe that 100 per cent course work is going to be on. I suspect that what we are talking about is something like eighty per cent course work with twenty per cent tests. That, may be, is the compromise towards which we would work. It is essential that some kind of course work, a significant proportion of teacher assessment, is there if we are going to be able to assess and validate what pupils are doing, particularly with Information Technology.

I think that one of the reasons why Information Technology has got a bad name and why the evidence that has come from across the waters and from here has suggested that actually it does not have an impact on language competence, which I think is what Bob Davis said, is partly because we have been doing the wrong thing with computers. We expected computers to enable us to do better some of the things that we were doing before. That is why I was a little sceptical about the potential for computers to teach reading.

However, while I am not a techno-freak, although I accept that I may give the impression of being the knight on the white charger, I suppose I am fighting a cause which is not about introducing technology but it is about saying: 'Let us recognise what is actually part of children's experience and let's make sure that the curriculum recognises that and validates that.' Whereas IT is the particular focus for that in the work that I am involved in, really what I am saying is we need to think again about a curriculum which recognises all aspects of the communications systems and the modes of expression and the vehicles for imaginative engagement that are available to children in our society today. That is why we need to look again at the English curriculum, not in order to get IT into the classroom.

The evidence that has come from the United States, that has come from programmed learning systems, seems to suggest that you can actually put children as individuals in front of computers and they will learn aspects of language, will learn to become competent language users. We all know that that is very unlikely to be successful. But computers can enable children to experiment and to investigate. It has been done in science and maths, and if it has been done in science and maths we have to be looking at how it could be done in English. If it is breaking the divide between English and media studies and communication studies, then we also need to look at how it is breaking the divide between other subjects in the curriculum.

Basically, we need to reconstitute the English curriculum so that IT is in its rightful place. As has been said, it is only one of the technologies that are to be used for communication in all the senses in which we communicate, and we need to be able to develop a critical language that enables us to deal with that and to decide when it is appropriate. We need to enable our children to do that, because however else we may feel it is there; it is there and it is not going to go away, and if we believe that education is about enabling children, among other things, to function competently and confidently in the society in which they live, then we cannot ignore it.

Farrukh Dhondy Judith Garrahan said that Buju Banton's lyrics are dangerous and harmful and then asked in the same question, whose values does one follow? Believe me, Buju Banton's lyrics have been defended to me by several Jamaicans of a Christian persuasion who think that homosexuality is much worse than any attack upon it. Obviously you do not share those values because you think that the song is dangerous. The fact is that there are some values which one ought to follow. Perhaps the best test is to follow those which do not interfere with the rights of others, whatever their gender, race, religious belief, or sexual preference. To take the case of Salman Rushdie, the problem is not racial, it is not imperialistic, but it is probably the largest divide over a book this century. The Muslims who want to kill him, or deny him the right to even publish it, fervently believe in his right not to write that particular book. I can leave you with that.

In talking about *The Bold and the Beautiful*, I believe that you have fallen into the school teacher trap – and remember I was one for nine years, a comprehensive school teacher – of thinking that that which has interesting things to be said about it is inherently of some value. It is the same trap that people who evaluate the Turner prize and evaluate other modern works of art have fallen into; that which can be talked about like a piece of art in a museum is not necessarily more beautiful than a Michelangelo, and I make a plea for the inherent values of things which can come out through discussion.

Michael Armstrong The only point I want to make is in relation to John Dixon's raising of the issue of the relationship between the imagination and practicality.

The reason why I stressed the imagination, as I hope was clear, is because I feel it is at the centre of everything else we try to do in schools and, conversely, that it is on the periphery of the National Curriculum. If you do not believe me yet – probably most of you who are teachers do – but if you do not I would remind you of a quotation which comes from the Cox report which has been presented to us, rightly I think, as by far the more encouraging of the two English curricula we have had foisted on us. The Cox report, in discussing writing, said:

> The best writing is vigorous, committed, honest and interesting. We have not included these qualities in our attainment targets because they cannot be mapped onto levels.
>
> DES, *English For Ages 5-16*, June 1989, para 17.31

A curriculum which denies you the opportunity to validate vigour, commitment, honesty and interest is not a curriculum which has very much interest for me. It is a curriculum which denies the significance of meaning in the evaluation of children's work, and to deny the significance of meaning in the evaluation of children's work is to deny them the significance which lies behind whatever it is that is most important that they themselves attempted to do. It is to deny their existence as thoughtful artists in any genuine sense.

That is also why I regard the issue of the basic skills as damaging not because I think that grammar, punctuation, spelling, knowledge of language, and the like are unimportant, quite the opposite, but because I think it is very dangerous to isolate those activities and skills from the activities within which they find their significance.

I would like to say in that respect that I would even regard theoretical discussion of language, contrary to what Colin MacCabe was saying, as both vital and totally plausible for all children. It seems to me to be essentially, though in the nicest possible way, insulting to children's intelligence to pretend that somehow they are incapable of discussing language in a theoretical way. Five-year-olds discuss language in a theoretical way the whole time. Any infant teacher will tell you. That can be done, I think, throughout a school career. But again it has to be done in the context of activities which are meaningful because they arise out of and sustain imaginative enterprise.

So in a way my response to John Dixon is that I think an education of the imagination ought to be able to cope with practicality and the questions of practicality you raised. I do not deny that there have been times in our recent educational past where that has not been the case, where for one reason or another teachers have confused the education of the imagination with somehow the opposite of practicality. That is simply a mistake. It may be a mistake for which many of us who have been teaching for a long, long time have ourselves to blame for having perpetuated it and now we are paying the rather heavy price, or more accurately our children are paying the rather heavy price. I very much hope that over the next twenty years we will be able to turn the tables.

Notes

1. Qawwali music developed around Sufi shrines in India and Pakistan. It is performed by a singer (Qawwal) supported by musicians, hand clapping and vocal chorus. Its popularity has been enhanced by the media and it is now often performed on stage, with fewer religious connotations; it is also becoming popular outside the subcontinent.

ADDITIONAL EVIDENCE

John Marenbon, Director of English Studies, Trinity College, Cambridge

I shall not try here to argue what should be the range of English as a subject. If it is not to beg more questions than it raises, any such argument would have to explore questions about the nature of culture and reason, and their relation to the individual – questions far too complex to be treated, or even usefully broached, in a few paragraphs. Let me, rather, confine myself to three general, preliminary points.

My first point is about the relationship between government and the English curriculum. There are minimum requirements for what should be taught as English at school which a government might reasonably impose, since the legal obligation on children between five and sixteen to attend school means more than that they should spend a certain number of hours in a building called 'school'. What as a whole should be covered by English at school is not, however, the proper concern of government or any branch of central or local officialdom. The aim of a Commission of Inquiry such as this one should not, then, be to provide a preferred view or compromise about the range of English as a subject which it would wish government to impose. Rather, the Commission should press government to allow individual parents, schools and pupils the greatest possible freedom to decide what, beyond the generally recognised basic skills of reading and writing, is taught in English lessons. Arguments about the range of English should be taken as addressed to those who teach English, not to those who draw up regulations. Their aim should be to persuade or, at least, give rise to thought, not to constrict and compel. They should be considered as part of an ideological battle, not a political one.

My second point is about the difference between the object of a discipline and the methods and material used to study it. A narrow and definitely specified object may be pursued by many diverse, wide-ranging methods. For example, my own preference would be to see the object of English at schools, besides learning how to read and write well, as the study of some of the recognised masterpieces of English literature. This view excludes from the object of English as a school subject most contemporary writing, as well as films and products of the media. Yet I would wish to insist that good teachers might well use any of this wider range of material as a method of teaching. When they should be used and how depends on the individual teacher and class: some teachers may not wish to use them at all, others may choose to use them frequently.

Third, and finally, I would suggest that there is no good reason to think that English as a school subject should be the same as its range as a subject at university. Universities, I would argue, are places for specialised academic study, whereas schools (although to some extent, from sixteen to eighteen; preparing pupils for higher education) are mainly concerned to teach areas of non-specialised knowledge and varieties of non-specialised understanding. It would, then, be very hard to justify basing a university course in English on the study of the great literary masterpieces of literature. For what could the student of English learn which a well-schooled economist or scientist would not also acquire, if he or she read carefully and avidly in his or her leisure time? Most university English departments are, indeed, keen to make their scope wide and to avoid any hint of amateurishness in the manner of their studies. Time may yet show that these aims cannot be realised merely by reconsidering and extending the range of work within English, but require a more general reorganisation of disciplines in which English would disappear altogether as a distinct university subject.

Professor Richard Hudson, FBA
Phonetics and Linguistics Dept, University College, London

The Tensions

1. Everybody agreed that it was important for children to learn to use English effectively and also to learn about the literary (and media) heritage; but these subject areas seem to involve different ranges of expertise and interest which would be hard to combine in one teacher. (I think of Andrew Webber's comment that he couldn't do any kind of grammatical analysis of the texts he studies.) A related tension is the problem of time: how to fit these two things into a single curriculum subject. It's relevant that English is the only subject that leads up to two separate subjects at GCSE (English language and English literature).

2. We considered two kinds of cultural heritage during the debate: the literary heritage and the linguistic one. But these questions turned out to be quite separate. Everyone agreed that children should learn to write and speak standard English, even if they were also encouraged to study their own non-standard or non-English variety; but when it came to the literary heritage I think most people opposed any idea of a fixed literary canon. Furthermore, we all agreed

that there is good and bad literature (and good and bad media texts), but it's dangerously easy to pass from this view to the view that the standard Language is inherently good, unlike non-standard varieties, simply because it is the medium of good literature. Most people (with the exception of Professor Scruton) seemed to agree that this leap was invalid, but it would be much less attractive if the two heritages were studied separately.

The Proposal

The school subject 'English' should be replaced by two independent subjects, 'Language' and 'Literature'. (Alternative names may be preferable, but these will do as temporary pegs to hang the ideas on.)

Language will deal with literacy skills in English at all levels, plus general understanding of language ('Knowledge About Language'). The over-arching aim is success in communication of all kind, but this presupposes some understanding of how language works.

Literature will cover the literary component of 'English', including the creative media and literature in translation – for instance not originally in English. The aim here is to let pupils explore feelings, morality, and so on, and perhaps also to develop their own creative abilities in this area.

Some Advantages of the Proposed Split

1. Two subjects can claim a larger portion of school time and resources than a single subject can (tension 1).
2. Teachers will be able to specialise and develop whatever expertise is needed (tension 1 again).
3. The role of standard English as the vehicle of great literature will be clearly separated from its role as the dialect which happens to have been chosen as our standard. This will make it much easier for the language teacher to treat local non-standard dialects with respect while teaching standard English as the dialect of school and the wider world (tension 2).
4. The language teacher will be free to deepen the pupils' understanding of language, which will arguably help them in learning foreign languages; this is 'one of the main planks in the platform of the 'Language Awareness' movement, which I was surprised not to hear mentioned by any speaker.
5. The language teacher will be able to pay some attention to the home languages of bilingual speakers, a gap which was pointed out by several speakers; it is harder to see a home for such work in a subject called 'English'. This too is part of 'Language Awareness'.
6. Literature teachers will be freed from responsibilities for language which many teachers of 'English' must currently find frustrating and irrelevant to their main interests. At the same time, however, it will be possible to bring the language of a text into focus because the pupils will have a deeper understanding of language.

7. The clearer focus on language will build on the existing demonstrated interest in language which has been uncovered by the new A Level English Language paper.

Possible Objections

(a) Other subjects will object to an apparent doubling of the territory covered by 'English', especially if the total resources needed turn out to be more than are currently dedicated to 'English'. However, the increase in work on language will benefit modern languages, and may even be taken from their current allocation since modern languages are where most 'Language Awareness' programmes are currently situated.

The language department will be responsible for the children's language development across the curriculum (whereas Margaret Maden suggested that other subjects should take this burden away from the English department). This has been tried out in the Wigan Project (mentioned by Jennifer Chew), and seems to have been extremely successful.

(b) Some 'English' teachers may object to the split in what they see as a seamless whole, as they enjoy teaching language and literature equally. However, this kind of situation can presumably be handled by cross-department appointments. There must be teachers who combine maths and physics, for example. There is no more reason to see the split as a denial of links than there is in the case of the maths and physics departments.

Laurie Smith
Graded Assessment Co-ordination Unit, King's College, London

I write as an experienced teacher of English, drama and media studies in schools, including ten years as Head of English. For three years I have provided practical school-based teacher training in assessing students' progress in terms of the National Curriculum, which involves working alongside teachers in a wide variety of schools each year.

The following observations concern the moving image only (currently cinema film, television and video, which for brevity I will call film), as use of print media and still images is usually integrated comfortably into English courses. Nor am I concerned with distinct media studies courses, often leading to an examination, of the kind lucidly described by Margaret Hubbard. These are valuable options for students. My concern is only to suggest that, in many schools, teaching using film is, in practice, displacing the teaching of literature. I would like to make three comments, in ascending order of significance as I see it. They are not made to criticise colleagues who are having to cope with delivering an overloaded English curriculum to students who respond much more readily to film than to print.

Use of Film Adaptations

The original place of film adaptations – back in the days when schools had to hire the 8 or 16 mm version of the film and project it – was for comparison after a novel or drama text had been studied. The arrival of video, with a much greater range of adaptations and much easier use, has led to three developments which I outline chiefly in the context of GCSE.

(a) Showing the adaptation before and during the reading of the text, sometimes the whole adaptation first and then sections relating to episodes in the text. The intention is to focus students' attention on certain elements of the text by bringing them alive through the visual version. Contrasting the treatment of text in written and visual media is also a legitimate element of GCSE course work. One result, however, is confusion between the written text and visual version. As Chief Examiners for GCSE English Literature comment from time to time in their reports, some candidates write about incidents or even dialogue that appears in the adaptation but not the text studied.

(b) Using the adaptation as an alternative to reading the *longueurs* of a novel. The adaptation is watched for narrative, character, setting, atmosphere, and so on, then significant episodes of the written text are read and studied in preparation for course work or examination. This approach is often used in schools which require study of a 'classic' novel or with modern novels, like Harper Lee's *To Kill a Mockingbird,* the length of which is daunting for some students.

This approach is now very common in years 7 – 9 where, for example, episodes of *Mrs Frisby and the Rats of NIMH,* would be read in relation to the brilliant cartoon version. Able readers would be encouraged to read the whole novel, but reluctant or limited readers would not be required or supported to do so.

(c) Using the adaptation instead of reading the written text. This development has been halted by the abolition of 100 per cent course work, so that examination questions have to be answered in relation to a written text. Previously it was not too uncommon for students to be shown a film that followed a written text reasonably closely (for example *One Flew Over the Cuckoo's Nest, The Elephant Man)* and to write a piece of course work on it using worksheets containing extracts from the text.

All three developments indicate a displacement of literature by film. This may be reversed by the backwash effect of the new requirement to answer GCSE English Literature questions in relation to written texts, but the consequence may equally be a reduction of the number of students entered for separate GCSE English Literature. The Commission is requested to be aware of this possibility and the likely cause of it.

Effect on Students' Engagement with Literature

There have always been students who, though competent readers, find literature and indeed, most fiction, uncongenial, probably for reasons of personality. Others take to fiction and, within their reading ability, to literature, with enthusiasm. There is a continuum between the two.

My impression, which is shared by numerous colleagues, is that students are increasingly reluctant to give their attention to elements of literature other than, in fiction and drama, action and realistic dialogue, that is, the very elements that are most evident in film. There is an apparently increasing reluctance to engage with description, reflection and unusual qualities of language. If left to themselves, many students will skip over these elements in a novel, seeking the next passage of dialogue and action. This is not surprising, as they are experienced consumers of film in which meaning is chiefly expressed through action and dialogue.

One result of this is that fiction read in schools, and provided in the teenage fiction sections of public libraries, approximates more and more closely to the qualities of film: clear plot, much dialogue, minimal description. To compare the novels most frequently read in schools twenty years ago with those used today makes the point very clearly. (A possibly related issue is that the attention span required to watch films has diminished. The average length of a shot is considerably less than thirty years ago, so that the pace of films from the past now seems slow. The invention of video also allows the watcher to speed the pace further. There are accounts of teenagers in Californian cinemas chanting 'fast forward' during more reflective passages of a film; they want to move onto the action, as they would when watching the film at home.)

The essential questions are whether there is a generally greater reluctance among school students to engage with the more demanding elements of literature; if so, how far this affects the effective range of their language and whether there is a genuine diminution of reading by young adults. I am not aware of any reliable research on these issues, but they seem fundamental and the Commission may wish to recommend that appropriate research is undertaken.

Social and Moral Cohesion

The effects of reading works of literature are recognised to be variable and somewhat unpredictable, each person responding personally and, in essence, privately. However, it also seems to be recognised that reading literature somehow promotes social and moral cohesion in a society, supporting shared values by suggesting that they are 'universal' or at least established in a particular society for a long time. It is presumably for this reason that all societies require their young people to read (in pre-industrial societies, to hear) the established fictions of their culture.

I request the Commission to consider whether literature is still valuable for this purpose in Britain and, if so, whether the purpose can be achieved equally by film. My own feeling is that it cannot, for four reasons:

148

(a) Literature requires greater commitment than film. First, of time: an accomplished reader may take more than thirty hours to read a Dickens' novel; its film adaptation would probably take less than two hours to watch. Second, of attention: one may watch a film attentively or one may not (the attention may wander, one may doze off, if at home one may give intermittent attention while doing other things); none of this is possible when reading – one reads with sufficient attention to grasp meaning or not at all.

(b) The reading of literature requires an engagement of the reader's imagination in order to make the work 'real' for him/her. This is less evident in film where all the essential elements are presented visually. While there may well be implications of plot, characterisation or symbol to which the viewer is invited to respond imaginatively, this is at a lower level than in literature. It is a common experience that the film adaptation of a good novel, however well done, is more shallow than the original.

(c) Film is limited to a narrow range of elements, chiefly setting, dialogue and action. The emotional effect of these elements normally has to be enhanced by various extrinsic effects – camera angles, lighting, music, and so on. (I am aware that film-makers would say that these are not extrinsic, but rather intrinsic elements of the total effect of the film. But the implausibility of this view can be shown by comparing the effect on the viewer of a live performance of a play and a film of the same play – a film using all the resources of film technique, not a film of the stage performance. The live performance, with relatively simple setting, lighting and costume, is likely to give much greater emotional impact and satisfaction than the film, however technically impressive. A comparison of almost any professional production of, say, *Hamlet* with any of the film versions will demonstrate this.)

It was this narrowing of emotional range that has led Jonathan Miller to compare film adaptations of Dickens to Crabtree & Evelyn soap wrappers – *ersatz* Victorian decoration covering an ordinary soap, and 'soap'.

(d) The growth of interactive technology, as outlined by Sally Tweddle, creates the possibility of adapting film for the individual's purposes. This is already available crudely with video, where the viewer can freeze, fast forward or rewind at will. When interactive technology is established, any possibility of film promoting social cohesion will disappear as consumers create and recreate their own versions. Although this will also be possible with text, for example, when whole novels are available on CD-ROM, there will presumably be little emotional incentive to rearrange sections of text.

The longer term prospects for social cohesion, if film replaces literature as the main medium for the transmission of cultural values but has no demonstrable cohesive effect, is a matter for concern.

John Higgins, Head of Media Studies
St Francis Xavier College, London

I write as a Head of Media Studies at a sixth form college, but one whose initial training was in English which I have taught for ten years and which I continue to teach now alongside media studies and classical civilisation at both GCSE and A Level.

Imagination

First, I must agree with Michael Armstrong that it is imagination that is most sadly lacking in the current debate about English teaching and in the structure of the National Curriculum. This was self-evident at the Commission of Inquiry itself with its emphasis on attempting to identify what is increasingly an impossible balance between the many competing demands for time under the banner of 'English' within the imposed constraints of the core curriculum. In these circumstances, it is hardly surprising that media education finds itself driven to the margins of the subject. Compare this situation with the one prevailing at a college such as this, where the curriculum is at least steered – if not driven – by demand and where media studies at GCSE and A Level has seen an increase in recruitment of around 1000 per cent over the last five years. This situation is mirrored at many colleges in the sixteen to nineteen age sector and increasingly in higher education too. Were it not for the strictures of the National Curriculum, it could safely be predicted that within a very few years, every secondary school in the country would be offering media studies as a popular option for its pupils resulting, no doubt, in an increasing downward pressure on primary schools to initiate media literacy.

I stray here outside of the context of the Commission – fixed, as it was, by an understandable determination to connect with current government policy – because it is important to observe that the situation would be very different if it were the government's concern to connect with, rather than simply train, students. The terms of the debate were in this sense too narrow.

English Literature and Media Education

The historically close juxtaposition of these two areas of study in the curriculum – often taught by the same personnel – has led, and did lead at the Commission of Inquiry, to some highly misleading assumptions about the textual focus in each case. It has become something of a truism to point out the qualitative prejudices associated with each area of study: whereas 'literature' is employed as a term to denote 'good quality', 'media' texts are assumed to be of the most vulgar kind. I think only Margaret Hubbard came anywhere near acknowledging the existence of a canon of challenging media texts, though her references, even then, were to David Mamet as a writer. This pejorative view of the focus of media education derives from several sources.

150

In part, it would have to be admitted, it derives from the excessive sociological zeal of some media teachers who emphasise only the broadest patterns of media experience – the generic paradigms, the social context and a uniform, passive audience – where only the institutional practices and (supposedly) collective responses are of interest. This is an unsurprising phenomenon, however. Had the technology for printing the written word been invented in the late 19th century and been developed with equivalent speed, perhaps our response to it would not have been dissimilar.

In part too, though, the prejudice is an expression of that form of cultural sneering that is the absolute antithesis of the educational spirit – what is simple or popular cannot, by definition, be worthy of our superior faculties. This hypocritical argument (or rather self-regarding posture) seems to suppose that we spring fully-articulate in English literature from the head of Shakespeare. The function of education is to look honestly to see where a pupil is, and then to build upon that experience. Failure to attend to that genuine, cultural process in favour of simply rolling out the time-honoured canon is a strategy roughly equivalent to marching your troops into unoccupied territory while ignoring the teeming cities en route. Life in them goes on untouched – it is often remarked that mass-market tabloids demand a reading age of only ten. We get the media we deserve.

It is a deep irony, therefore, that education itself has periodically conspired – viz. the Newsom Report – in what is in essence an anti-educational ethos. If film and television are 'powerful forces in our culture', then it is the business of us all, not simply those of lower than average ability, to learn from and about them. I regret that at least one of the Commissioners referred to distinctions between 'high' and 'low' culture in a way that shifted the debate back some thirty years to Leavisite days. British society is infinitely more complex now in its production of a continuous spectrum of multi-cultural artefacts from the accessible to the arcane, so that any attempt to re-introduce such incongruous, hierarchical notions of value represents an educational, though not a political, irrelevance. The Commission of Inquiry, I note, endeavoured to interpret its brief within a political consensus.

One Cultural Panic Followed by Another

I shared Alan Howarth's disappointment at Phillippa Giles' responses as a representative of television drama. This, together with Andrew Webber's exuberant but undisciplined performance, appeared to inspire Professor Butler's closing remarks on the positive role of media texts within English as a 'bridge' for gaining the access to the canon of English literature necessary for the moral evaluation of the commercial culture of the media. Again, no suggestion that the media themselves produce film, television or printed texts that evaluate human behaviour or indeed offer a critique of the very industries from which they spring. This, despite the fact that film is perhaps the most self-reflective medium. Forget Eisenstein, Welles, Renoir, Hitchcock, Ford, Fellini, Buñuel,

151

Hare, Potter. Literature is, it seems – to adopt a commercial phrase – 'the real thing'. Yet where are the questions and doubts about its social origins and cultural contexts? What limits can be placed on its values, accessibility and relevance today? Who is selling it and why?

What made me panic at the Commission of Inquiry was the number of individuals who were happy to declare their ignorance of Information Technology. Anthony Smith was also pleased in his conclusion to identify the demand by employers for flexibility as a red herring derived from the rapidly changing patterns of technology. These responses seem quite inappropriate in a society where we are struggling to ensure that Information Technology serves us rather than vice versa and where the Romantic notion of the slow and organic growth of the individual (best charted, it seems, with a quill!) has in reality been displaced by a fragmented, if noble, endeavour to pick up the available pieces and display them in as coherent a manner as possible. If the study of English cannot offer the electronic skills necessary to express and survive as well as the relevant insights into the psychology of the 21st century then it is the study of English that will wither away. The only way to preserve what is of contemporary value in the canon is to test it vigorously and dispassionately in current contexts. Nostalgia and imposition born of moral rectitude will consign it to history.

Cultural Studies

I'd like to finish by a return to the educational context. The one thing that was quite clear from the three days of the Commission was that both English and media studies have pressing tasks to carry out and that they cannot all be adequately undertaken within the current framework of English as defined by the National Curriculum, let alone by the revised Orders. Margaret Maden made a series of excellent points in relation to the transactional aspects of the subject and these alone could easily occupy much of the available time. However, those transactional skills will only be transferred from generation to generation if the literary and cultural imperatives are compelling. Margaret Maden sat on the National Commission on Education which has, in truth, set the real agenda for the changes which could achieve this – freeing up the National Curriculum in consultation with tutors and the introduction of the broader and more flexible baccalaureate style GED qualification. Discussion about the warring priorities of English and media studies in too narrow a curriculum slot runs the danger of legitimising the current structure which, in the long term, will be damaging to both subjects.

If I may end on a personal note, I regard myself as extremely fortunate in being able to teach classical civilisation, English and media studies alongside one another: three subjects that I daily consider as a single subject extended over a broader chronology than is usual. How does Tony Harrison's *V* redefine Gray's *Elegy*? Why is one poem regarded as part of the canon and the other not? Is this a matter of value or style? Who is Harrison's readership and is it the same as his audience for a televised reading of his verse? Where is his poetry placed in the television schedules and why? Is Harrison's a tragic vision? Should we read Harrison's 'dramatic' translation of the *Oresteia* in preference to Fagles' 'poetic' one? Although from time to time I do find that I am teaching a student in all three subjects, in many more cases these three subjects account for one or two of a student's options. Broadening what is now the A Level curriculum would enable students to make much more sense of the cultures with which they live and the same would be true if the choice of learning programmes were more flexible at fourteen to sixteen.

So, to conclude, the question of a National Curriculum clearly carries more than a pedagogical significance. Are we to travel backwards in search of a discarded core in the (vain) hope of imposing social cohesion through a species of narrowly-focused cultural induction? Or would we not be better off providing a less prescriptive framework within which students can make intelligent choices, grope their own way forward with our guidance and do justice to their interests in both English and media studies? That is the real question.

Paul Moore, Chairperson, Education Committee
The Northern Ireland Film Council

Controversy has always been a prime factor in the development of English as a school subject. In the late 19th century when 'English' did not yet exist as a separate subject, it was associated with working class and women's education while the classics dominated universities, public schools and grammar schools.

By the 1860s worries that standards had fallen below acceptable levels prompted a move towards funding based on performance, in the hope that the much quoted German system of education might be emulated. By the turn of the century, however, a Commission of Inquiry had found that payment by results had led to falling standards.

It was not until the early 20th century that English established itself as a subject in its own right, although it was still taught by classicists heavily influenced by German linguistics who based their lessons on Latin. Throughout the early part of the 20th century, school inspectors bemoaned the fact that even the most intelligent pupils were inferior to the previous generation, with the Norwood Report in 1943 blaming falling standards on the schools.

By the 1960s English was established as a central subject and, with the educational emphasis now on personal growth through pupil-centred, 'experiential' learning, a series of papers culminated in the consensual notion that standards were falling, the blame being laid this time at the door of the newly formed comprehensives.

The discourse of 'falling standards' has sustained the call for educational reform through the Bullock Report, the Kingman Report and the Cox Report, leaving us in 1990 with a curriculum order which sees English as an entitlement for all and as 'recursive', 'holistic' and 'heuristic' combining knowledge about language, literature, drama, media and giving a new priority to oracy.

This brief over-view of the development of English as a central and discrete study area is offered not only as a means of grounding the present debate, but also as a reminder that there is nothing new or radical about addressing these issues or about the Government's attitude towards them. What is new, perhaps, is that they are being addressed in an intellectual climate where any attempt to understand the present is, as Fredric Jameson points out, an 'attempt to think the present historically in an age that has forgotten how to think historically in the first place'[1], a forgotten skill often regretted by those in Northern Ireland who have to educate in a society where a one-dimensional atavism passes for historical process and thinking.

Given that the role of the Education Committee of the Northern Ireland Film Council is to promote media education across all educational sectors in the region, it is both fitting and important that it should contribute to this Commission of Inquiry into English, since for over twenty years, debates about cultural heritage, identity and the ideological role of English as a subject in schools have often been resolved on the streets rather than in the classroom.

Despite the presence of division, however, it is ironic that most people in Northern Ireland would answer the Commission's question as to what English is for with the reply that it was supposed to create a notion of British national pride (initially a product of empire) by emphasising a common, unifying cultural heritage, with English teachers functioning as missionaries. The 'supposed' should be emphasised here, since neither tradition would have been content with this notion of English given that as Seamus Deane puts it, 'It is Ulster's peculiar fate – to be neither Irish nor British while also being both.'[2]

This notion of cultural heritage may hide a more important question, however, in that it assumes a common definition of culture and its role in society. The common definition may further contain often unspoken assumptions relating to the consensual notion of culture as a civilising influence, with the cultural guardians from Matthew Arnold, through Leavis to more recently David Hare, ready to defend us against the emerging philistinism of each new social era.

It is useful to challenge this accepted wisdom and remember the Raymond Williams definition of culture as a 'lived experience', a dynamic process concerned with relationships of inequality and power and the kinds of lives people can lead, given these apparently innocent processes, even the most innocent ones like reading literature. If culture is seen in terms of these primary social relations, then cultural heritage needs to be concerned with issues of class, gender, race, nationality, ethnicity, sexual difference, age and ability/disability. By addressing these social relationships, the teacher can attempt to make alliances which might go some way to creating an educational climate where real cultural and social transformation might take place. Nowhere is this more important than in the Northern Irish context where the roots of the conflict are seen to lie in a confusion of abnormal and problematic values, attitudes and beliefs. It is essential that the dialectics of the relationship between the structures of society and the culture be recognised in order that the conflicts do not become merely subjectified, trapped by the notion that a change of ideas through education can solve them. As Joseph Ruane and Jennifer Todd have argued in the Northern Irish context (although their basic position has a wider relevance):

> Northern Irish culture deviates little from mainstream Western culture on such issues as myth, nationalism, religion, compromise and violence. The basic motivations and interests which sustain conflict are not romantic nationalism or sixteenth-century theology, but concerns with equality, security and distribution of power. In other words, ordinary liberal democratic concerns produce conflict in the structural context of Northern Ireland. The roots of the conflict lie in ordinary social relationships, not in perceptions. The conflict is ultimately about conflicting interests, not conflicting ideas. It arises because the structure of the situation is such as to place the two communities in a bind in which their fundamental interests are irreconcilably opposed.[3]

It might well be argued that these issues are concerned with the teaching of cultural studies rather than English but the fact remains that, as with media education, in most schools it is the lot of the English teacher to confront these debates. This is particularly true, for example, in literary theory where (after much often bitter debate) it is accepted that the forms of subjectivity discovered in literature have a much wider social significance. It has also been the lot of the English teacher to confront many of what Roger Scruton, the New Right's leading philosophical guru, refers to as 'the second order subjects', areas such as film, television, black studies, women's studies, communication studies and basic levels of sociology and psychology.

To acknowledge this situation is in no way to condone it, either in pedagogical terms or in terms of the burden it places on an English teacher, but it is to highlight the crucial role an English teacher's view of cultural analysis can play in constructing a platform where these fundamental debates about difference can take place. One example from the local context will underline this. The Northern Ireland Office has recently been screening three short films aimed, it would seem, at encouraging the 'general public' to play a more active role in combating terrorism. Martin McLoone in a short, but brilliantly incisive article,[4] has argued that these films, related as they are to the thriller genre (a Canadian visitor apparently thought they were a trailer for a thriller called 'Confidential Telephone') are the beginnings of an attempt to create a discourse about paramilitary violence, a discourse which hints at the scrutiny of the strategies of the paramilitary organisations in political rather than simplistic or moralistic terms. It may be that the English teacher is the only person in a school with the knowledge and scope necessary to exploit such cultural insights, insights which are at the centre of any hope for cultural heritage progress.

It is difficult to divorce these issues from the question of whether English can unite a fractured society, if only because the 1988 Education Act was based on some of the cultural assumptions criticised above. The distinctions honoured in the National Curriculum, not only between subjects but in the meta-categories such as the split between the academic and the vocational, are unlikely to create an educational environment where fractures are healed. This is especially true if the role of English is to be seen as the vanguard of the move towards a new form of cultural imperialism. It is ironic that commentators on education and 'standards' from Richard Hoggart onwards have been bemoaning the impact of American popular culture on the 'English way of life', since in many ways this notion is at the heart of the programmes for English particularly with regard to literature. In fact, the very act of discussing this issue is itself ironic since as John Tomlinson pointedly remarks:

> There is a sense in which writing in English, and drawing primarily on English language sources, may be reproducing the practices of cultural imperialism in the very act of discussing them. My writing and your reading in English helps to maintain this whole debate as the cultural property of the English-speaking world. And this is not merely accidental: a whole history of global dominance – of imperialism and colonialism – stands behind our present privileged discursive position.[5]

The best we can do in this situation is to remember the story of the man shipwrecked on an island where the inhabitants mistook him for their lost king, and he accepted this role, on the condition that he constantly reminded himself that he had it through an infinity of chances and not through any personal merit or natural worth.

As Tomlinson has shown, cultural imperialism is an extremely problematic concept but it is relevant here in that it contains as one of its elements a discourse of nationality, a discourse which assumes that ideas of authenticity, historiocity and identity are shared in some 'common sense' fashion. It could be argued, however, that English can only remain relevant to any debate about uniting society if it recognises the principle of cultural autonomy. To accomplish this, the national will have to be seen in the broader terms of the global, historical advance of modernity and it will have to be accepted that the notion of particular cultural values needs to take second place to the more urgent question of how cultural meaning can be generated in the conditions of social modernity.

The final answer to this question depends on your reading of the National Curriculum. If there is an openness and flexibility in the workings of the various subjects, then there is a possibility that English might be an area where fragmentation and fracture could be confronted and partially resolved. If, how-ever, as initial developments would suggest, the National Curriculum is merely a attempt at political control of the curriculum, then it will be as Richard Johnson warns 'not a recipe for cohesion, but for the renewal of divisions'.[6]

It might appear from the above arguments that this paper has already found a position on the issue of English remaining a separate subject. On the question of its status as a central element in the core curriculum, this is indeed so, but on the wider issue of its relationship to media education and cultural studies the debate is far from closed. The previous remarks about the role of the English teacher reflected the reality rather than the ideal and the relationship between English and media studies remains problematic. This is evident in the position of media education in Northern Ireland. On the one hand, English teachers continue to address media issues in a professional and meaningful way, making use of relevant staff development as it becomes available (for example BFI courses and Education Board INSET days).

Alongside these English teachers, there are many staff now involved in media-related learning as a specialism, particularly in the secondary and further educa-tion sectors. Their work is reflected in the growth of organisations such as the NIFC Education Committee and NIMEA, the Northern Ireland Media Education Association, organisations whose members are teaching both GCSE and A Level programmes and whose work is supported by a number of enthusiastic and active education authority advisers. The number involved is evidenced by the fact that a Media Education Officer for Northern Ireland has just been appointed, funded jointly by the BFI and the five education authorities.

Nevertheless, the very numbers involved underlines the fact that many of the key issues have not yet been theorised to the extent where those involved have a position strong enough to embed media education fully with students, teachers, local education authorities and the Department of Education for Northern Ireland.

Programmes of study are a case in point. It is generally felt that the position of media education is stronger in Northern Ireland than on the so-called 'mainland' because everyone involved accepts that programmes of study are 'a good thing'. It may be time, however, to challenge this growing orthodoxy and to problematise the question of programmes of study, especially in the light of what has happened to other study areas (not least English) which have gone through this process. Might tablets of stone undermine the flexibility crucial to good media education, or would they embed media education in the system as a further core element? They may indeed emerge as a 'good thing' but they will be better for a period of focused and rigorous theoretical analysis.

The same is true of the continuing debate about the relationship between media studies and media education. Most of the work done on media in English lessons is of the media studies category where the media are seen to have pre-dominantly negative effects, manipulating and deceiving readers into accepting false values, through mechanisms they are powerless to resist. It is unlikely that English teachers apply the same ideological critique to the literary texts they ask children to confront. On B/TEC programmes, the emphasis may be entirely different, with students being given the opportunity to develop skills in media presentation whereby they can attempt to produce media texts which contain alternative strategies for the presentation of meanings. This debate is no longer just a philosophical one with the advent of GNVQ. Leaving aside the issue of the Government's unseemly haste to bring GNVQs into operation, the claim that they will combine, in a meaningful way, media education and media studies makes a resolution of this issue a matter of paramount importance, especially since the new qualification will be available to both schools and colleges.

Then there is the perennial issue about the relationship between English and media studies. Those involved in media studies, such as Len Masterman,[7] are adamant that English teachers neglect context through their concentration on texts which are too dependent on the Leavisite concept of 'discrimination' to be really useful in teaching the media. Such a position may be too extreme, but the fact remains that there are fundamental differences in pedagogic practice in the two areas. Two recent articles in *The English and Media Magazine* by David Buckingham[8] defined the differences (texts, concepts and practices) and the similarities (knowledge about language, distinction between fact and fiction, cultural values) and came to the conclusion that 'the National Curriculum documents present a number of opportunities for developing media education – although we may have to read between the lines to find some of them'.[9] The position of those involved in media education in Northern Ireland is that a separate provision for the programme area might be useful, provided the subject does not become 'ghettoised', but that in the final analysis (and without ducking the issue) there is no reason why media education should not take place in all these contexts provided it is well resourced, well taught and well supported at Department level.

What this paper would argue for is something more radical. Colin MacCabe, in a recent article in the *Times Educational Supplement,* suggested that the premises society makes regarding basic literacy skills may now be obsolete since most people (certainly most young people) now communicate through a literacy system which is media and technologically based. If Colin MacCabe is correct (and one suspects time will prove him so) then media education needs to be viewed as an entitlement, a right for all, to be taught to all individuals, throughout the curriculum and their educational careers, in order that they might be able to communicate with confidence in a rapidly developing global media-scape.

To some extent the arguments have come full circle with media education taking up the position English held as a subject in the late 19th century. How should this position impact on our future visions? It is extraordinary that a project like the National Curriculum, a project which was until recently highly controversial, can so readily have become acceptable. This does not mean, however, that concerns about the government's ability to recruit progressive slogans for reactionary policies have disappeared. It may merely reflect the tiredness of teachers in the face of continual change, and the 'loss of morale' which some government supporters are keen to label a lack of professionalism. To combat these tendencies, English teachers (all teachers!) must continue to find ways to control what goes on in their own schools and classrooms, and to develop strategies to cope with the cultural uncertainty which will accompany the evolution of what Paul Willis calls the 'Common Culture':

> The strengthening, emerging, profane common culture is plural and decentred but nevertheless marks a kind of historical watershed. There is now a whole cultural and social medium of interwebbing common meaning and identity-making which blunts, deflects, minces up or transforms outside or top-down communication. In particular, elite or 'official' culture has lost its dominance. It has certainly always been honeycombed with subterranean resistances and alternatives but now the very sense, or pretence, of a national 'whole culture' and of hierarchies of values, activities and places within it, is breaking down.[10]

Notes

1. Fredric Jameson, *Postmodernism, or the Cultural Logic of Late Capitalism* (London: Verso, 1991), Introduction, p.ix.
2. Quoted in Eamonn Hughes (ed.), *Culture and Politics in N. Ireland* (London: Open University Press, 1991), p.3.
3. Joseph Ruane and Jennifer Todd, 'Culture, Structure and the Northern Ireland Conflict' in Eamonn Hughes (ed.), *Culture and Politics in N. Ireland* (London: Open University Press, 1991), pp.39-40.
4. Martin McLoone, 'The Commitments' in *Fortnight*, no. 321, October 1993, pp.34-6.
5. John Tomlinson, *Cultural Imperialism* (London: Pinter Publishers Ltd, 1991), p.28.
6. Richard Johnson, 'Cultural Studies in a Strong State' in *The English and Media Magazine*, no.22, pp.10-14.
7. Len Masterman, *Teaching the Media* (London: Routledge, 1989), p.49.
8. See *The English and Media Magazine*, issues 23 and 24.
9. David Buckingham, 'English and Media Studies – Getting Together' in *The English and Media Magazine*, no.24, p.23.
10. Paul Willis, *Common Culture* (London: Open University Press, 1990), p.128.

Jean Walker, Teacher and Teacher-Trainer
The Dyslexia Institute, Middlesex

I would like to comment on Roger Scruton's assertion that 'through rule-guided activity, freedom becomes possible', and John Hickman's remark that he must 'begin where the students are'.

The dyslexic school students with whom I work have difficulty with the symbols and sequencing of written language. They are alienated from the society of school. They may cope well with English at the oral level, but struggle inexplicably with reading, writing, and many of our information systems. For dyslexic students, the use of a dictionary, telephone directory, or index, is a mystery.

They certainly need structured teaching, though at a level much more fundamental than Roger Scruton can envisage. They need to 'begin' at several different levels: orally and conceptually, they may function at a competent level; in terms of literacy, they may be several years behind their peers.

I know that my dyslexic students are grateful to English teachers who teach them in a lively and enthusiastic way using a variety of texts and media, and provide the means for them to record their responses in different ways. With such teaching, they learn about their own culture and that of others, and stretch their imagination, emotions, and intellect.

However, as they and the adults whom I teach will tell me, there is no substitute for the ability to read and write to the level of one's social and intellectual group.

I would therefore make a plea that in training (initial and in-service) we equip teachers with more practical skills to help the struggling, possibly dyslexic, pupil. Of course, all teachers of English should be familiar with the grammatical structures of our language so that they may use them well, and teach them to students when it is appropriate to do so.

However I feel that there are two much more fundamental skills which every teacher of English needs:

a) Firstly, a good knowledge of the phonology and spelling structure of English, so that he or she can help students to spell better; can give reasons for a particular spelling, and can point out the patterns and regularities of the written language. This would give some order and structure to a student's learning about language, and would be useful to all pupils in all schools.
b) Secondly, that English teachers should be better acquainted with the complexities of the task of learning to read and spell, and the reasons why some may fail, so that they can give to pupils more than sympathy and ways of getting round the problem.

My final plea would be on behalf of the youngest learners and those who are struggling with English: that they be taught this most crucial and important part of the curriculum by highly-trained specialist teachers. If we get it right for children in the early stages, the English curriculum will be more rewarding for both teachers and children in secondary school.

THE DEBATE

Competition, Coherence and Control:
Education in the Next Ten Years

Anna Ford   Good evening and welcome. I hope that this will be the first of
very many public debates on the topic of education. It is an enormously wide
subject, and we cannot possibly cover it all here. I know that all of you will want
to speak, and therefore I will keep my remarks very short. The speakers tonight
are all going to speak at the beginning of the debate for five minutes each, simply
outlining some of the thoughts they have on this topic.

This is, of course, the first session of a two-day Commission looking at English, looking at coherence, competition and control, and looking at education in
the next ten years in this country. It is a debate in which politicians, teachers, parents, industry and children themselves are fiercely interested, and one which I
feel we should pursue to the right conclusions (whatever they may be) because at
the moment it seems to me that we are in a terrible muddle. It is a prominent concern of all of us. Four Secretaries of State have held office since 1987, and over
the same period, three major pieces of legislation have transformed every aspect
of education from infant schools to universities. The rhetoric of free choice in the
market-place has flourished alongside an unprecedented centralisation of control
over both curricular content and assessment.

Have these upheavals improved education? Can there be a consensus about
what improvement would mean, or is it simply too soon to tell? Do we any longer
have a common culture when twenty per cent of twenty-one-year-olds have only
the most rudimentary of numerical and literary skills? And how far should this
debate be about values? It is first on the agenda of the Commission, and it will go
on over the Commission. You are all invited to come back and spend as much
time as you can until the Commission is over.

In 1976, James Callaghan called for a 'great debate' which would develop a
vision of what education might be in Britain, in an industrial nation, at the close
of the 20th century. Despite all reforms and legislation, despite all institutions

and agencies that have been established and re-established, can it really be said that this great debate has ever taken place?

We have heard a great deal about education over the last few years, and two themes seem to predominate: first, the need to open up education institutions and services to the ethos of free market competition; and secondly, the need to exert greater control over what is being taught. Can these two themes form the basis of a coherent national policy for education? Can competition and control produce a vision of what and how the children of the 21st century will be learning, or do we still need to have that great debate? How can we ensure that we create an education system for the next century?

The debate has been widened by the contribution of *Learning to Succeed*, the report of the National Commission on Education which I am sure many of you have seen already, which points out that all too often our own progress here in Britain is overshadowed by the success of other nations. As you have heard, the organisers of these proceedings believe that the need for responsible and informed debate has never been more pressing. We are going to listen first of all to three distinguished speakers from different walks of life, each of whom has his perspective on recent events, and his own vision of what ought to happen over the next ten years. Then the floor will be yours, not only to question and comment on their points of view, but also to contribute your own.

Tonight's proceedings are being recorded and will form part of the Report on the Commission of Inquiry into English. The report will be sent to the Secretary of State for Education, to the School Curriculum and Assessment Authority and to a wide range of people and institutions concerned not only with education but with our social, industrial and cultural future. We all hope that the views of everyone who speaks here will be taken seriously by that audience.

I intend to ask each of our speakers to speak for five minutes, and then I will open the floor to take as many contributions from you as I can before I return to the speakers. It has been my experience of situations where there are a lot of people on a platform, and even more people in the audience, that the audience feels the proceedings are very much weighted in favour of the people on the platform. They and I, and the people to whom the Report is going to be sent, would like to hear what you, the experts, have to say.

The first speaker this evening will be Sir Malcolm Thornton, who is, and has been since 1983, the Conservative MP for Crosby in Liverpool. He was previously Leader of the Wirral Metropolitan Council, PPS to the Secretary of State for Industry and for the Environment and Chairman for the Parliamentary Select Committee on Education, Science and the Arts since 1989.

Our second speaker will be Eric Bolton, who has been Professor of Teacher Education at the Institute of Education in London since 1991. Professor Bolton was formerly an English teacher, an inspector of schools and most recently Senior Chief Inspector of schools between 1983 and 1991.

Finally we have Professor Alan Smithers, who is Director of the Centre for

Educational Employment Research at the University of Manchester which undertakes work for industry, government departments and other bodies. He is an honorary Fellow of the Society for Research into Higher Education and a chartered psychologist. He was a member of the National Curriculum Council and serves on committees of the Royal Society, the Engineering Council and the Business and Technology Education Council.

Sir Malcolm Thornton   Thank you, and good evening, ladies and gentlemen. As a Select Committee Chairman, it gives me perhaps a unique role in parliament in the sense that I can stand back somewhat from the party political debate in education, and for nearly thirty years, at both local and national level, I have been involved in education. There are one or two things that I have learned and I would like to share them with you.

I believe very fundamentally in two things. One is the evolutionary processes which bring about the changes in education, and should bring about necessary changes. But also I believe very strongly – and this is fundamental to my present role as Select Committee Chairman – in trying to achieve a consensus. I believe (and I am sure that everyone in this room will understand this) that because the leads and lags of education legislation are so long, bad legislation that has been ill-thought through, ill-prepared and does not actually address all the points of view which are there, is like a time bomb which is just ticking away, set to explode years in the future. In the meantime, we have seen perhaps a generation of children, and certainly many years of education for children, set at considerable risk.

I believe too that legislation at its best should be very much a framework for what happens, and not a strait-jacket. It should be a framework within which people can work, and not a strait-jacket which binds them into a particular series of thoughts or ideologies.

It is also important to remember that the implementation of legislation is not done by politicians. It is done by the practitioners. Politicians can pontificate as much as they like, but at the end of the day, it is the teacher or lecturer in front of his or her class who actually delivers those reforms. Unless those very people feel a strong sense of ownership of what they are doing – the ownership of the reforms, and ownership of the system – then I believe that the system is indeed in jeopardy, and so often of late that feeling of ownership has, in my view, been sadly lacking.

One of the references which is made in the report, which is in the preamble to the conference programme talks about a 'climate of uncertainty'. We have seen, and Anna Ford has referred to, Claus Moser's report. I am glad to be able to tell you that the Select Committee hopefully will be talking to Claus Moser and his colleagues very shortly, to examine with him the implications of his report and to actually further discuss the points that he will be raising there, which are an important part of what is very much an on-going debate. Some of them quite clearly will be more acceptable to some people than others, but that does not make them any the less worthwhile in a debate which should be joined by all sides.

And what is the underpinning of this? It is very much quality education for all. It is often said, and I sometimes think I share the view, that the biggest success of the British education system has been to institutionalise failure for far too many of our children. It is a system which benefits only the top thirty per cent and does not actually address the real needs of the other seventy per cent, and it has led us to face very firmly the sort of conclusions that Claus Moser has been bringing forward.

I personally am very unhappy about the belief that somehow market forces will solve all these problems. I cannot see that 24,000 schools, bobbing around like corks on a market sea, are going to have very much in the way of coherence or vision.

In future, we will be seeing a whole new regime as local education authorities' influence continues to diminish and schools with delegated budgets often find themselves having to make unenviable choices which are not always in the interests of their pupils.

So my conclusion is that as we face this massive political, technological, and economic change (and in particular I do not think that we have come to grips with economic change, because of events that have been happening around the Pacific Rim and the OECD projections of what this will mean in terms of GDP for European countries), education is central to this whole debate. It is central to equipping our young people with not only the skills that they will need for the jobs that are available and that are going to be available in the near future, but also to actually appreciate all these changes that are there and that are going to be facing them. It is central to equipping them with basic skills for life, which is what education should be very much about.

In all this I feel as passionately about this one thing as I do about anything else: there is an enormous wealth of experience that exists right throughout education. That does not mean to say that every teacher's views are ones that are right, but there is a wealth of practical experience. If we ignore that experience, if we do not draw upon it, then the chances of actually getting the basics right in our education system are very much reduced indeed.

Eric Bolton Thank you and good evening. Towards the end of the Vietnam war, after a particularly bad defeat for the Americans, at a press briefing an American general was reported to have cried out: 'The future is not what it was', and I think any of us who have been involved in education for any length of time would say that that is a pretty fair statement of the education service. Malcolm Thornton has touched on some of the reasons why that is so. But if those of us who have been involved think back to 1983 or 1984, and certainly the beginning of the 1980s, although many of us foresaw important and necessary changes, I think we would have seen an education system that would have been, in terms of its organisation and management and governance, rather like the one we had then. It would have been peopled by education authorities and teachers who were employed by them and so on. Yet here we are now, with the two key centres of power and influence in our public education service being central government, with a control of the strategic direction (which is probably right anyway) but also with the most detailed involvement in what is going on in schools; and as the other centre, about 25,000 individual schools, all with a much greater level of autonomy than they have had previously.

What I want to do now is to sketch briefly how I think we came to that point and what sort of debate we are now in. I would like to give you three dates to try and post the way through that enormously detailed territory in such a short time. The dates are 1986, 1988 and 1992.

In 1986, Keith Joseph was the Secretary of State, as he had been for some time. Unbeknown to most of us then, he was coming to the end of his time. He produced his White Paper, entitled *Better Schools.* That White Paper had the stated aim of setting out to raise standards at every level. It was the end result of a typically Keith Joseph exercise of a long, rather cerebral analysis of what were the strengths and weaknesses of the English public education service. That exercise was conducted by what I suppose could be called the guru of the 'less government rather than more' and the market economy Conservative Party.

I believe that that analysis of the strengths and weaknesses of our system was sound and correct. Broadly speaking, it was that we performed as well, if not better, than most other people with academically bright and capable pupils. We also had just about the same number of virtual non-starters – a very small proportion – as any other similar country. But we failed seriously the broad mass of ordinary people, the whole centre ground. I remember seeing at that time some graphs which gave a picture of the achievement of children across the compulsory school age in various countries. The graph for Japan between the brightest and the non-starters was an absolutely straight line. Our graph was an almost concave feature. Our two points were the same as the Japanese at top and bottom, but failure and poor performance started very high in our ability range.

Sir Keith Joseph (of all people) in his White Paper accepted, on the basis of that analysis, that we needed to do something to establish a national framework for the curriculum. There was far too much variation and choice in every aspect; what was offered, what was achieved, what was paid for it and everything else. Significantly large numbers of pupils simply lost touch with important parts of it far too early; in other words, we specialised at a ridiculously early age. Most girls lost all contact with sensible, worthwhile science at about the age of twelve or thirteen, for instance. So Keith Joseph took us as far towards legislation for curriculum and assessment as you could go on the basis of that analysis, but he was not a legislation man himself because that would have meant more government rather than less. So his White Paper called for a national agreement about what we should teach, what children should learn, know, understand, master and experience in their education, and stressed the need (again on the basis of the national and international comparisons) for a broad, balanced and relevant curriculum for the compulsory years.

One of the lessons that came from comparisons with other countries – and those lessons are always dangerous to translate across national boundaries – was that all of our more successful comparators kept a larger proportion of their young people in a broad general curriculum for longer than we did, as well as keeping a lot more people staying on beyond compulsory school leaving ages.

In 1988, Kenneth Baker and the 1988 Reform Act took that further. In fact, he brought the curriculum legislation into being. It was very similar to what was in the White Paper, and there was consensus about that. There was virtually no disagreement in the House of Commons between the parties about the curriculum part of that legislation. But the 1988 Reform Act introduced something that was nothing to do with the great debate that had gone on, but was to do with the macro philosophy of the Thatcher Government. That was to introduce an education market, and all of the other things we now know as opted-out schools, funding going to school level, open enrolment, choice for parents and so on, which was designed to produce, as near as could be done, informed users of the system with a lot of people providing within it and a lot of choice within it, so that you would get near to a market. Nonetheless, within the curriculum and the assessment as it was being worked out through those years, there was a great deal of national agreement, not about the way of doing it, but about the need for it.

By 1992, we had had a general election. John Major was Prime Minister, and we had John Patten as the Secretary of State. Following on promises made by Kenneth Clarke, his predecessor, prior to the election, a new White Paper led to a massive piece of legislation. It was called *Choice and Diversity,* and if you look at that legislation, it was concerned almost entirely with the second part of the 1988 Reform Act. It was concerned with mechanics and the easing of the passage for the system into the new market-style education service. There was virtually no mention of curriculum and such matters within it.

At the same time as the opening up of that particular issue, the consensus that had been reached on various aspects of the curriculum began to be systematically unpicked. It was being unpicked on the basis not of the curriculum agreement but out of the problems arising from assessment. In whatever way we move ahead, it is vastly important to distinguish between the curriculum itself and its assessment. The focus of both those activities – both the market notion for schools and what they should do and the unpicking of the consensus that had been arrived at after years of debate about the curriculum – was to take us into a fundamental debate about the values that should underpin our society's institutions and behaviour, with education to play a large part in that.

Therefore, I think we need to look carefully and we need to have that debate. We now have no choice as to whether we have it or not, but I think we need to recognise, particularly when we are discussing issues in English, that it is not wholly or even mainly the issue itself that is in contention. It is what it represents and stands for in terms of values that is the important issue. Therefore, phonics or look and say in reading, progressive education or traditional learning, Shakespeare or *Neighbours,* are value arguments and they are about how different polarities of the present debate see the system. I think we had better treat that as being the subject of the debate if we are to win through, as we must eventually, to a sensible working compromise.

Alan Smithers   I want to underline what Malcolm Thornton and Eric Bolton have said, and open up two lines for debate this evening. First of all, I want to explore with you why it is so hard to agree on a National Curriculum, particularly in English; and then, assuming that we can come to some kind of consensus, ask how we can get young people to make use of it. It is all very well for us to say that children are supposed to be in school from five to sixteen or, as Sir Claus suggests, from three to eighteen, but how do we get them to want to make use of the opportunities that are available to them?

First, as regards the curriculum itself, I think there is widespread agreement that the National Curriculum is a good idea on the basis that we want to set out what no child should miss out on. We want to guarantee to every child a good start in life, and there is a core of skills, knowledge and understanding that is too important to leave to whim or circumstance.

So far so good. It is when we come to try and identify what is really important that things become difficult. In a society where there is general agreement about the purpose of life and an over-arching set of values, then it is not so difficult. If, for example, we are agreed that the purpose of life is to achieve salvation and that the way of achieving it is through the worship of God, then the curriculum follows logically from that. But in a pluralist society like our own, it is by no means obvious what should be required learning. There is no absolute version of the curriculum. What it is that is to be learned has to be arrived at through debate and consensus.

Therefore, it is a great pity that the way that the National Curriculum is described in documents is very obscure. It is very hard even for specialists to get their heads round just what is the prescribed content. That is because it comes out in the funny language of attainment targets, statements of attainment and programmes of study. Even the Education Act of 1988 is confused about what these are.

Moreover, it is an assessment-driven curriculum. The shape of it is determined by the recommendations of the Task Group on Assessment and Testing. I am delighted to see Paul Black here, because he can actually present the alternative point of view. That group proposed a ten-level scale to cut across the eleven years of schooling, and the curriculum, instead of being simply listed, is framed in terms of the criteria for those ten levels. So instead of the hard issues being tackled head-on – such as, what part has film to play in the English curriculum, and what part has drama to play in it, and what part has food to play in the technology curriculum – a tremendous amount of effort has gone into differentiating these ten levels. So if one takes the communication description, Level One is: 'Give simple, audible explanations, narratives and descriptions' (I am delighted, actually, if I am operating at that level tonight!) There are ten fine gradations which go all the way up to: 'Speak with confidence, flair, creativity, in a range of complex situations'.

A tremendous amount of effort has had to go into coming up with a form of words which separates out those ten levels, and that is one of the reasons why it has been difficult to agree on the National Curriculum in English or any of the other subjects. These ten levels have distracted both the curriculum makers and ourselves from the heart of the issue.

That is not the only problem as far as English is concerned. I have written in my notes: 'English is of course not one but several subjects'. That is a matter that is going to be debated during the Commission, but English is a number of different things and it relates to the fundamental purposes of education in different ways. So one of those purposes is to teach young people the conventions of the society into which they are born. Among those conventions is the way their own language is written down on paper, so spelling and punctuation and other conventions are important. It seems perfectly reasonable to prescribe those in a National Curriculum.

On the other hand, another important purpose of education is to develop a sense of meaning and purpose, and since it is by no means obvious what life is about, each of us has to work it out in our own way. Literature, along with drama, art and music, are very important ways of discovering that sense of meaning and purpose. What we are doing in education there is saying: 'Look, these things have helped a lot of people to work out what their lives are about, to give them a sense of meaning and purpose. We would like to share them with you and see if they help you'. Clearly there are no prescribed outcomes here. It is a process of sharing, and so one does not want to be in the business of trying to set out the outcome in terms of a set of levels. That is why it is perfectly appropriate to prescribe some parts of the English curriculum. But in other ways, one is just wanting people to enjoy the experience.

Above all else (and this applies not only to English but to other aspects of the curriculum), it ought to be in a language that we can all understand. By 'we', I mean not only students and teachers (and professors of education also find it very hard to understand), but also parents, employers and the general public. We need to be able to discuss what it is that we are requiring our young people to learn, and to reach consensus on it. So I hope that one thing that will go out from this debate and the Commission is a statement to Sir Ron Dearing, who even now is drafting his final report of his review of the National Curriculum, which says that we would like the National Curriculum to be set out in the simplest possible way so that we can understand what is there and what is not.

Assessment is a secondary issue, but a step in the right direction for a more simple statement would be to get rid of those ten levels.

Let me just underline one other point, and I will deal with that very briefly. We have always to ask ourselves what is in education for the children. It is all very well for the three of us here or the Commission or Sir Claus's commission or SCAA to say: 'This is what we think is desirable for you', but how do we get young people involved? I think we have a lot to learn from other countries about the way they use both intrinsic and extrinsic incentives. By intrinsic incentives, I mean arranging the learning in a way that young people can cope with it. I think we do them no favours by pushing them up in lock step by age, without discovering if they are ready for that next stage of education. I was struck, in a programme I watched, how a persistent truant was transformed when he discovered a level of learning which he could really enjoy.

By extrinsic incentives, I mean that learning needs to be organised around something that people find has meaning and is realistic. The justification for education is often that it is important for its own sake or that it is enjoyable. If people do not think it is important for its own sake (and sadly the truancy tables and the low regard for education in this country suggests that a lot of people do not), then we have to create a focus and an incentive. That means that education can be organised around work, around the performing arts or whatever can give relevance to the forms of knowledge.

Therefore I hope that another message that can go to Sir Ron is: 'Can we differentiate education and have different pathways?' and the two questions I want to open up are: what should be the curriculum and how can we have it set out simply; and above everything, how can we get young people to become involved in it?

Anna Ford   Thank you. Can we open our discussion up to the floor.

Bob Davis   You may be able to tell by my accent that I am from Scotland. I want to question an assumption which all three contributors seem to share, and I do this from a Scottish perspective. It is the assumption that legislation is a good thing and brings unity of purpose.

The most conspicuous distinction between the Scottish educational system and the English educational system is the absence of legislation in Scotland. Scottish education is governed by legislation to a much lesser extent. We do not have a National Curriculum, which commands the assent and the consent of the whole community. We do not have opted-out schools. We do not have national testing. We do not have a perfect system, but in the visits I make frequently to England as a teacher trainer, I am dismayed at how politicised the legislation of the past six years has made your system. Incidentally, I speak from a culture in which the term 'English' carries deep ambiguities. I speak also from a culture where there are eleven Conservative MPs and no Conservative local authorities.

Judith Garrahan   I am a teacher in a school in the north-east of England. I enjoyed Sir Malcolm Thornton's comment about bad and ill-thought out legislation being a potential time bomb, because I think truancy rates and the tables we have now for children failing to come to school are quite closely connected. The bad legislation I am thinking about is all this nonsense that we have had with the Key Stage 3 examinations in 1992 that thankfully teachers managed to defeat, and also the new examinations that we have to confront in the coming year at Key Stage 4, when all the very good practical work developed over the last four or five years with GCSE course work is now out of the window, and where we have to test kids again and put them into levels and stream them and do all sorts of things that de-motivate them and make them run away from school in their hundreds.

The second point I want to make is that I suspect that Malcolm Thornton is rather more on our side than is his colleague Mr Patten. If that is the case, would you please ask him to leave, because we can do without him.

Another point I would like to pick up is what Professor Bolton said about the number of Secretaries of State for Education that we have had over the last few years. We have had four, the most recent of which is trying to undo absolutely everything that was devised by the first, Sir Keith Joseph. I am no great Conservative fan, as you may guess by what I am saying now, but Keith Joseph was trying, I believe, to make access to quality education a bit more equal by saying that we are not going to have the divisive O Levels and CSEs but rather across-the-board GCSEs open to many more children. That is being changed, and we now have to start dividing different levels at Key Stage 4, and I think that is a big mistake.

The last point I want to make is to do with enjoyment and students learning because they want to learn and having some kind of say in what they are learning. I would like to give a brief personal example of something that happened in my classroom. I have decided to say to hell with Key Stage 4 at the moment with my year ten students, and I have offered them private individual reading for the last week. I have said to them: 'Bring a novel, from the school or public library or from your own homes, and we will spend a lesson reading'. I have brought my own. I am reading Henry James. They are reading everything from *The Outsiders* to *Jurassic Park,* and in the last week I have three, one hour and ten minute sessions of absolute, total and engrossed silence. One child who has come into this class is a habitual truant. He came in one Monday. I offered him a book to read. He picked it up and said, 'It's boring'. Then he sat for the rest of the hour with his nose buried in it, telling people next to him to shut up if they so much as moved. For the rest of the week he has not moved from his seat. This child does not go to other lessons, but he is now coming to English to read a novel.

Hilary Lloyd   I am a Celtic cousin of the first speaker. I am from the University of Wales and I am a teacher trainer. I think we can answer the question of why we have had so much legislation. I will throw my political hat in the ring immediately and say that education is a form of social control, and that is why we have such a tightly controlled curriculum at the moment. It is about, even now, separating those who have from those who have not. That is what league tables are about. That is in the context of the whole debate on education.

The second point is about the teaching of English. We say in Wales that a country without language is a country without soul. I am sure that what is happening is that the revised Order for English is very much about controlling the soul of the people through its language. English is my second language, but it is a beloved one, and I do not like to see it being put into the strait-jacket that it looks as if it will be in under the revisions. We need to watch very carefully what is happening to English, because through it you control what people say, and when you control what people say, you control how they behave.

Anna Ford   Thank you. Malcolm, I will throw that back to you in a moment, because you said specifically that education should be a framework and not a strait-jacket, and that there should be quality education for all.

Michael Stern   I chair the National Literacy Association. I would like to disagree profoundly with one remark of Eric Bolton's, and that is that the decision between phonics and look and say, which he gave as an example, is a matter of values. I do not believe that to be true. I believe that the debate about literacy has been bedevilled by the introduction of questions of value into what should be a technical discussion. It should be accessible to research, because there is more research on the development of literacy than on any other topic in education. People have done training studies. They have been able to evaluate the effectiveness of approaches. If more of that sort of work was done, we would find that more of the discussion, which is a discussion of values, is accessible to that sort of investigation. I do not, for example, think that the question of grammar and linguistics, and the effectiveness of it, the need for it or the age at which it should be introduced, should necessarily be a question of value. We can compare children given different training studies, and we can investigate how that affects their writing. The end result of that may well be a question of value, but curiously there is not much disagreement about the ends. The values have been introduced into the means.

I accept completely that the question about whether there should be a canon of excellent literature and many other questions are questions of values, but not, surely, the technical questions.

The other point I would like to make is that the National Curriculum is largely about content, but there is insufficient differentiation between the different functions that a National Curriculum bears, and I would like to suggest that content, for most people who are going on to the age of eighteen, at ages much below fourteen, is relatively unimportant. We should see the curriculum more as a vehicle than as an end in itself, and a great deal of the work that has been done and the passionate arguments about content, I would suggest, have been in effect a waste of time. By the time we are adults, the content of our curriculum at the primary level is pretty irrelevant to us.

171

Sarah Mumford I am an advisory teacher for media education in Wakefield. I want to come back to what Alan Smithers said when he talked about the purpose of education and gave two purposes for education. One was to teach young people the conventions of the society into which they are born. The second was to develop a sense of meaning and purpose. He gave examples, none of which, I noted with interest, included a reference to the media. As far as I understand the purpose of this two-and-a-half-day debate, it is that we are actually looking at what we mean by English. What is English in the late 1990s and the early 20th century? Is it about print on paper, if we are talking about communication and how we make sense of the world? How far are we now to take into account technology – television, films, newspapers, radio, computer games and videos – by which we receive our information and education? The move I think we are looking to make is to appreciate that this is 1993. It is not the past. Shakespeare has his place, but the future is important, and we should be taking our children towards that future. We should be investing in that future.

We need to be addressing the notion of media education within English, which I know is already a statutory part of the English National Curriculum, and I am very concerned about the fact that it may be removed, but I do not believe that it will be. Whatever comes out of this Commission, one of the strong messages has to be that media education is absolutely vital. I wonder whether media or communications studies or whatever we decide to call it will become the subject rather than English.

Anna Ford Thank you. Would anybody like to follow on that whole broad question of the use of the media in teaching? Having been asked to teach media studies myself in Belfast in my first year of teaching, I know how incredibly difficult it is to devise a curriculum when one does not exist.

Brian Stevens I am a director of the Banking Information Service, which is a specialist unit working on behalf of the banking industry with the education services throughout Britain. Could I go back to the macro-organisational points made earlier on. I think there are key ones here, and it follows from what our colleague from Scotland said. I entirely agree with what he said, and it is a pleasure for me to go North of the Border to work in Scotland. But I have to point out as well that that is with a population of five and a half million. It is relatively easier to work in a smaller community than it is in the very large and diverse communities of England and Wales. If, as Sir Malcolm Thornton mentioned earlier on – and this is a base tenet of all the work we are concerned with, and there is a business drive for it – we are looking for a mass education and training system of quality and not a continuation of the elite form of education that we have had for so long, then we will inevitably move into the organisational problems that beset not only education but the Training and Enterprise Councils and many businesses themselves: that is, moving the level of responsibility down to a region. The question there is that, when you empower people in the regions, how is that to be managed from the centre? It is a massive organisational problem, and I do not think we can duck it.

Steve Medway   I travelled up to be here from Somerset, where I teach in a rural school with a small number of pupils but a large number of statemented children. Backing up what was said earlier, may I say that for me, using the media is one of the most vital methods of getting children involved in literature, film, plays or whatever. It is a way for us to get children excited and interested. Someone mentioned enjoyment earlier, and I find that some of the strictures of the National Curriculum are making my teaching staid and boring. We as teachers are being constricted, strangulated – even herniated! – in getting children involved. As regards the comment about reading lessons, it is one of my favourite times of the week when I say, 'Look, go and read this, because you will enjoy it'. The truant may come in and say: 'I am not going to enjoy this' but you put him with a Stephen King, and it is like watching a firework go off. My problem is my lack of time, and if we can find a way around that I think we will make great progress here.

Anna Ford   Thank you. Perhaps we can ask Sir Malcolm Thornton what can be done about that.

Sir Malcolm Thornton   Sir Ron Dearing, of course, is trying to address this particular problem. It was quite interesting that in front of the Select Committee we have had both OFSTED and the Audit Commission and we were talking about the disparity of funding between primary and secondary education, which I do not wish to touch on at the moment, but one of the things that came out of that was a question as to what sort of percentage reduction one should be looking for in times terms of the curriculum. Clearly I share the view – I would want to be on record as saying this – of those who believe that the National Curriculum, rather like legislation, should be a framework. There should be certain basic things in the National Curriculum, but there should still be the time – and the last speaker, Steve Medway, talked about the need for time – to be able to do other things. The excitement of education is quite fundamental.

I would also accept what was said about media studies. It is total nonsense to believe that you can suddenly change the whole culture that a child has been used to by using modern communication and technology, and the fact is they are computer literate in a way that I could never hope to be, and say that that does not matter. One has to maintain the impetus and the excitement of learning so that other things can be fed in and will be picked up as and when students are ready for them. In that way, I believe you get the roundness in education.

If I can just pick up two other points, certainly I think that regarding the Scottish experience – agreeing, of course, with what Brian Stevens says about scale – there is nevertheless legislation there, but it is the sort of legislation that I was trying to refer to in my remarks. It is a legislative framework and not a strait-jacket. Within that limited amount of legislation, certain other good things happen.

I would like to make one final point. I cannot possibly agree with the lady from Wales who spoke about the underlying purpose of the legislation. I have disagreed with aspects of the legislation; it may be arising from muddled thinking or lack of consensus. I do not believe that it has the sinister motivation that you attribute to it.

Anna Ford   May I ask you a question on behalf of the lady who put that point? You appear to be out of step with Education Minister, John Patten. If that is so – and you do not have to say yes or no – how would you influence changes?

Sir Malcolm Thornton   I am tempted to say: 'You can ask that; I could not possibly comment'. But I am not as out of step as it is often fashionable to portray me as being, as far as John Patten is concerned. I talk with him a lot. To some extent, as I think Eric Bolton said in his earlier remarks, John Patten has inherited a pattern of legislation which he has, in my view, the unenviable task of actually seeing through. There are some basic flaws there. It is too prescriptive; it has gone too far. But some of the underpinning principles, as Eric Bolton has already said, are ones on which there is a remarkable degree of consensus. It is when you try and carry that too far, when you push it and tell people what they should do and cross all the Ts and dot all the Is, that you start to have problems. So I would not want anyone to think that I am standing here saying that everything that is happening in legislative terms is and has been bad and all the statements that are coming out of the DFE are ones with which I disagree. What I have criticised has been the implementation of policy, and that is where the debate needs to be opened up much more. That is what I believe Ron Dearing is addressing, first of all in his interim report and hopefully in his final report.

Anna Ford   Alan Smithers, you were criticised for not having mentioned the media.

Alan Smithers   Yes, I apologise for that! When I was talking about the need to confront the issue of content head-on instead of in terms of criteria, this was the kind of issue that I was thinking should be explored. But I have come here to learn, so can I put a question to you, as other participants in the debate, and ask, is it reasonable to suppose that we think that the National Curriculum is a good idea, or would you prefer not to have a National Curriculum at all? How many of our audience think that the National Curriculum is a good idea in principle? [pause]. And who would think we would be better off without it? [pause]. Thank you, so it therefore was a reasonable assumption that there is agreement that we need a curriculum in place to guarantee to every child a certain essential core of skills, knowledge and understanding.

Anna Ford   Well, you say we need a National Curriculum in place, but it needs to stay in place long enough, does it not, for people to be able to learn how to teach it. Certainly where I work there comes over a tremendous amount of disaffection from teachers with the system in that they are under an enormous amount of pressure.

Sir Malcolm Thornton   I would accept that.

Anna Ford   I wonder how their concerns are being addressed.

Sir Malcolm Thornton   My mail bag, during the course of debate – or the lack of debate – which led to Ron Dearing being asked to conduct his review and the Secretary of State's statement at the Box over Key Stage 3 testing, was massive. It was, perhaps uniquely in my experience, the one issue where it was very difficult to find any friends for a particular course of action outside the DFE. With parents, governors, counsellors, teachers and pupils as well, I had a mail bag of nearly 3,000 letters from around Britain. I was in no doubt whatsoever about their views.

It is interesting that we have just seen a strong expression of opinion supporting what Eric Bolton was saying in his original remarks, that there was a remarkable degree of consensus for a National Curriculum. Where the consensus has broken down is over what form that should take, what should be in it and what percentage of time the National Curriculum should take. That is where we have lost the debate on the consensus side of it, and that is what we are trying to get back through Ron Dearing. He has a very felicitous turn of phrase, ladies and gentlemen, and we were very impressed by some of the very simple things that he said at the Select Committee, such as that he was in the business of listening and learning, and it showed.

Eric Bolton I think Michael Stern is being disingenuous, really. Of course all questions, if they are handled at a technical level, are technical. But the point I was making was that in the way those issues are currently being debated, they are being used as icons for particular stances in the current debate. If you doubt that, Michael, then remember that both you and I know that what works in schools that are successful in teaching reading to young children is a mixed economy, a planned and structured mixed economy, with high expectations from teachers. Yet that carries little weight in the public debate. If you doubt that, read Kenneth Clarke's missive sent out just before the election that led to the 'three wise men' and all of that. Therefore, phonics is on one side of a particular fence and 'real books' is on another. Teacher assessment is one side of the fence and external testing is on the other.

Of course if a thing is sensibly and quickly tested by external tests, that is the way to do it. If it can only be assessed – and that is the point at which Keith Joseph arrived and he was the great supporter of course work and teacher assessment because he conducted a very public argument with the examination boards about science and one or two other subjects – in situ and not by written tests because (and these were the words of Keith Joseph and not some ridiculous left wing lobby) he said that if the examination boards are allowed to test practical science and technology and art and music through written papers, it will cease to be practical science, technology, art and music. That is true, but that is not the debate that we are currently having. Teacher assessment for certain sides of that debate is anathema. Tests for other sides of that debate is equally anathema. The reality of the practice, as you rightly say, is finding out what works. And as you say, in most of these matters, we know what works. Paul Black and his research teams at King's College, London, can tell you what kind of assessment leads to improved performance by pupils. But you cannot get funded for it!

Paul Black I am Professor of Science Education at King's College, London. I want to make two types of comments. One starts with what Alan Smithers said about wanting content and not criteria. I cannot understand that, because a simple

175

statement of content without some form of explanation of what it is that the children should know and understand, which gets you into criteria, is absolutely meaningless.

But I want to go behind the ten-level discussion – and I resist the temptation to turn this into yet another ten-level debate – and say that the underlying problem will not go away whether the ten levels are abandoned or not. Any curriculum which is to span five to sixteen for children has to have some sort of structure. That structure has to correspond in a meaningful way to the way in which children progress in learning. Otherwise, that structure does not provide a helpful framework. That is the problem that we have to tackle.

Any such structure has to respond to some evidence, and one of the pieces of evidence to which I draw your attention is that in a wide range of subjects, children at any one age, taking a group of children across ability ranges, show a very wide range of achievements. Some are three or four years ahead of the norm and some are several years behind. That was established in mathematics; I have done it myself in science; I know people who have done it in geography and history; I am pretty sure that will be true in English. That indicates that if you want to attend to the needs of all the children in any one age group, you have to have a structure which is fairly flexible in responding to the very wide range of needs.

Finally, any such structure has to, in some way, create a language by which we can report in a meaningful way on what children can do, and that language has to be a language which can help the different teachers of the same child across the year in a school, between years in a school, between different schools, to communicate in some common way. Otherwise that child's interests cannot be looked after properly.

Now whatever structure you get for a curriculum has to meet those needs. All I will say about the ten-level system was that it was the best way that we could find of meeting those, and I have not heard of a better, and indeed I have not heard of a serious attempt to put up an alternative to meet those sorts of needs, and an end of the key stage thing does not begin to do that.

Alan Smithers himself referred to the truant who was transformed when he found something that he could do. That is exactly the skill of the teacher, to find out what a pupil can do and then in terms of progression in that subject to move from the pupil's success. That is my first type of point.

The second type of point I wish to make is rather different. I agree entirely with what Eric Bolton said about values, but there is one thing that makes me very angry, and that is, in our education debate, the sheer neglect of any evidence. Let me quote some bits of evidence which are neglected. The statement is made that we have progressive education in our schools and it has caused a lot of trouble. Eric Bolton and his colleagues have pointed out in vain that we have hardly any progressive education in the schools so it could not have caused much trouble! That is completely ignored. We have Anthony O'Hear writing for the Centre for Policy Studies a pamphlet attacking John Dewey, and what do we find six months later? Amazing! The British Prime Minister declaring to the public in one of his speeches about the damage that John Dewey has done to education, followed within a couple of weeks by the Minister for Education declaring what a dreadful thing John Dewey has done for education. I tell my friends in the United States about this and they are absolutely amazed. They say: 'What are your politicians doing, do they study John Dewey?' No, they do not; they study pamphlets by Anthony O'Hear.

Another example is the alleged unreliability and invalidity of short external written tests. It is said that they give results that you should not trust. And yet, in spite of all the evidence about that, it is yet the one thing that is to be trusted. The corollary of that is the rubbishing of teacher education. It is appalling to be able to report to people overseas that a British Prime Minister stood up and said there was too much teacher assessment and we had to reduce it. When we are asked: 'What was the enquiry, what was the evidence on which he based it?' I have to say we do not know. There was no debate, no consultation, and it came out of the blue; he just said it. As a result, the great progress made, particularly in English education, from 100 per cent teacher assessment has been rubbished. Why was it done? Where was the debate about that? Nowhere! That makes me angry.

Then the assumption is made that short tests do not damage teaching and do not interfere with the way teachers work when we know jolly well that they do, and every piece of research about the effect of high-stage tests on teaching is of an oppressive and negative backwash. But most of all, there is the failure to understand that the key to raising standards is in teachers' formative assessment of how their pupils knit into their learning programme, so that they have a programme which is informed by what their pupils are doing, modified by those achievements of their pupils and tuned to the different needs of different pupils. Good formative assessment built into teaching is the one way to raise standards that we have not fully exploited at all, and there is ample research evidence in many countries of the world on that issue. I do not buy statements such as: 'We do not want an assessment-led curriculum'. I want a curriculum in which assessment is intrinsic to improving learning, and it is in the daily practice of teachers. If there is one tragedy after the Task Group on Assessment and Testing's ten-level scale that I regret more than any other, it is that the plea for a substantial programme to support teachers' formative assessment was never heeded. All the investment of resources was put into external tests. That is a very big mistake in terms of any programme to raise standards. ·

Elizabeth Atkinson   I am a lecturer in education in Sunderland. Following on from what Professor Black said, of course we need some sort of structure, and it would be fine if the Government took the ideas about the ten levels being used for structure as long as they also took in the points that he has just made about the fact that any one year group of children is going to include children at a huge range of levels. But instead of that, they take each of the levels and say: 'In this year, children should be at that level'. If they are not, then they are seen to be underachieving. This is where the problem seems to arise, in that no account whatsoever has been taken of the spread, the range of ability, the range of development among children in any one year group, so that the whole debate about below average achievement has come up in a totally inappropriate way.

Mike Clarke I am a curriculum adviser for media education in Essex. I begin by saying, at some risk to my future safety from my colleagues, that I am a strong supporter, in principle, of the National Curriculum, but I must say that my view is somewhat different on that as we find it at present. It seems to me its importance is largely as a ground for debate and development. What we need is a curriculum which is alive and which offers motivation and enjoyment to children. We also need stability without continual major shifts by government dictat. But within that stability we need scope for evolution through consensus. It seems to me that this demands restraint from government, and a willingness to listen and take account of experience – very much the sort of stance taken by Sir Malcolm Thornton, and, so far as we know, by Sir Ron Dearing at other times. The problem with education at present is the Government's refusal to listen.

I would like to close by saying that it seems to me that one of the things we could do with is a return to Victorian values, but what I mean by that is the sort of values which I found in teachers who teach in Australia in the state of Victoria a couple of years ago at a conference organised by the British Film Institute. What they have there is an imposed state curriculum, but it is developed largely by teachers and it is widely supported by everybody. I think those sorts of Victorian values would be very welcome here.

Victoria Dunacre I am a teacher training lecturer at Middlesex University. Concerning media education, I think it is about questioning images, audiences, producers and so on. It is about helping to empower children to develop their own best skills, some of which they have already developed before they even touch school, such as visual literacy and indeed questioning. Has media education been revised (so-called) to the point of exclusion because media education would empower children to question the National Curriculum itself? I would like to celebrate our National Curriculum literacy heritage, and go back about three years and write media back in.

Anna Ford Could I put that question to you, since it was posed in the form of a question, Malcolm?

Sir Malcolm Thornton The one thing I cannot do is speak for people who may have their own particular agenda. Certainly from my point of view, as I think I have already made clear, I would wish to see media studies and the use of media methods very much part of, if not central to, the curriculum, and particularly in the early years, because for many children that will be the bulk of their experience. To help them to develop on from that and get the excitement from it is very worthwhile.

It is always easy to go looking for Reds under beds, and I do not believe for one moment that there is anything sinister in trying to exclude this. Eric Bolton, if I may use the examples he gave before, has touched on that. What has happened is that the middle ground in the debate has been lost. You have a view here and a view there; but the sensible view is somewhere in the middle and it is a bit of all things. The illustration that he gave about reading is a classic example of this. The Select Committee did its own enquiry into reading and came down very strongly in favour of mixed methods producing the best results, which actually underlines things which have been happening for a very long time.

So I think that is yet another casualty of the present debate, which has become far too polarised, and that area of consensus from which we should be looking is one which we must go after with renewed vigour.

Eric Bolton   Briefly, I want to support Malcolm Thornton and say that my experience of working closely with politicians is that the idea of conspiracy falls down because they cannot keep any single thing running for long enough!

Sir Malcolm Thornton   Absolutely right!

Eric Bolton   There are so many issues, you see. But what we need to distinguish between, and not just on the media issue but on many things that are happening within the National Curriculum, is to the extent that they are being handled very prescriptively, in the minutest detail, that happens and is possible, through the fact that the Secretary of State has to approve every single assessment order. The Secretary of State is actually not allowed, by law, to go into the curriculum debate in that kind of detail, if it is a curricular debate, though he can express an opinion. But he actually can write in, in the closest detail, as you saw, not just Shakespeare but the specific Shakespeare. Generally speaking, in the debate over this Commission and more widely, there needs to be some sharp distinction, in the problems that teachers face and that you have from whatever angle you come at the curriculum, between those that are to do with assessment and the way that is being operated, as distinct from the curriculum orders and the programmes of study, which do not seem to me to be arguably narrowly restrictive and prescriptive.

John Dixon   I am a retired inner city teacher and college lecturer. I hope the panel feel, as I do, in reading the National Education Commission report that the key issue that we have to think about, not just here but in the next year, is the critical condition of the British economy and the contribution that education must make in the next decade to changing that position. It seems to me that if that is the case – and I would be glad to be shown to be wrong – then there is no question as to the necessary strategy. We have been quite clear since the Parliamentary Select Committee report of 1977 that it is not the top forty per cent of our kids who we have to look at and see what we can do to raise standards with, but the other sixty per cent. League tables and things of that kind are actually totally irrelevant and what we need is a consensual position about what can be done concerning that sixty per cent.

I want to address a point made earlier about what we can do to regionalise something that must have coherence and a degree of national guidance. We want a consensus very badly if we are going to raise standards at the speed that we need to raise them. We need to have not only that consensus but also room for the kind of teachers who have spoken here, who are experimenting in their classrooms and who are finding ways to motivate their students. We need them to be given prominence in their role in that movement. We therefore need to have forms of regional curriculum going on of a kind which have not been tried in Britain before, though we have had partial movements in many of the main subjects.

I want to remind people here that when I started teaching in 1950 in Islington, the idea of a National Curriculum would have been laughed out of court as unthinkable. Two generations of teachers have produced the position we are in now, where it is the most obvious thing to have. That is an achievement, but the difficulty is that unless we get a consensual movement forward in the next decade, I see Britain as sunk. It is terrible to think of that, when we consider that during the late 1960s and 1970s, people across the world wanted to know what was happening in English classrooms in England, Scotland, Wales and Northern Ireland.

Inda Garon I am a confused parent but I have taught in the past. I always understood 'debate' to be something about divergence of views, and it is very refreshing to see that from the platform there is some consensus. Let us hope that we get a national consensus as well.

I wish to ask a question about the English curriculum which is based on my discussions with my two children. Their expectation is that any debate in this Commission will take English in three distinct contexts. One is the context which is being played out here, which is to do with communication skills, identity and media, and there is no disagreement that all those components are very important. But there are two components missing from the debate today. The first concerns 'English' becoming synonymous with 'language'. We work out our identity in communication through language and that is not the English language necessarily. There are now more Punjabi speakers in mainland England than speakers of Welsh. That raises issues of bilingualism and the skills of English teachers.

The other thing that my children would very much like to be on the agenda is the national perspective. Are we the custodians of the English language? Can my children go to India, Australia, South Africa and have a meta-language which makes sense of the different varieties of English languages both in this country and abroad? Thank you.

Anna Ford Thank you very much indeed. I am a confused parent as well! Briefly, I will ask the panel to make their final contributions at the end of the debate. Eric Bolton?

Eric Bolton I think we ought to be very thoughtful about legislation and its usefulness. It seems to me as silly to believe that everything can be achieved through legislation as it is to dismiss it utterly. One of the great and undoubted successes of recent years in English and Welsh education – the GCSE – was a situation where the optimum combination of good, grass roots knowledge of what kind of things worked combined with legislation and built on that, and there was then the insistence through legislation that it would happen everywhere. Lo and behold, overnight those things began to happen in the fourth and fifth years in schools all across the country. So there is a very real argument for legislation but it is how you use it that is the crucial question.

Alan Smithers   May I just underline two points. The first is to do with stability and change in the curriculum and all the changes that seem to have been taking place since 1988. There is a real dilemma here that if it has been got wrong, do you live with it or do you try to change it? If media studies is not given sufficient prominence within the English curriculum, do you soldier on with something which is unsatisfactory to maintain stability or do you campaign for change?

I think I agree with the person who said that we want restraint and we want minimum prescription in the National Curriculum just to guarantee to every child what we think they should not miss out on, and that there ought to be room for evolution for teachers to make use of their particular circumstances, develop their particular interests, and develop the particular interests of their pupils. The stability needs to come with this essential core, and we need to hammer out what belongs to it.

The second thing I have heard here is that we need to improve education for the ordinarily intelligent child. We do pretty well by those who are academically able. But those who are ordinarily intelligent tend to miss out in the English education system – and I use that form instead of the British system – and what we have to do (and it may be painful) is to face up to the considerable differences in aptitudes and interests of young people. The logic of the ten-level scale or any level scale may be that we have to group young people much more by ability and that we do not try to cope with a wide spread of abilities by moving people forward by age. But whatever we do, I think we have to organise it so that people are not pushed forward for areas of education for which they are not ready. We have to ensure that every child masters a level of education before moving to the next. That would be the way in which we could improve the opportunities of all young people and improve the performance of the education system as a whole.

Sir Malcolm Thornton   We were asked to give an over-view of education in this public debate against which the Commission will take places during its course, and at the risk of perhaps stretching the consensus that our last speaker referred to, I would like to underline the central points which I believe have come out in this debate. One was made by Eric Bolton and one was made by Alan Smithers. First, there is the need to have legislation coming after the debate, discussion, agreement, and testing some of the models and seeing if it actually works, and then making certain that the legislation is a light rein to allow people to actually develop within that legislative framework.

The second point, which is equally fundamental and in the longer term must be addressed, is the graph which Eric Bolton showed us of the huge dip in the middle, showing the failure, the poor expectations that we have. HMI reports have shown that even teachers have poor expectations of that group, so they must also examine what way they are going as far as that particular middle mass of our school population is concerned. Unless we tackle this problem and evolve a system which gives to all pupils throughout the education system, starting perhaps as early as three and right through the education system, that high quality which gives them all a chance of exposure to the best forms of education and teaching, then we are going to reap a bitter harvest. We can see that harvest there today in terms of social problems in terms of educational under-attainment, and in cases of the sheer waste of young talent and lives that the education system is supposed to be there to encourage.

If we can take those two messages away from a debate like this and address those as fundamental to any debate about education for the future, then we stand a chance of regaining that consensus and rebuilding something which we need vitally if Britain is going to move forward properly into the next century.

Anna Ford Thank you all very much for asking such fascinating questions and getting the Commission off to such a good start. I would like to thank the panel on your behalf, and say that it is clear that we have the wherewithal in this country to have the best education system in the world. Let us hope that we can achieve it within the lifetime of this rather disaffected new generation. Thank you all very much indeed.

INDEX